MAKING HOME FURNISHINGS

THE ART OF SEWING

MAKING HOME FURNISHINGS

BY THE EDITORS OF TIME-LIFE BOOKS

TIME-LIFE BOOKS, NEW YORK

TIME-LIFE BOOKS

FOUNDER: Henry R. Luce 1898-1967

Editor-in-Chief: Hedley Donovan
Chairman of the Board: Andrew Heiskell
President: James R. Shepley

Vice Chairman: Roy E. Larsen

MANAGING EDITOR: Jerry Korn
Assistant Managing Editors: Ezra Bowen,
David Maness, Martin Mann, A. B. C. Whipple
Planning Director: Oliver E. Allen
Art Director: Sheldon Cotler
Chief of Research: Beatrice T. Dobie
Director of Photography: Melvin L. Scott
Senior Text Editors: Diana Hirsh,
William Frankel
Assistant Planning Director: Carlotta Kerwin
Assistant Art Director: Arnold C. Holeywell
Assistant Chief of Research: Myra Mangan

PUBLISHER: Joan D. Manley
General Manager: John D. McSweeney
Business Manager: John Steven Maxwell
Sales Director: Carl G. Jaeger
Promotion Director: Paul R. Stewart
Public Relations Director: Nicholas Benton

THE ART OF SEWING
EDITORIAL STAFF FOR
MAKING HOME FURNISHINGS
EDITOR: Fred R. Smith
Designer: Virginia Gianakos
Assistant Designer: Elaine Zeitsoff
Text Editors: Betsy Frankel, Anne Horan,
Gerry Schremp
Picture Editor: Ed Brash
Chief Researcher: Wendy A. Rieder
Staff Writers: Sondra R. Albert, Don Earnest,
Marian Gordon Goldman, Angela D. Goodman,
Susan Hillaby, Marilyn Kendig, Sandra Streepey,
Reiko Uyeshima
Research Staff: Laura James,
Lyn Stallworth, Cinda Siler,
Ginger Seippel
Art Staff: Anne B. Landry (art manager),
Angela Alleyne, Penny Burnham,
Patricia Byrne, Catherine Caufield,
Jean Held
Editorial Assistant: Anne Gordon

EDITORIAL PRODUCTION
Production Editor: Douglas B. Graham
Assistant Production Editors:
Gennaro C. Esposito, Feliciano Madrid
Quality Director: Robert L. Young
Assistant Quality Director: James J. Cox
Associate: Serafino J. Cambareri
Copy Staff: Eleanore W. Karsten (chief),
Kathleen Beakley, Ricki Tarlow,
Florence Keith, Pearl Sverdlin
Picture Department: Dolores A. Littles,
Susan Hearn
Traffic: Carmen McLellan

THE CONSULTANTS
Henrietta Blau owns Delta Upholsterers, Inc., a
custom workroom for draperies, slipcovers and
upholstery in New York City. Her expertise in making decorative home furnishings is derived from
22 years at Delta and 15 years of training prior to
that at the well-known workroom of Thomas Di
Angeles in New York.

Gretel Courtney taught for several years at the
French Fashion Academy in New York City. She
has studied patternmaking and design at the
Fashion Institute of Technology in New York and
haute couture at the French Fashion Academy.

Tracy Kendall has for many years designed sets
and costumes for commercial films and advertising. She is currently a fashion stylist.

Julian Tomchin is a textile designer who has re-
ceived the Vogue Fabric Award and a Coty
Award of the American Fashion Critics. A grad-
uate of Syracuse University's Fine Arts College,
he has been chairman of the Textile Design Department at the Shenkar College of Fashion and
Textile Technology in Tel Aviv and now teaches
at the Parsons School of Design in New York.

Valuable assistance was provided by these
departments and individuals of Time Inc.:
Editorial Production, Norman Airey; Library,
Benjamin Lightman; Picture Collection, Doris
O'Neil; Photographic Laboratory, George Karas;
TIME-LIFE News Service, Murray J. Gart;
Correspondents Dorothy Bacon (London), Ann
Natanson and Deborah Sgardello (Rome),
Martha Green (San Francisco), Giovanna Breu
(Chicago), Lois Armstrong (Los Angeles),
Josephine Du Brusle (Paris), Elisabeth Kraemer
(Bonn), Traudl Lessing (Vienna), Joyce Leviton
(Atlanta), Mary Martin (Ottawa).

CONTENTS

1
INTERIORS
WITH
STYLE

According to psychologist Milton B. Saperstein, "There is no time at which a woman is more apt to go to pieces than when she is engaged in decorating her home." The prospect of putting her taste on public display so unnerved one of his patients that it took her five years to redecorate her home —and she spent two of those years in psychoanalytical treatment for what Saperstein has described as "hysterical stupor."

TURNING THE DREAM INTO LIVE-IN REALITY

The psychic trauma brought on by a decorating project is almost as common, regrettably, as it is unnecessary. Common sense and some confidence in personal taste make the job fun; some tricks of the trade from seasoned professionals make the job easier. Women who sew have a head start, for they already know how to deal with a major part of the problem—the part that involves fabrics. Curtains and draperies, window shades, slipcovers and bedspreads often make the crucial difference in transforming a room from a tired cliché into a fresh and inviting environment. Fabrics help realize the dream by introducing new colors, textures and designs. They can dramatize or disguise the lines of a piece of furniture, frame a lovely view or erase a bleak one. They can cover upholstery that is worn or dull, and they can ensure a longer life to upholstery that is brand new.

There are excellent reasons for making these fabric furnishings at home, as opposed to buying them ready-made. Maximum advantage can be taken of a fantastic variety of fabrics, styles and techniques. The results will look better because such projects can be made to fit exactly, using the same methods employed by the workrooms that serve high-priced decorators. Not least of the many benefits of home-sewed furnishings is economy; often they will cost no more than inferior ready-made products and they can cost about a third of the price of those made to order.

Few special skills are demanded in making fabric furnishings. Most of the sewing is done with straight seams on the sewing machine, and basic techniques are easy to master. But producing a perfect fit on a slipcover or a perfect drape on a curtain does take patience and care. Measurements have to be meticulous, and mathematics must be accurate; there are no paper patterns to serve as guides in cutting and sewing — the seamstress is strictly on her own. Additionally, the sheer size of a project like a slipcover can be intimidating. It means dealing with huge quantities of fabric, running up countless yards of welting — enough, it may seem, to enclose a football field. Indeed, the hardest part of the project may be finding a space large enough to spread out the cloth for cutting, and for placing lengths of cloth side by side to match the design. The living-room floor might well be the only place.

When it comes to choosing the fabrics to use, the amateur decorator might well take her cue from Elsie de Wolfe, the American actress who became Lady Mendl and is recognized in both Europe and America as the originator of the profession of interior decorator. Lady Mendl, whose clientele included the likes of coal baron Henry Clay Frick, French banker Fritz Mannheimer and movie star Gary Cooper, wrote: "Good taste is suitability! *suitability! SUITABILITY!*" By her definition, suitability started with the nature of the life that went on in a house. "When I am asked to decorate a new house, I study the people who are to live in this house, and their needs, as thoroughly as I studied my parts in the days when I was an actress."

Furnishings were also suitable and tasteful to Lady Mendl when they complemented the architectural style of the house and followed a central color scheme, preferably one that flowed from room to room but varied enough in each room to take into account its exposure. She was always amazed, she said — writing in 1913 — that there were people who did not realize that a blue color scheme made a north room look bleak and that red and yellow were all wrong for a room flooded with sunshine. She advised people with hot tempers not to use too much red in their homes. For those who took a childish delight in patterns of red roses on green backgrounds, she suggested a scheme that stuck to neutrals for furnishings and depended for color accents upon flowers, bookbindings and open fires.

Considering that her clients were exceptionally well off, Lady Mendl was surprisingly sensible about fabrics. She was deeply enamored of chintz, which at the time cost only 20 cents a yard, and she used it so often that she became known as the Chintz Decorator. Not only were its bird and flower patterns bright and colorful, she observed, but its glazed surface defied dust. She was also enchanted by the decorative possibilities of the slipcover (pages 120-121) at a time when it had come to be regarded by most people as a loose-fitting utilitarian covering for parlor furniture when the parlor was not in use. Under her aegis, the slipcover regained status as a substitute for upholstery, to be changed to suit the season. "One's room may always be clean and inviting" if covers are used, she wrote, "and their color will give glory to the darkest day."

Though chintz no longer costs 20 cents a yard, Lady Mendl's commonsensical approach to fabric furnishings still holds good. Modern decorators also like simple fabrics that behave well. Chintz is back in style for the same reasons Lady Mendl used it: its patterns are fresh and pretty and its glaze repels dirt. Printed fabrics are popular for slipcovers because, as London decorator David Mlinaric observes, "you don't notice so much if the covers move about." Synthetic fabrics make upkeep easier and stand up to all sorts of climatic conditions. Decorators, on the other hand, often prefer natural fabrics because they seem to age more gracefully. In fact, many decorators welcome fading because it softens colors and gives fabrics character—although their clients do not always agree.

Indeed, the look of a fabric matters as much as its performance, and here the same rules that women instinctively apply to their wardrobes can be applied equally to their homes. If a woman is small she does not wear jazzy, aggressive patterns, and the same is true of small rooms. If she is mixing colors, she makes one color predominant and uses other colors as accents—a scarf sets off a dress, curtains set off a wall. And though in rooms as in clothes the choice of color combination is largely a matter of personal preference, certain colors just naturally work well together.

David Hicks, the British decorator, says that the easiest color scheme to use is one that combines "no-colors"—beige, off-white, dark brown, gun metal, oatmeal; to these basic neutrals, Hicks likes to add splashes of Chinese yellow, shocking pink and flame orange. In fact, the idea of choosing color according to family is one of his favorite devices. "All reds work with all other reds and pinks," he observes, "all oranges work with all oranges and with browns and yellows; all blues work with each other and with green. And while two particular reds might work together on their own, it is nearly always safe to say that the more shades of a particular color you put together, the better the result will be."

The principles that guide color selection can also be adapted to the often puzzling blending of patterns. There is no need to hold back from using several in one room. Clashes can be avoided if color as well as design is considered. Howard Dilday, an American decorator working in Rome, picks his busiest print first, one with three or four colors; then he repeats those colors alone or in groupings around the room.

Color can also be picked up in the choice of trimmings. Tapes, braids, fringes and welting can, by matching or contrasting to other fabrics, pull together the design of a room. But decorators caution that these trimmings should be used logically: braids should outline the natural configurations of a furnishing; fringe should occur at the nat-ural point of termination. Rome decorator Stefan Mantovani likes to trim a sofa by out-lining its contours with a border print —which he calls "re-inventing" fabrics.

The opportunity to attempt such inven-tions is the main attraction of sewing fabric furnishings at home. When they work, they create a living atmosphere with an entirely new dimension. When they do not work, they can usually be reconstructed fairly eas-ily. And even seeming failures should not be abandoned hastily. Mantovani once cov-ered a chair with the wrong side of the fab-ric out. "But it turned out all right because the fabric looked better that way—and the client preferred it that way too."

A lavish use of fabrics marks a fashionable bedroom of the mid-19th Century. Awash in chintz ruffles and roses, it contains slipcovered chairs, a fringed and flowered bedcover, and a staircase curtained with a fabric swag —perhaps to veil from the vulgar gaze the ankles of descending females. A needlepoint rug lies in front of the hearth and the workbasket on the carpet contains what may be the needlework of the lady of the house.

A harmonious use of fabric

Like the chameleon that changes its skin color to suit its surroundings, a room can transform its personality with fabric. Slipcovers, draperies, curtains and pillows—if inventively used—underscore the best features of an interior, hide those that are bad, give a lift to worn furnishings and pull together a random mix of periods. Fabric can also alter the mood of a room. And, to cap all these qualities, most fabric furnishings are readily removable for cleaning.

Cheeriness and a sense of comfort are suggested by glazed chintz, peony-printed and quilted for stability on the chair and sofa slipcovers, ribbon

printed for a lamp-table cover. Yellow taffeta curtains match the walls, and the plump cushions pick up the pink of the chintz blossoms.

Five small controlled prints, all different but color related, combine to enliven the corner of a small sitting room without being obtrusive: the sofa's

The café curtains hang from rods slipcovered in the same fabric, which is also repeated on several of the pillows. The table cover is a circle of felt. 17

Two fabrics and a calico-patterned wallpaper work together in an all-blue farmhouse bedroom. At the windows, one fabric is the light curtain; the

A single bold pattern helps a bedroom double as a sitting room: the bed covering, pillows and window curtains (reflected in the mirror of a Regency

armoire) are all made of a cotton printed in an 18th Century design to match the wallpaper. On the floor is a needlepoint rug, worked in squares.   21

2
WONDERS
BY THE
YARD

Not far from the royal compound of Versailles, in the French village of Jouy, an ambitious Bavarian businessman named Christophe-Philippe Oberkampf set up a factory for producing cotton prints, in 1760. Soon he was delighting aristocratic customers with fabrics, printed in brick red or French blue, showing scenes from the life of the peasants and *petite bourgeoisie.*

Today, copies of Oberkampf's *toiles de*

A WORLD OF FABRICS FOR FURNISHINGS

Jouy (Jouy cloth) are still much in demand, part of a remarkably diverse repertory of fabrics for home furnishings. Traditional and modern, printed and textured, designed to cope with every condition of use and every desired esthetic effect, the fabric available for draperies, curtains and furniture coverings far exceeds in variety that for clothes.

Along with this greater selection go some unfamiliar concerns in determining which fabric to buy. Factors such as dye lot, durability and ease of care matter as never before. So do stability of weave, fastness to sun, resistance to mildew and even the interval at which the pattern is repeated.

Home furnishings fabrics are purchased in yardages seldom encountered in dressmaking. A slipcover for a couch and two pairs of matching draperies can consume as much as 48 yards of 48-inch-wide fabric. And since that much material may have to be cut from more than one bolt, the color may not match unless both bolts carry the same dye-lot number—look for it on the hang tag. Yardage also makes the size of the pattern repeat an important consideration. The larger the repeat, the more fabric will be needed to make the pattern match across drapery panels, or fall in the center of slipcover cushions. Even the quantity itself can raise problems. Sometimes the only substitute for a large enough cutting board may be the floor.

Figuring in the fabric choice will be the kind of wear it gets—and the fact that slipcovers and draperies are cleaned less often than garments. Soil- and stain-resistant finishes like Zepel and Scotchgard prolong the freshness of fabric by holding soil on the surface, where it can easily be sponged away. When a fabric has been treated for soil resistance, this fact is generally noted on the selvage and on the bolt-end label.

Also on the bolt label or selvage is information useful in gauging a fabric's resistance to fading. If the label reads sunfast it means that the color will withstand a minimum of 60 hours of sunlight without fading; if it reads sun-resistant, it will withstand sun for at least 40 hours. But a curtain in a south window will surely get many more hours of sunlight than that, and will inevitably fade unless it is lined. One fabric that is especially vulnerable to sun is silk, whose fibers literally rot from the sun's ultraviolet rays, making blinds or shutters obligatory protection for silk draperies in sunny windows, even if they are lined.

Mildew attacks home furnishings fabrics in humid climates, natural fibers more quickly than synthetic ones. And humidity may also affect the stability of natural materials. Some linens expand and shrink so much with changes in moisture that, in one classic example, an irate customer complained that the linen curtains in her seaside home drooped when the tide was in and shrank when the tide went out.

Obviously, the sturdiest fabrics are those that are most firmly woven. But sturdiness alone does not guarantee long life. The synthetics, for instance, are generally very tough. Yet, one expert maintains, they may not age gracefully. And when printed they may not hold their color well—especially when the printed surface must take the abrasion of human bodies. Indeed, one decorator who claims he "never uses anything but miracle fibers," identifies those fibers as "cotton, linen, wool and silk."

Whether a miracle of nature or a miracle of chemistry, every home furnishings fabric has something to recommend it. Overleaf, the choices are examined in terms of how they look in use; in the charts on pages 34-37, characteristics of the fibers and weaves are described with an eye to performance.

The rich range of drapery

Opaque or airy, multicolored or monochromatic, fabrics intended for curtains and draperies must meet two criteria: they should fall in graceful folds, and patterns, and textures should adapt to the inevitable loss of certain areas of design within the folds. There is only one way to judge these qualities—lift and gather the fabric and look.

These six hangable fabrics capitalize on pattern: left to right, a jungle-printed sailcloth; a woven-checked gingham; an allover floral design on a linen-cotton blend; a Mondrian arrangement of lines on cotton; a dense paisley; and a cotton voile strewn with flowers.

Some of the textures that can be draped into subtly shadowed folds of fabric include *(from left to right):* a light-as-air acrylic leno that looks very much like linen; an iridescent silk shantung; a diamond-patterned silk damask; a polyester-and-cotton eyelet; a nubby cotton homespun; and a cotton-and-rayon moiré faille with a satin stripe.

Well suited for sitting

Fabrics that cover furniture, unlike those used for draperies, are viewed flat and often at close range—conditions to keep in mind when choosing them. Patterns should be compatible in size with the scale of the object being covered; be wary of stripes that may create weird optical effects as they curve over contoured surfaces. Textured fabric should be closely woven—loose weaves wear badly and can snag on jewelry.

Stretched taut to show how they would look in use, patterns for sitting (*top to bottom*) are a silk warp print, a rayon faille with colored satin stripes, a glazed chintz, a linen-cotton check and a ticking-striped cotton duck.

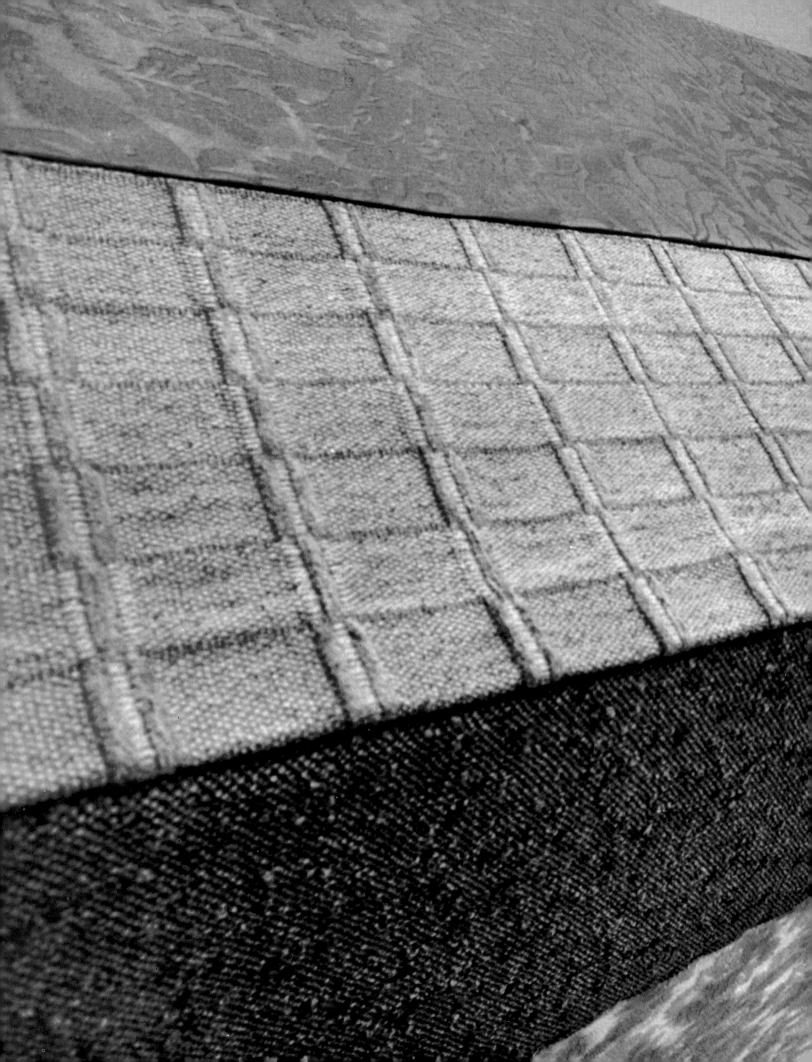

Textures that take well to flat surfaces *(top to bottom)* include an elegant silk damask with a stylized floral motif, thick cotton accented with shiny rayon and chenille, two-tone rayon and cotton tweed, cotton and acetate damask printed on its warp threads alone to give a shadowy effect, and an alternating thick-and thin-waled cotton-rayon corduroy.

A check list for fiber qualities

Since fabrics for the home must last many years, how they will wear is the first question to ask. Such properties as ability to take abrasion, resistance to sunlight and reaction to humidity are often determined by the fiber (or fibers) from which a fabric is made.

The three major categories of fibers are the natural animal and plant fibers; the cellulosics, which are made from plant fibers reduced to a chemical broth and then respun; and the noncellulosic synthetics, most of which are made from petroleum. The chart at right explains the advantages and disadvantages of fibers in each of these categories.

However, in blended or specially treated fabrics, the disadvantages of a fiber are often minimized or canceled out. Also, fibers do not always exhibit the same properties in clothing and furnishings: wool, for instance, wrinkles more when used for clothing than when used for draperies or slipcovers. The chart includes suggestions for adapting each fiber type to specific home furnishings uses, and information on the care of each. Many fibers are washable, but decorators often recommend dry cleaning since all fabrics shrink somewhat in laundering, and slipcovers and draperies often have trims and linings with different washing properties.

FIBER	ADVANTAGES
ACETATE Lustrous cellulose fiber	Drapes well; resists mildew and moths; remains free of static electricity. Economical. Dyes easily, giving a good color range.
ACRYLIC Resilient synthetic fiber (Acrilan, Chemstrand, Orlon, Zefchrome)	Abrasion-resistant; resists mildew, moths, fading and wrinkling; not damaged by sun; easily cared for. Holds color well. Feels soft.
COTTON Absorbent versatile natural plant fiber	Strong and durable; abrasion-resistant; free of static electricity. Feels cool. Easily cared for. Dyes easily, giving excellent color range.
GLASS Nonabsorbent silicate fiber, especially spun for sunproof curtain fabrics (Fiberglas, PPG Fiber Glass)	Resistant to damage by sun, moths and mildew; colorfast. Will not shrink or wrinkle; remains free of static electricity. Flameproof.
LINEN Absorbent, lustrous, natural plant fiber	Strong and durable. Excellent color range. Feels cool. Easy to care for.
MODACRYLIC Nonabsorbent, synthetic fiber noted for resilience; most often used for fake furs (Dynel and Verel)	Resists wrinkles, damage from sun, mildew, moths, acids and alkalis; flameproof. Holds creases well; resists oil and airborne dirt; colorfast. Good color range. May require special care.
NYLON Nonabsorbent, resilient synthetic fiber; exceptionally strong (Antron, Cadon, Caprolan, Enkalure, Qiana)	Durable, abrasion-resistant; resists moths, mildew, oil and airborne dirt. Recovers shape if stretched and resists wrinkling. Dries rapidly. Usually easy to care for. Good color range.
OLEFIN Nonabsorbent synthetic fiber (Herculon, Marvess, Vectra)	Strong, abrasion-resistant; resists moths, mildew, stains and wrinkling. Withstands weather and often recommended for use outdoors.
POLYESTER Nonabsorbent, resilient synthetic fiber (Ancron, Chemstrand, Dacron, Quintess, Trevira, Vycron)	Strong, durable; wrinkle- and abrasion-resistant. Not damaged by moths or mildew. Holds shape well and stays crisp. Resists sunlight. Easily cared for. Dyes moderately well, giving reasonably good color range. Adds easy-care properties to natural fiber blends.
RAYON Absorbent, lustrous cellulose fiber	Drapes well; does not pill; is not affected by bleaches and household chemicals. Excellent color range. Relatively strong. Feels cool.
SARAN Nonabsorbent synthetic fiber	Resists sun, abrasion, fading and mildew; fireproof. Resilient; weatherproof. Often can simply be wiped clean.
SILK Natural animal fiber, absorbent, resilient, lustrous and luxurious	Particularly strong, permitting thin but durable fabrics. Resists mildew and wrinkles. Feels cool. Exceptional color range, on which all other fiber colors are based.
WOOL Exceptionally absorbent and resilient, natural animal fiber	Strong; resilient; resists wrinkles; not damaged by sun. Abrasion-resistant in tightly woven fabrics. Excellent color range. Crease-resistant in home furnishings use.

DISADVANTAGES	SUGGESTIONS FOR USE	CARE
Injured by abrasion; weakened by sunlight; melts at low heat. Dissolved by perfumes and nail polish remover. Fades unless labeled "solution dyed." Usually not washable.	For draperies, interline, or line with sun-reflective fabric. For hard-wear covers, use blends containing a more abrasion-resistant fiber, such as a synthetic.	Dry-clean, unless otherwise labeled. Press with warm iron.
Accumulates static electricity; tends to pill.	Very good for curtains and draperies because it holds its shape. For covers, use blends containing nylon or polyester for firmness. Pile fabrics need special care.	Dry-clean. If labeled washable, launder gently by hand or machine; tumble dry. Use fabric softener to control static electricity.
May wrinkle or shrink, if not treated. Weakened and faded by long exposure to strong sunlight, unless lined; attacked by mildew.	Excellent for all home furnishings. Look for fabric that is preshrunk and treated for crease resistance. Blends with synthetics also tend to crease less.	Dry-clean. If labeled colorfast and preshrunk, may be washed. Press with a medium-hot iron.
Poor abrasion resistance; may crack along folds if creased; may splinter and scratch when handled. Limited color range. Requires special care.	Suitable only for curtains. Do not use for curtains that are touched often, or where small children can handle it or chew it, for glass fibers may scratch.	Wash gently by hand, using rubber gloves; do not twist or fold; hang to dry. Do not press or dry-clean.
Wrinkles easily and shrinks unless treated; subject to mildew and may stretch and shrink in damp climates; may crack along creases. Colors tend to fade in sunlight and intense colors may run in laundering.	Draperies should be lined if placed in direct sun. In damp climates, use a blend that includes a nonabsorbent synthetic fiber; for pleated curtains, use a blend that includes a more resilient fiber.	Launder gently if labeled colorfast and preshrunk; press while damp on both sides to restore luster. Excessive starching makes fiber break. Dry-clean if untreated.
Poor abrasion resistance; not very strong. Melts at low heat; accumulates static electricity.	Excellent for easy-care draperies and curtains. Furlike fabrics require special care.	Dry-clean. If labeled washable, launder gently. Drip dry; press with a cool iron. Furlike fabrics should be dry-cleaned only.
Accumulates static electricity; pills; fades and tends to weaken in sunlight.	Line draperies; use reflective lining with medium and dark colors. For covers, choose a blend that includes an absorbent fiber to aid release of static electricity.	Dry-clean. If labeled washable, launder separately, as nylon picks up other colors. Use fabric softener to control static electricity. Remove from dryer immediately to avoid heat-set wrinkles; press with a warm iron.
Melts at low heat; accumulates static electricity. Retains heat from sun. Limited color range. Requires special care.	Excellent in blends with other synthetics for slipcovers that get heavy use or are exposed to weather.	Dry-clean. If labeled washable, launder gently and dry on low-heat setting, but do not dry in commercial or gas-fired dryers; remove from dryer immediately. Use fabric softener to control static electricity. Pure olefin should never be ironed. Iron blends with a cool iron.
Pills; accumulates static electricity.	The major fiber for easy-care curtains, and the top priority fiber for all home furnishings. For covers, choose a blend with natural fiber for absorbency.	Dry-clean. If labeled washable, launder gently and separate whites from other colors, as polyester picks up loose color easily. Remove from dryer immediately to avoid heat-set wrinkles; press with warm iron. Use fabric softener to control static electricity.
Lacks resilience; injured by abrasion; damaged by sun; attacked by mildew. Wrinkles easily. Cannot be laundered.	For draperies in direct sunlight, interline or use a reflective lining. For covers, choose a blend that contains a stronger fiber for better wear.	Dry-clean only, unless otherwise labeled. Press with a cool iron.
Lacks strength and is stiff; melts at low heat. Limited color range. Requires special care.	Often used alone for curtains and outdoor furniture webbing. In blends, it makes fire-retardant draperies. Must not be used within two inches of heating unit.	Hand wash gently, do not fold or twist; hang to dry. Do not iron. Do not dry-clean.
Weakens and fades in sunlight; damaged by abrasion; spotted by water. Delicate in weights and constructions generally used.	For draperies or curtains in sun, interline, or line with reflecting fabric. Not recommended for slipcovers subject to heavy use.	Dry-clean only. Press with a warm iron.
Shrinks unless labeled shrinkproof; soft weaves may pill under heavy use. Damaged by moths and mildew. Feels warm; may be prickly. Cannot generally be laundered. Tends to accumulate static electricity.	Line and interline loosely woven draperies to retain shape. Use tightly woven fabrics for covers, and blends containing synthetics for added wear.	Dry-clean only. Press with warm iron or steam press.

A glossary of fabric usefulness

The characteristics of a fabric that determine its use in the home may depend less on the fibers from which it is woven (*preceding page*) than on the way these fibers are spun into yarn and woven into cloth—the same fiber can make a diaphanous voile, a rough homespun or an elegant satin. Weight and weave control not only looks but also practicality. Most pile fabrics and satins, for instance, are not recommended for slipcovers on furniture that gets a lot of wear. Sheers, loose weaves and laces are primarily curtain materials, though when stabilized with lining a few are suitable for such applications as bedcovers or pillows, where a coordinated look is wanted.

In the glossary at right the most frequently encountered home furnishings fabrics are categorized according to their usefulness. The sturdiest weave, when closely woven, is the plain weave, in which lengthwise and crosswise yarns crisscross each other evenly, one for one. Less durable weaves are twill and satin weaves, in both of which the lengthwise yarns pass, or "float," over several crosswise yarns (or vice versa). In twill, this float yarn is staggered to create a diagonal effect; in satin, it jumps over as many as eight crosswise yarns, creating a luxuriously smooth surface—but one that "picks" very easily when subjected to any rough object, such as a jewelry clasp.

MULTIPURPOSE FABRICS

These fabrics can be used for curtains, draperies or covers of all kinds. Most wear well and are easy to clean. None are difficult to sew.

Chambray: A durable, medium-weight plain weave traditionally made of cotton. The lengthwise yarn is a color while the crosswise yarn is usually white or off-white; when both yarns are colored, the variation is called iridescent.

Chintz: A crisp, glossy, tightly woven cotton plain weave that, when printed, is often in old-fashioned floral patterns. A coating is applied to give the smooth glazed finish. Also called polished cotton.

Corduroy: A sturdy, medium- to heavyweight plain weave, traditionally cotton, with pronounced pile ribs, called wales, of various widths, running lengthwise.

Cretonne: A medium-weight plain weave printed in patterns similar to chintz (*above*), but not as finely woven and without chintz's glossy finish.

Denim: A heavier twill-weave version of chambray, usually cotton. It is characteristically made of light-colored crosswise yarns and darker lengthwise yarns.

Duck: A strong, medium-to-heavy plain weave made of evenly spun, closely woven yarns; traditionally cotton. Also called sailcloth and, in a heavier weight, canvas.

Gabardine: A durable, medium-weight cloth whose twill weave creates a noticeable diagonal cord or rib; traditionally cotton or wool. A heavier version is called whipcord.

Gingham: A light- to medium-weight plain weave in which lengthwise and crosswise stripes of colored yarn intersect to form a checked pattern; traditionally of cotton.

Herringbone: A medium- to heavyweight fabric whose twill weave alternates to create a distinctive zigzag pattern; traditionally cotton or wool.

Homespun: A fabric made from rough-textured yarn woven to reproduce a loosely woven hand-loomed look. Also called hop sacking, monk's cloth and crash.

Muslin: A serviceable medium-weight plain woven fabric, traditionally made of cotton. Coarse muslin is often used as a basic covering for upholstered furniture. Fine muslin is used for sheeting and printed cloth.

Percale: A finer version of muslin made of fine-combed, closely woven yarn. Often used for quality sheets.

Poplin: A medium-weight plain weave, with a very slight crosswise rib produced by interweaving a heavier crosswise yarn with a finer lengthwise yarn; traditionally cotton; also called ribbed cotton. When it has a more pronounced rib, it is known as rep.

Sateen: A very smooth, sleek medium-weight fabric whose weave creates a lustrous finish. Made in imitation of satin, but more durable and easier to sew; traditionally cotton.

Seersucker: A puckered, light- to medium-weight plain weave with a distinctive pattern of striped or checked puckers; traditionally cotton. A very similar fabric is called plissé.

Ticking: A strong, medium-weight twill weave especially woven for bedding of all kinds; traditionally of cotton. Characteristically, it has a woven pattern of colored stripes of varying widths.

Tweed: A weave made by using rough-textured, randomly

colored yarns. Best known in wool, it is now frequently made of cotton or linen.

LIMITED-USE FABRICS

Less durable than the preceding group, these fabrics are suitable for curtains, draperies, bedcovers and pillows, but they should not be used for slipcovers subject to heavy use. Most of these fabrics require care in sewing. Nap direction must be considered on the pile fabrics, and the slippery satin weaves require careful pinning and basting.

Bouclé: Any fabric made from a nubbly, or bouclé, yarn that gives it a spongy surface.

Brocade: A very formal, medium- to heavyweight satin weave—originally of silk or rayon—with a multicolored woven pattern similar in look to embroidery. When the pattern is raised, the cloth is called brocatel.

Chenille: Any fabric woven from the looped or fuzzy yarn called chenille, producing a textured or piled surface. Most often associated with bedspreads.

Damask: A reversible, medium- to heavyweight satin weave with a woven pattern created by a change in the direction of the long "float" yarns, from lengthwise to crosswise; traditionally cotton, linen or silk.

Faille: A medium-weight plain weave similar to poplin or rep except for the glossy yarn of which it is made.

Moire: A light- to medium-weight faille impressed with a wavy pattern.

Pongee: A nubbly, medium-weight plain weave with an irregular rib produced by uneven crosswise yarns; traditionally made from wild silk in its natural beige color.

Satin: A lustrous fabric, available in many weights, whose lengthwise yarns "float" over many crosswise yarns (or vice versa). One variant, called antique satin, is a double-faced fabric whose textured surface results from a shantung backing.

Shantung: A plain weave with an uneven texture created by a nubbly yarn; traditionally made of a naturally slubbed silk yarn, it is now often reproduced by artificially texturing such yarns as cotton.

Taffeta: A crisp, rustling, tightly woven light- to medium-weight plain weave made from very fine yarn; traditionally made of silk.

Terry cloth: A soft, highly absorbent, medium- to heavyweight fabric with a looped pile; most often used for toweling; traditionally woven of cotton.

Velvet and velours: Smooth, fine-textured medium- to heavyweight fabrics traditionally made of such dissimilar fibers as silk, rayon or linen. In crushed velvet the pile has been crushed by rollers to produce a randomly shadowed textured surface; in cut velvet, a design is created by selectively weaving some areas of the cloth without pile.

Velveteen: A pile fabric similar in appearance to velvet but with more body; usually made of cotton.

CURTAIN AND DRAPERY FABRICS

These fabrics, mostly sheers and loose weaves, are best suited for curtains and draperies. But the function of eyelet or lace can occasionally be extended to coverings that receive little wear, provided that the covering is lined.

Burlap: A rough-textured, medium-weight plain weave made of very coarse, loosely woven yarn, usually jute.

Dotted swiss: A crisp, lightweight sheer plain weave, traditionally cotton, characterized by a pattern of raised dots —woven into cotton, imprinted on synthetics.

Eyelet: An openwork embroidered design on fine-textured, lightweight plain weave; traditionally cotton.

Gauze: A soft, extremely lightweight fabric made of fine, loosely woven yarns; traditionally linen or cotton.

Lace: A fabric made by knotting and interweaving yarns to create designs on a netting background; traditionally linen. The designs are customarily floral in the same color as the net, though abstract designs are also available.

Leno: An open-mesh fabric produced by the special leno weave, which combines airiness with strength. In this weave, pairs of lengthwise yarns, often much thinner than the crosswise ones, intertwine each other over the crosswise yarns, forming figure 8s.

Marquisette: A very fine version of leno (above), usually made of cotton or nylon.

Net: Any open-mesh material, from very fine to very coarse, made of yarns knotted or twisted together in the manner of fishing nets.

Ninon: A soft sheer plain weave made of fine yarns, usually nylon, in a very open mesh.

Organdy: A crisp, airy, almost transparent plain weave, which is made of very fine, closely woven yarn; it is traditionally cotton.

Voile: A soft, fluid plain weave made of fine yarns, closely woven; traditionally cotton. A less fine-textured version is known as scrim.

LINING, INTERLINING AND STIFFENING FABRICS

These fabrics are used to give body and shape to draperies and coverings, and to add such characteristics as sunproofing, lightproofing and extra warmth.

Buckram: A coarse, almost rigid woven fabric made of white cotton or brown jute and stiffened with heavy sizing. Available in various weights. For use in curtain and drapery headings.

Crinoline: A lighter-weight, finer-textured version of buckram; usually made of cotton or a blend, and usually available in white only. For use in curtain or drapery headings.

Flannelette: A soft, napped medium-weight plain weave, most often cotton or a blend. Used mostly for interlining lightweight draperies to give them body and shape.

Nonwoven stiffeners: Fabrics made of matted synthetics that look like a stiff lightweight felt. Available in neutral colors in a wide range of weights, under such brand names as Pellon, Interlon, Nonwoven Shapeflex.

Reflective lining: A medium-weight twill or satin-weave fabric coated on one side with a metallic or white finish that protects draperies by reflecting heat and sunlight.

Sateen lining: A less refined version of the sateen listed under Multipurpose Fabrics (above), available in white or pale neutral shades for lining draperies and covers, and in black for use as a light-blocking interlining.

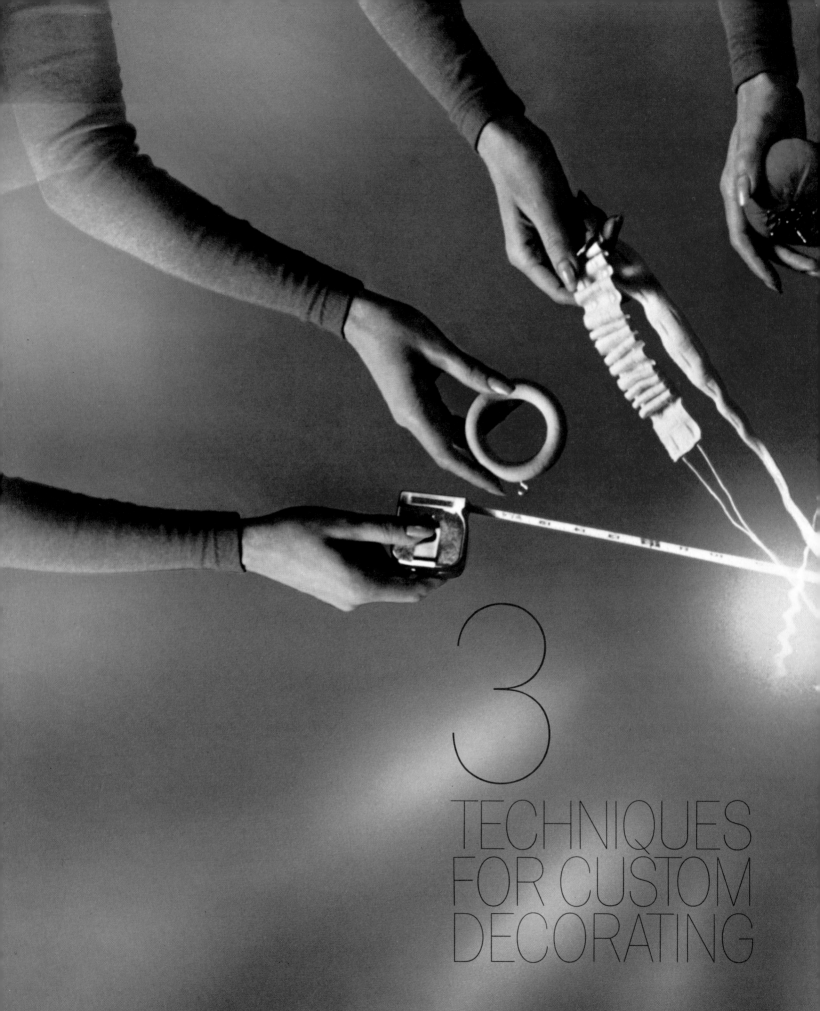

3
TECHNIQUES
FOR CUSTOM
DECORATING

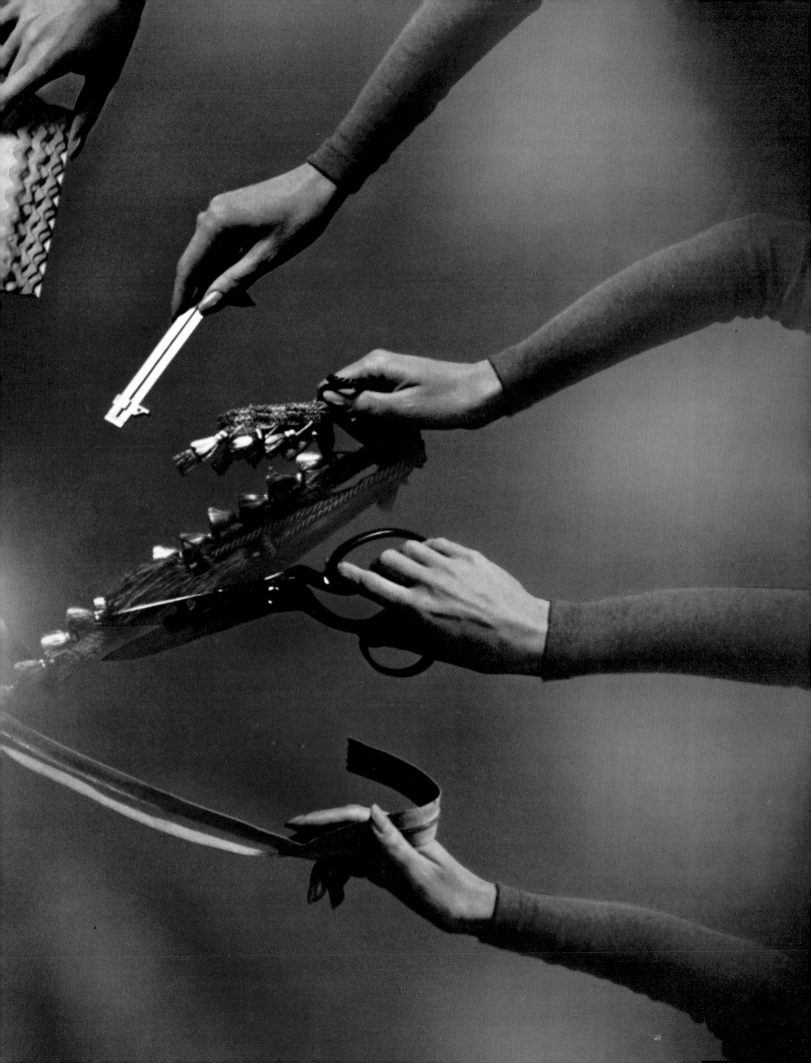

Sometime in the 1950s a Swiss engineer named George de Mestral came home from an Alpine walk to face—like many another hiker since time immemorial—the exasperating chore of ridding his clothing of burrs. Inspired to put one of the burrs under a magnifying glass, de Mestral found the secret of its tenacity: its tiny prickles are hook-shaped, and adhere to cloth. As an engineer, de Mestral was singularly well

THE DETAILS THAT MAKE THE DIFFERENCE

equipped to make a practical application of his discovery, and he went on to invent a new kind of fastener consisting of two tapes —one with hundreds of burrlike hooks, the other with hundreds of loops—that lock when pressed firmly together (the best known is sold under the trade name Velcro). Today his discovery serves to hold in place all sorts of materials, including removable skirts for bedcoverings and swaths of fabrics for valances.

Efficient fasteners such as hook-and-loop strips, heavy-duty zippers and snap tapes are often taken for granted, but they make possible smooth fit and easy removal of fabric coverings for cleaning or even for seasonal changes. Such details and their proper application give home furnishings the extra touches that mark the best work of custom decorators.

Not all of the details of well-made home furnishings are hidden from sight. Some of them form the most visible part of the design while serving practical purposes of structure as well. Pleats and their softer counterparts, shirrings, are used to control the upper edges of curtains and draperies and cause them to fall in graceful folds. If the draperies will be frequently pulled back and forth (opened to let in light during the day and closed to keep out prying eyes at night) pleating or shirring will counteract the tendency of the fabric to bunch, and help to distribute the folds evenly as the draperies are drawn to and fro.

Welting, too, serves a dual purpose. It outlines and defines the contours of cushions, sofas, chairs and bedcovers. But it also serves to reinforce seams and guard against fraying, for the very edges that mark the contours of a chair are the ones that get the most wear. One welcome new item on the market for making welting is polyester cord, which does not shrink as old-fashioned cotton cord does, and therefore withstands washing better.

A dual function is also served by the use of decorative trims such as embroidered tapes or braids with tassels or ball fringe. Not only do they accentuate the color and texture of home furnishings but they can also emphasize the architectural elements of a room. Vertical tapes on Roman shades, for example, increase the feeling of height in a room. Most decorative trims are available in an astonishingly wide spectrum of colors and designs and many of them are shrink-controlled or made with synthetics that will hold their shape in cleaning.

Finally, there are details that simply give a finished look, the decorative touches that add character to a room in which they appear. Dentil edges, for example, with their squared-off regularity, have an architectural and masculine look. Gracefully curving scallops on the other hand suggest femininity. Both lend themselves to firm fabrics such as linen and sailcloth and to unpleated curtains, table covers or bed skirts.

The making of home furnishings begins and ends with these details, visible or invisible, decorative or purely functional. Whether the project is a casual café curtain for a country breakfast room or draperies for a formal dining room, whether the material is gingham at a bargain $1.98 a yard or silk brocade at an extravagant $99.98, it is the care put into the making that separates the custom look from the ready made.

"Even when you use such products as Velcro and snap tapes, patience pays off," says Henrietta Blau, who runs an upholstery and drapery workshop that supplies made-to-order fittings to some of New York's most elegant homes. "Every bit of effort put into the details returns extra dividends of practicality and appearance."

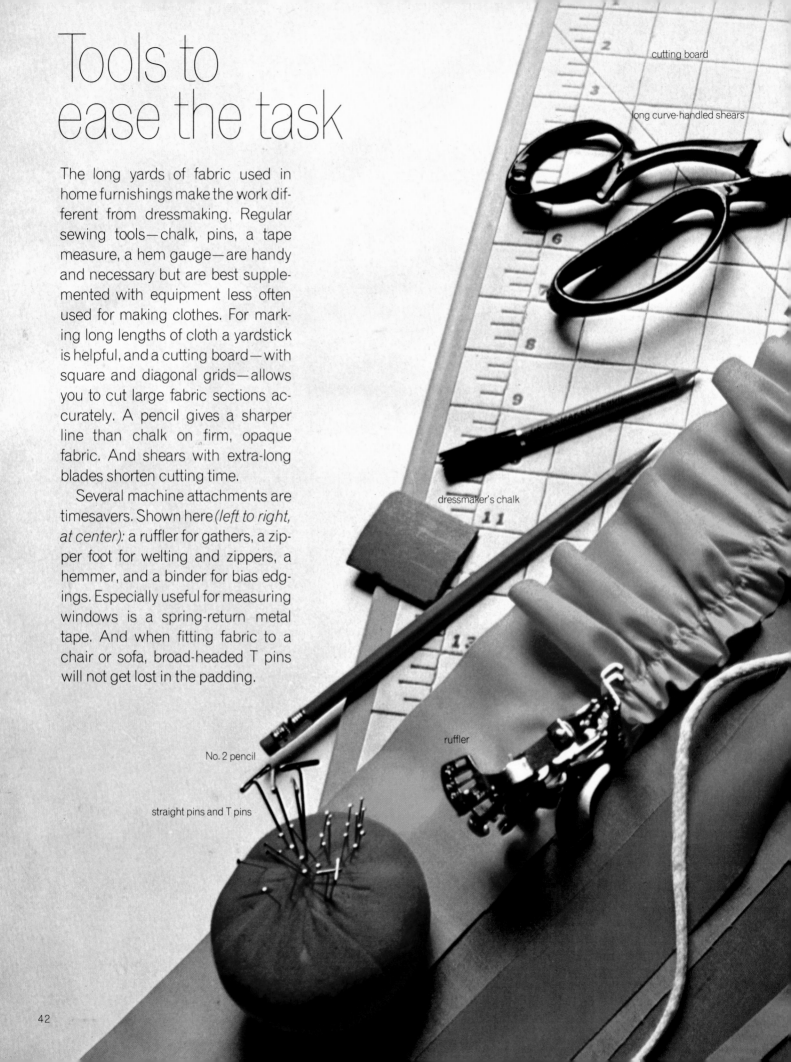

Tools to ease the task

The long yards of fabric used in home furnishings make the work different from dressmaking. Regular sewing tools—chalk, pins, a tape measure, a hem gauge—are handy and necessary but are best supplemented with equipment less often used for making clothes. For marking long lengths of cloth a yardstick is helpful, and a cutting board—with square and diagonal grids—allows you to cut large fabric sections accurately. A pencil gives a sharper line than chalk on firm, opaque fabric. And shears with extra-long blades shorten cutting time.

Several machine attachments are timesavers. Shown here *(left to right, at center):* a ruffler for gathers, a zipper foot for welting and zippers, a hemmer, and a binder for bias edgings. Especially useful for measuring windows is a spring-return metal tape. And when fitting fabric to a chair or sofa, broad-headed T pins will not get lost in the padding.

cutting board

long curve-handled shears

dressmaker's chalk

No. 2 pencil

ruffler

straight pins and T pins

zipper foot

hemmer

binder

metal measuring tape

yardstick

tape measure

hem gauge

Austrian
shade
tape

drapery head
stiffening

pull cording

welt cording

drapery return
ring and hook

tieback hook

curtain
rings

weights

drapery hooks

buckram
stiffening

nonwoven stiffening

reflective
lining

flannel
interlining

Velcro tape

snap tape

Roman
shade
tape

shirring
tape

pleater tape

upholstery
zipper

Indispensable underpinnings

The professional look of slipcovers and draperies comes largely from things never seen. The luxurious body of rich folds and the sleek smoothness of flat surfaces are achieved with a variety of woven and nonwoven stiffeners, linings and interlinings (some do double duty —one reflective lining is a heat insulator). To make draperies hang straight, there are weights, strung on tapes for inserting in hems or used singly to ballast corners.

To simplify the making of home furnishings, there are clip-on curtain rings, tapes prefitted with cording and rings for Roman and Austrian shades, and shirring tapes for gathered curtain headings. One alternative to the luxurious custom pleating explained in this book is ready-made pleater tape, with woven-in pockets that pleat automatically when hooks are slipped into them.

Finally, for achieving smooth fit there are sturdy zippers designed especially for home furnishings, and either snap tape or the intertwining Velcro mesh tape for attaching dust ruffles to box springs or skirts to dressing tables.

45

Useful welting, fancy trims

Welting—whether plain or shirred (as on the pillow at right)—is both a decorative and a practical addition to slipcovers, bedspreads and valances. It delineates the shape like an artist's line. At the same time, it strengthens the seams and reduces wear on the edges of furnishings.

Plain welting is usually cut on the bias, and the tubular method (*page 50*) makes it easy to cut the long lengths needed for slipcovers and bedspreads. Shirred welting (*following page*) is usually cut with the grain and is best made from light- or medium-weight cloth.

For a speedier finishing touch, ready-made trims are an alternative. Ribbon and braid trims are added to the fabric sections before any lining is attached. Fringe can be applied in the same way, but it is also frequently inserted in a seam, like welting.

SHIRRED WELTING

A CUTTING AND JOINING WELTING STRIPS

1. Place the fabric wrong side up and trim off the selvages.

2. To determine the length of the fabric strip required, first measure the seam into which the welting will be sewed and add about 12 inches. Then, for heavy fabrics, double this figure; for lightweight fabrics, triple this figure.

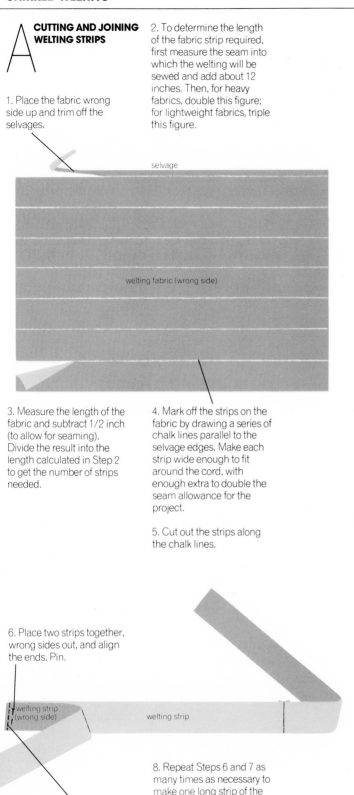

selvage

welting fabric (wrong side)

3. Measure the length of the fabric and subtract 1/2 inch (to allow for seaming). Divide the result into the length calculated in Step 2 to get the number of strips needed.

4. Mark off the strips on the fabric by drawing a series of chalk lines parallel to the selvage edges. Make each strip wide enough to fit around the cord, with enough extra to double the seam allowance for the project.

5. Cut out the strips along the chalk lines.

6. Place two strips together, wrong sides out, and align the ends. Pin.

welting strip (wrong side)

welting strip

7. Machine stitch 1/4 inch inside the ends and remove the pins.

8. Repeat Steps 6 and 7 as many times as necessary to make one long strip of the length required.

9. Press open the seams.

B MAKING THE WELTING

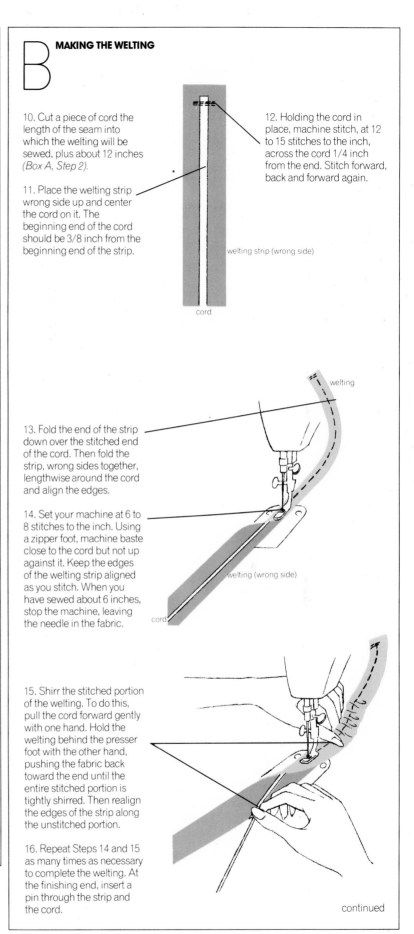

10. Cut a piece of cord the length of the seam into which the welting will be sewed, plus about 12 inches (Box A, Step 2).

11. Place the welting strip wrong side up and center the cord on it. The beginning end of the cord should be 3/8 inch from the beginning end of the strip.

12. Holding the cord in place, machine stitch, at 12 to 15 stitches to the inch, across the cord 1/4 inch from the end. Stitch forward, back and forward again.

welting strip (wrong side)

cord

welting

13. Fold the end of the strip down over the stitched end of the cord. Then fold the strip, wrong sides together, lengthwise around the cord and align the edges.

14. Set your machine at 6 to 8 stitches to the inch. Using a zipper foot, machine baste close to the cord but not up against it. Keep the edges of the welting strip aligned as you stitch. When you have sewed about 6 inches, stop the machine, leaving the needle in the fabric.

welting (wrong side)

cord

15. Shirr the stitched portion of the welting. To do this, pull the cord forward gently with one hand. Hold the welting behind the presser foot with the other hand, pushing the fabric back toward the end until the entire stitched portion is tightly shirred. Then realign the edges of the strip along the unstitched portion.

16. Repeat Steps 14 and 15 as many times as necessary to complete the welting. At the finishing end, insert a pin through the strip and the cord.

continued

ATTACHING THE WELTING TO THE MAIN PROJECT FABRIC

17A. If the welting will end at the edges of the fabric piece or at a hem or seam line, place the main project fabric wrong side down and lay the welting along the edge to be seamed. Align the cut edges of the welting with the project fabric edge and line up the beginning end of the welting against the hemline, seam line or the end of the fabric, as required. Pin at the end.

18A. Set the machine to the normal stitch length and attach a zipper foot.

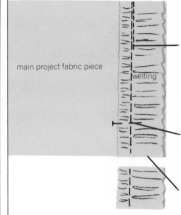

19A. Place the fabric, wrong side down, in the machine and insert the needle at the end of the welting just outside the machine basting.

17B. If the welting will be joined around a continuous edge, place the main project fabric piece wrong side down and select an unobtrusive place for the joining, such as the center back on a cushion. Do not join at a corner. Place the beginning of the welting at the place selected for the joining and align the cut edges with the fabric edge. Pin at the end.

18B. Set the machine to the normal stitch length and attach a zipper foot.

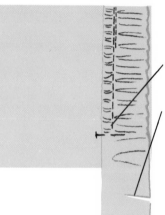

19B. Place the fabric, wrong side down, in the machine and insert the needle 2 inches from the end of the welting just outside the machine basting.

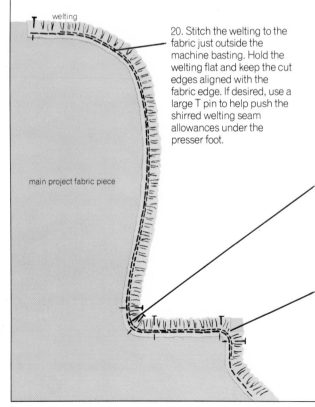

20. Stitch the welting to the fabric just outside the machine basting. Hold the welting flat and keep the cut edges aligned with the fabric edge. If desired, use a large T pin to help push the shirred welting seam allowances under the presser foot.

21. Stretch the welting seam allowances around outside curves and ease them slightly around inside curves. Keep the cut edges aligned with the fabric edge.

22. To attach the welting around an inside corner, stop the machine 1 inch from the corner, leaving the needle in the fabric. Shape the welting with your hand, pinching the cord into a point at the corner. Pin. Sew straight to within a few stitches of the corner, then stitch in a sharp curve —pivoting several times.

23. To attach the welting around an outside corner, follow Step 22, but before shaping the welting with your hand, clip the welting seam allowances 1/2 inch from the corner—cutting up to but not into the machine basting.

ENDING THE WELTING AT A FABRIC EDGE

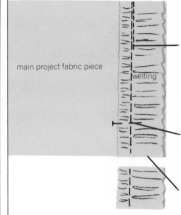

24. If the welting will be joined around a continuous edge, skip to Box E. To end the welting at a seam, hemline or fabric edge, stop the machine 2 inches before that point, leaving the needle in the fabric.

25. Insert a pin into the welting strip fabric and through the cord about 1/2 inch from the desired ending point.

26. Trim off the welting at the desired ending point.

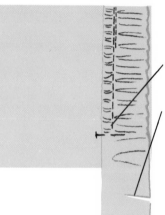

27. Pull out the welting strip fabric beyond the pin, eliminating the shirring.

28. Remove the machine basting on the welting up to the pin.

29. Trim the welting strip fabric 3/8 inch beyond the desired ending point.

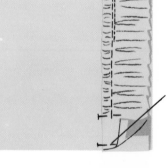

30. Open out the welting strip and fold the end over the end of the cord. Then refold the strip around the cord and align the cut edges.

31. Insert a pin into the welting strip and through the cord near the folded end. Then remove the pin inserted in Step 25.

32. Adjust the shirring so that it continues to the end of the welting.

33. Machine stitch the remaining portion of the welting. Remove all pins. Skip to Box F.

JOINING THE WELTING AROUND A CONTINUOUS EDGE

34. Stop the machine 2 inches before reaching the joining point, leaving the needle in the fabric.

37. Pull out the welting strip fabric beyond the pin, eliminating the shirring.

38. Remove the machine basting on the welting from the pin to the cut end.

39. Open out the end of the welting strip.

42. Fold under the cut end of the welting strip fabric 1/4 inch.

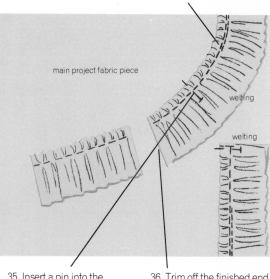

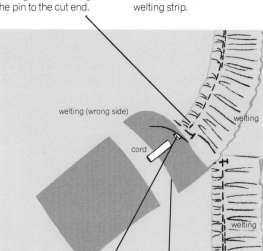

35. Insert a pin into the welting strip fabric and through the cord about 1/4 inch before the point where the two ends of the welting will be joined.

36. Trim off the finished end of the welting 3/4 inch beyond the joining point.

40. Trim the end of the cord so that it will butt against the beginning end of the welting when the two are joined.

41. Trim the finishing end of the welting strip fabric 3/4 inch beyond the joining point.

43. Lap the folded finishing end of the welting around the beginning end. Pin.

44. Machine stitch the open portion of the welting and remove the pins.

ATTACHING THE SECOND LAYER OF PROJECT FABRIC

45. Place the welted fabric piece wrong side down and lay the second project fabric piece, wrong side up, on it. Align the edges to be seamed.

46. Pin along these edges. Insert the pins so they enter and emerge from the fabric on either side of the ridge formed by the corded part of the welting. Pins should not catch the first, or bottom, layer of fabric.

47. Turn the project so that the first, or welted, fabric piece faces up.

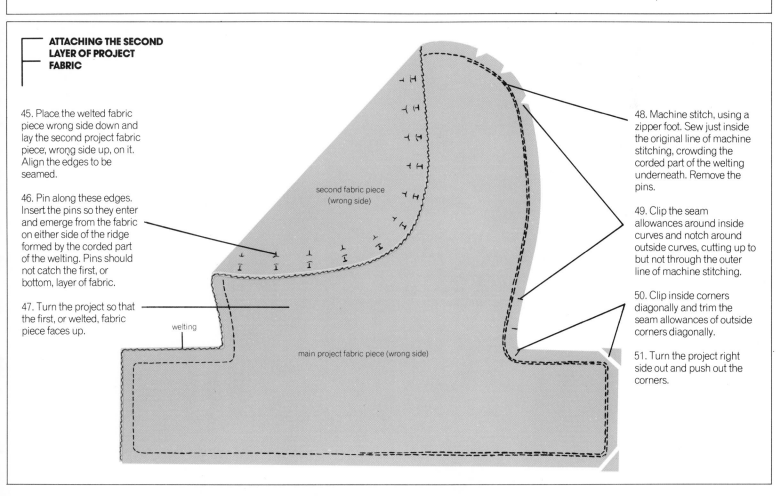

48. Machine stitch, using a zipper foot. Sew just inside the original line of machine stitching, crowding the corded part of the welting underneath. Remove the pins.

49. Clip the seam allowances around inside curves and notch around outside curves, cutting up to but not through the outer line of machine stitching.

50. Clip inside corners diagonally and trim the seam allowances of outside corners diagonally.

51. Turn the project right side out and push out the corners.

PLAIN WELTING

A MAKING BIAS STRIPS FOR SMALL AMOUNTS OF WELTING

1. To determine the total length of the fabric strip needed, measure the seam into which the welting will be sewed. Then add about 12 inches.

2. Fold the fabric for the welting diagonally, wrong sides together. Make sure the fold is on the true bias (Glossary). Pin the edges.

3. Cut along the diagonal fold. Remove the pins and the top piece of fabric, then trim off both selvages.

4. Measure the length of the diagonal edge and subtract 1/2 inch (to allow for seaming). Divide the result into the length calculated in Step 1 to get the number of strips needed.

5. Mark off the number of strips determined in Step 4 by drawing a series of chalk lines parallel to the diagonal edge. Make each strip wide enough to fit around the cord, with enough extra for double the seam allowance of the project.

6. Mark a 1/4-inch seam allowance across the ends of all the strips.

7. Cut out the strips along the diagonal chalk lines.

8. Place two strips together, wrong sides out, and align the seam lines so that the strips form a V. Pin.

9. Machine stitch along the seam lines and remove the pins.

10. Repeat Steps 8 and 9 as many times as necessary to make one long strip of the length required.

11. Press open the seams and trim the extended points of the seam allowances.

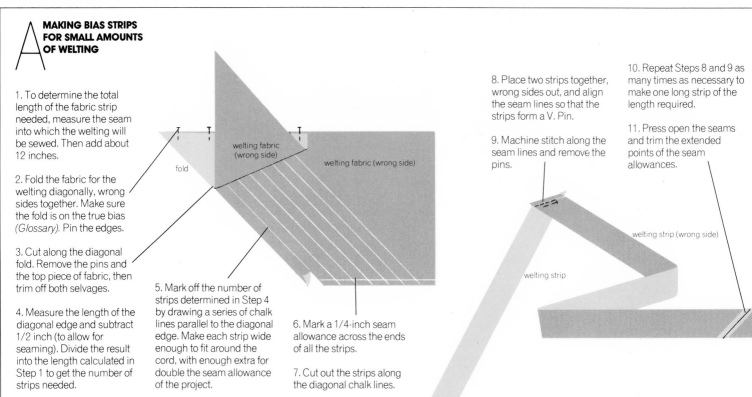

B MAKING BIAS STRIPS FOR LARGE AMOUNTS OF WELTING

12. Prepare the fabric as shown in Box A, Steps 1-6, but mark off strips all the way to the bottom right corner of the fabric.

13. Trim off the unmarked triangular portion of the fabric along the last diagonal chalk line.

14. With the wrong sides out, pin together the shorter ends of the fabric piece along the seam lines. Match at the markings for each strip and be sure that one strip width extends beyond each edge.

15. Machine stitch along the seam lines and remove the pins.

16. Press open the seam.

17. Cut along the markings around the cylinder to form one long strip.

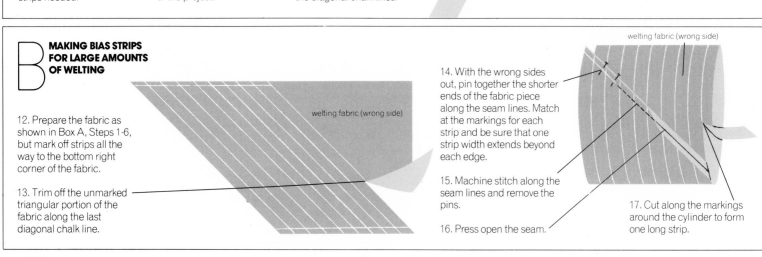

C MAKING THE WELTING

18. Cut a piece of welting cord and a fabric strip the length needed (Box A, Step 1).

19. Place the fabric strip wrong side up. Center the cord on the strip with the first end 3/8 inch from the end of the fabric. Then fold the end of the strip down 3/8 inch over the end of the cord.

20. Fold the fabric strip, wrong sides together, around the cord and align the edges. Pin at the end.

21. Using a zipper foot, machine baste at 6 to 8 stitches to the inch, close to the cord but not up against it, as shown for shirred welting (Box B, Step 14). Hold the edges to keep them aligned as you stitch.

D ATTACHING THE WELTING

22A. If the welting will end at the edges of the fabric or at a hem or seam line, begin to attach it following the directions for shirred welting (page 48, Box C, Steps 17A-19A).

22B. If the welting will be joined around a continuous edge, begin to attach it, as shown for shirred welting (page 48, Box C, Steps 17B-19B), but leave several inches of welting extending beyond the joining point and insert the needle 2 inches from the joining point.

23. Stitch the welting to the main fabric piece as shown for shirred welting (page 48, Box D, Steps 20-23).

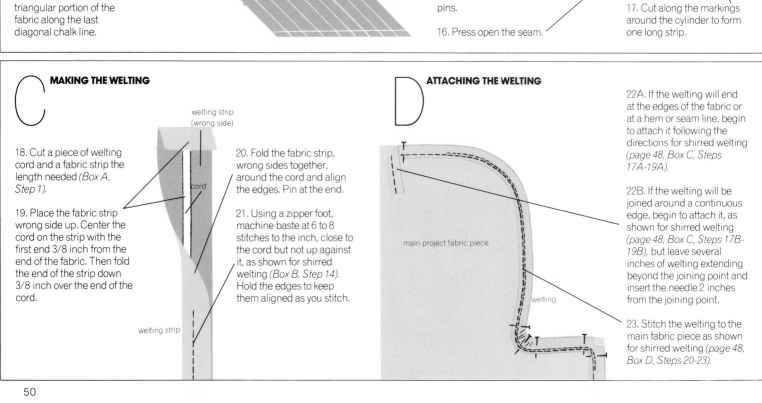

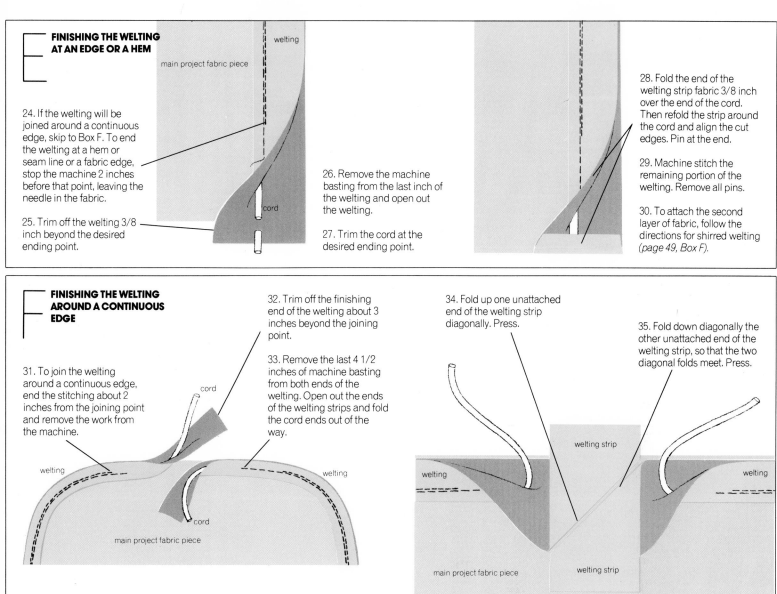

FINISHING THE WELTING AT AN EDGE OR A HEM

welting

main project fabric piece

cord

24. If the welting will be joined around a continuous edge, skip to Box F. To end the welting at a hem or seam line or a fabric edge, stop the machine 2 inches before that point, leaving the needle in the fabric.

25. Trim off the welting 3/8 inch beyond the desired ending point.

26. Remove the machine basting from the last inch of the welting and open out the welting.

27. Trim the cord at the desired ending point.

28. Fold the end of the welting strip fabric 3/8 inch over the end of the cord. Then refold the strip around the cord and align the cut edges. Pin at the end.

29. Machine stitch the remaining portion of the welting. Remove all pins.

30. To attach the second layer of fabric, follow the directions for shirred welting (page 49, Box F).

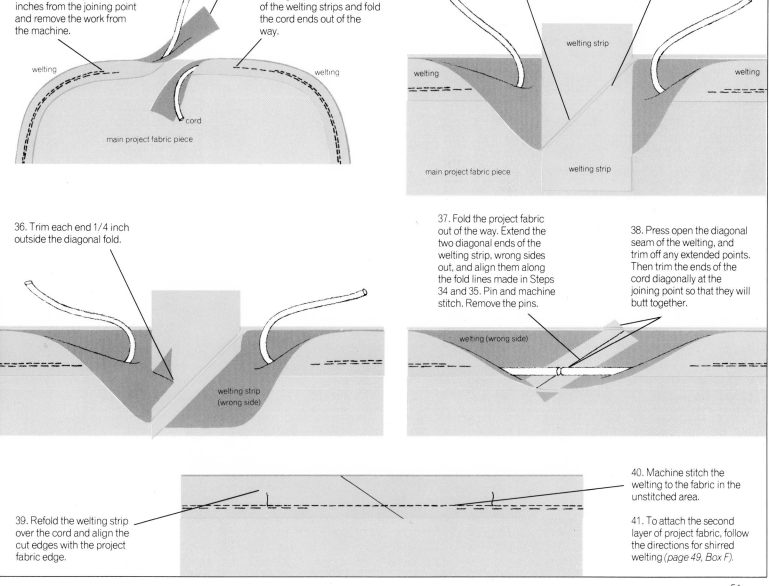

FINISHING THE WELTING AROUND A CONTINUOUS EDGE

31. To join the welting around a continuous edge, end the stitching about 2 inches from the joining point and remove the work from the machine.

32. Trim off the finishing end of the welting about 3 inches beyond the joining point.

33. Remove the last 4 1/2 inches of machine basting from both ends of the welting. Open out the ends of the welting strips and fold the cord ends out of the way.

cord

welting

welting

cord

main project fabric piece

34. Fold up one unattached end of the welting strip diagonally. Press.

35. Fold down diagonally the other unattached end of the welting strip, so that the two diagonal folds meet. Press.

welting strip

welting

welting

main project fabric piece

welting strip

36. Trim each end 1/4 inch outside the diagonal fold.

welting strip (wrong side)

37. Fold the project fabric out of the way. Extend the two diagonal ends of the welting strip, wrong sides out, and align them along the fold lines made in Steps 34 and 35. Pin and machine stitch. Remove the pins.

welting (wrong side)

38. Press open the diagonal seam of the welting, and trim off any extended points. Then trim the ends of the cord diagonally at the joining point so that they will butt together.

39. Refold the welting strip over the cord and align the cut edges with the project fabric edge.

40. Machine stitch the welting to the fabric in the unstitched area.

41. To attach the second layer of project fabric, follow the directions for shirred welting (page 49, Box F).

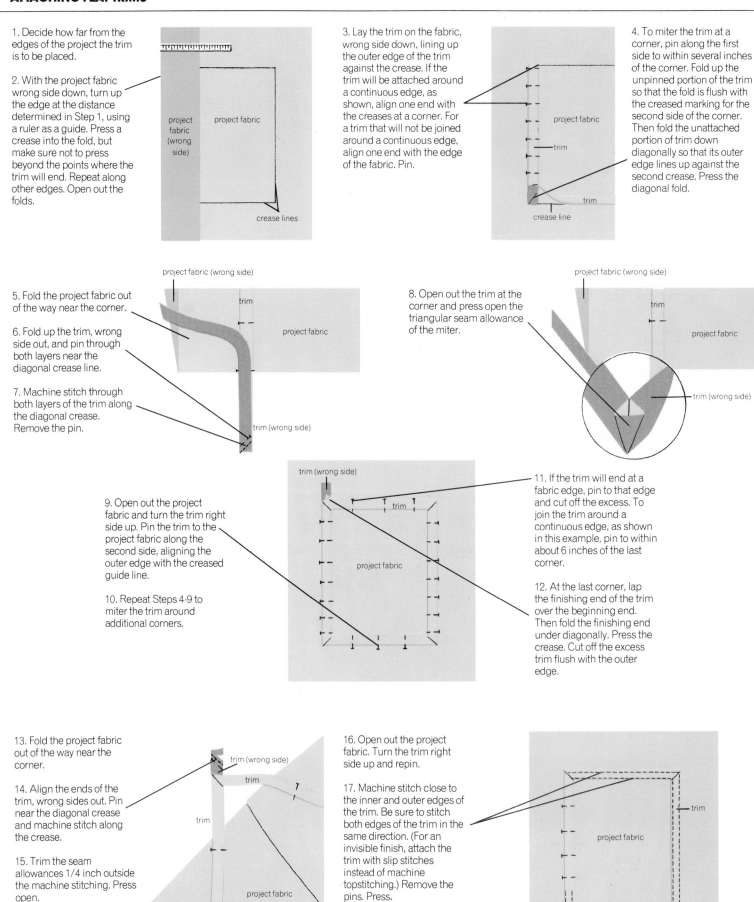

1. Decide how far from the edges of the project the trim is to be placed.

2. With the project fabric wrong side down, turn up the edge at the distance determined in Step 1, using a ruler as a guide. Press a crease into the fold, but make sure not to press beyond the points where the trim will end. Repeat along other edges. Open out the folds.

3. Lay the trim on the fabric, wrong side down, lining up the outer edge of the trim against the crease. If the trim will be attached around a continuous edge, as shown, align one end with the creases at a corner. For a trim that will not be joined around a continuous edge, align one end with the edge of the fabric. Pin.

4. To miter the trim at a corner, pin along the first side to within several inches of the corner. Fold up the unpinned portion of the trim so that the fold is flush with the creased marking for the second side of the corner. Then fold the unattached portion of trim down diagonally so that its outer edge lines up against the second crease. Press the diagonal fold.

5. Fold the project fabric out of the way near the corner.

6. Fold up the trim, wrong side out, and pin through both layers near the diagonal crease line.

7. Machine stitch through both layers of the trim along the diagonal crease. Remove the pin.

8. Open out the trim at the corner and press open the triangular seam allowance of the miter.

9. Open out the project fabric and turn the trim right side up. Pin the trim to the project fabric along the second side, aligning the outer edge with the creased guide line.

10. Repeat Steps 4-9 to miter the trim around additional corners.

11. If the trim will end at a fabric edge, pin to that edge and cut off the excess. To join the trim around a continuous edge, as shown in this example, pin to within about 6 inches of the last corner.

12. At the last corner, lap the finishing end of the trim over the beginning end. Then fold the finishing end under diagonally. Press the crease. Cut off the excess trim flush with the outer edge.

13. Fold the project fabric out of the way near the corner.

14. Align the ends of the trim, wrong sides out. Pin near the diagonal crease and machine stitch along the crease.

15. Trim the seam allowances 1/4 inch outside the machine stitching. Press open.

16. Open out the project fabric. Turn the trim right side up and repin.

17. Machine stitch close to the inner and outer edges of the trim. Be sure to stitch both edges of the trim in the same direction. (For an invisible finish, attach the trim with slip stitches instead of machine topstitching.) Remove the pins. Press.

FRINGED TRIM

A ENCLOSING FRINGED TRIM IN A SEAM

1. Decide how much of the fringed trim heading you wish to be visible on the finished project. Subtract this figure from the total width of the heading.

2. To determine how far from the edge of the project fabric to place the edge of the fringe heading, subtract the figure arrived at in Step 1 from the width of the project seam allowance.

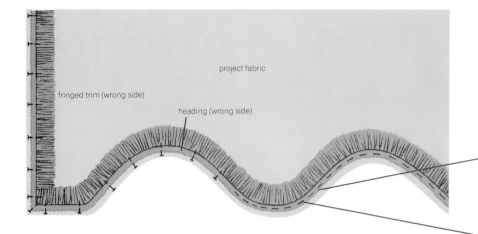

3. Place the project wrong side down. Place the trim, wrong side up, on the project, with the heading edge of the trim closest to the fabric edge. Align the edge of the heading at the distance from the fabric edge determined in Step 2. Pin.

4. At corners, pinch the heading into a point.

5. Stretch the heading slightly around outside curves, and ease it slightly around inside curves.

6. Machine baste the trim to the fabric at 6 to 8 stitches to the inch. Sew 3/8 inch or 1/2 inch inside the fabric edge, depending on the width of the seam allowance of the project.

7. Place the facing or lining for the project wrong side down and place the trimmed fabric on top of it, wrong side up. Align the edges to be seamed. Pin.

8. Machine stitch at the normal stitch length just inside the line of machine basting made in Step 6. At corners, pivot and take several stitches across the point. Remove the pins.

9. Trim the seam allowances diagonally at corners.

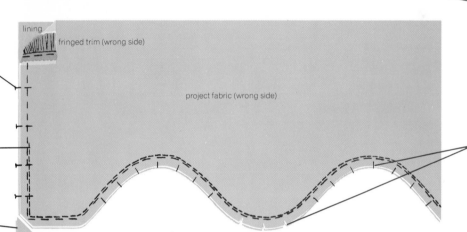

10. Clip the seam allowances around inside curves and notch them around outside curves.

11. Turn the project right side out and push out the corners. Press.

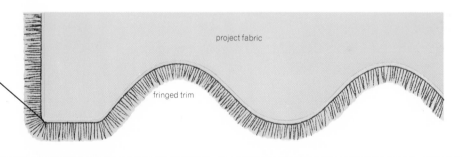

B ADDING FRINGED TRIM TO THE OUTSIDE OF THE PROJECT

12. If the fringed trim will be attached by hand with slip stitches, attach the facing or lining to the project before adding the trim. If the trim will be machine stitched to the project, sew it in place before attaching the facing or lining.

13. Place the lined or unlined project wrong side down and lay the trim on it, wrong side down, with the fringed portion outward. Align the edge of the heading at the desired location—usually near the finished edge or the seam line so that the fringe will extend partially or fully beyond the fabric. Pin.

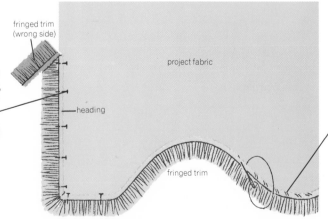

14. At corners, pinch the heading into a point.

15. Ease the heading slightly around outside curves and stretch it slightly around inside curves.

16. Attach the trim by hand with slip stitches or with machine topstitching. Remove the pins.

Shirring and ruffles

For prettiness nothing compares to shirring and ruffles, both of which release fullness into a froth of dainty folds. Shirring need not be as fragile as it looks. If gathered over rows of encased cording, as shown here, backed with a stiffening material and tucked to anchor drapery hooks, it is completely stabilized and forms one of the most luxurious drapery finishes imaginable.

Both shirring and ruffles work best on light- and medium-weight fabrics and, depending upon the weight, generally need fabric two and a half times the finished width. Shirring is used primarily for controlling the fullness of curtains and valances; ruffles can either skirt a slipcover or bedspread, or they can softly trim curtains and pillows.

HANDMADE SHIRRING WITH A BANDED BACKING

A ‖ PREPARING THE FABRIC

1. To calculate the width of fabric the shirring will require, determine the width of the area the shirring must cover. Multiply that figure by two and a half and add whatever seam allowances the project requires.

2. To calculate the length of fabric required, decide how many rows of shirring you want and how high each row will be. Multiply these figures, then add the height of the heading plus 1/2 inch for two cords on the first shirring row and 1/4 inch for one cord on each additional row. Multiply this sum by two to determine how much fabric to add to the length of the project.

3. Complete the project up to the point where the side seams are hemmed. Then spread out the project fabric, wrong side up, with the top edge nearest you.

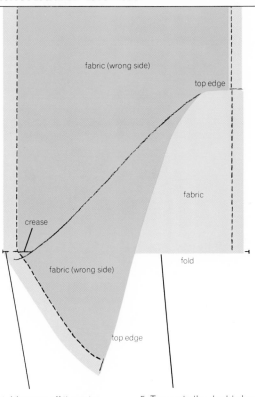

4. Measure off the extra length allowance figured in Step 2 from the top edge of the fabric down each side seam and insert a pin.

5. To create the double hem required for shirring, first fold up the fabric at the pins and press a crease into the fold. Remove the pins.

6. Unfold the fabric, then fold it up again—this time to the crease made in the previous step. Press.

7. Fold the doubled fabric on the first crease. Press.

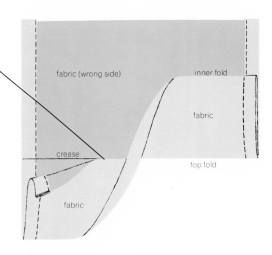

8. If a design on the back layers of the hem will show through the front on the finished project, cut out a piece of solid-colored fabric about 1/4 inch smaller than the hem in both dimensions. Slip the solid-colored fabric between the doubled hem and the front fabric.

9. Pin the hem along the inner fold.

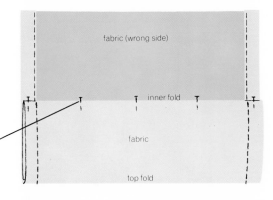

B ‖ INSERTING THE CORD

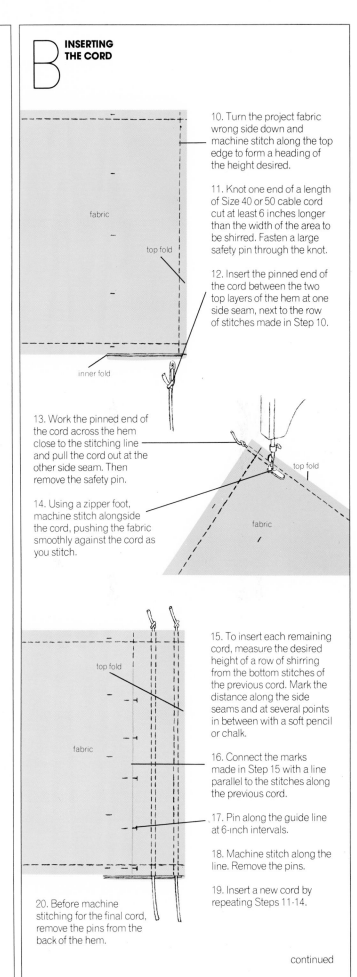

10. Turn the project fabric wrong side down and machine stitch along the top edge to form a heading of the height desired.

11. Knot one end of a length of Size 40 or 50 cable cord cut at least 6 inches longer than the width of the area to be shirred. Fasten a large safety pin through the knot.

12. Insert the pinned end of the cord between the two top layers of the hem at one side seam, next to the row of stitches made in Step 10.

13. Work the pinned end of the cord across the hem close to the stitching line and pull the cord out at the other side seam. Then remove the safety pin.

14. Using a zipper foot, machine stitch alongside the cord, pushing the fabric smoothly against the cord as you stitch.

15. To insert each remaining cord, measure the desired height of a row of shirring from the bottom stitches of the previous cord. Mark the distance along the side seams and at several points in between with a soft pencil or chalk.

16. Connect the marks made in Step 15 with a line parallel to the stitches along the previous cord.

17. Pin along the guide line at 6-inch intervals.

18. Machine stitch along the line. Remove the pins.

19. Insert a new cord by repeating Steps 11-14.

20. Before machine stitching for the final cord, remove the pins from the back of the hem.

continued

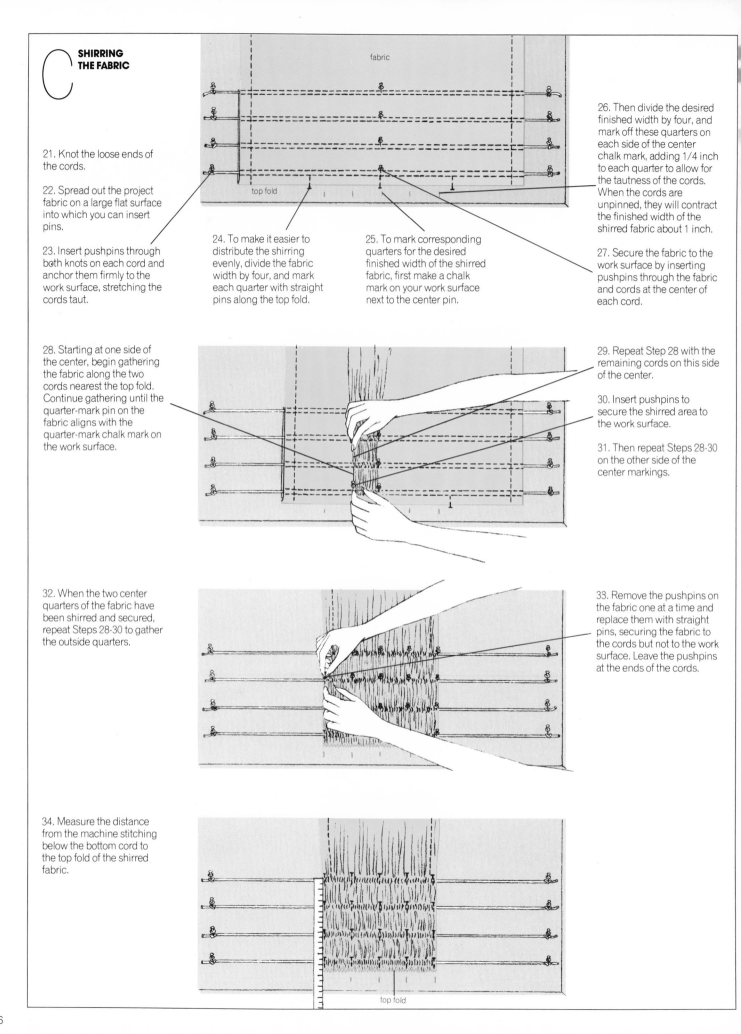

21. Knot the loose ends of the cords.

22. Spread out the project fabric on a large flat surface into which you can insert pins.

23. Insert pushpins through both knots on each cord and anchor them firmly to the work surface, stretching the cords taut.

24. To make it easier to distribute the shirring evenly, divide the fabric width by four, and mark each quarter with straight pins along the top fold.

25. To mark corresponding quarters for the desired finished width of the shirred fabric, first make a chalk mark on your work surface next to the center pin.

26. Then divide the desired finished width by four, and mark off these quarters on each side of the center chalk mark, adding 1/4 inch to each quarter to allow for the tautness of the cords. When the cords are unpinned, they will contract the finished width of the shirred fabric about 1 inch.

27. Secure the fabric to the work surface by inserting pushpins through the fabric and cords at the center of each cord.

28. Starting at one side of the center, begin gathering the fabric along the two cords nearest the top fold. Continue gathering until the quarter-mark pin on the fabric aligns with the quarter-mark chalk mark on the work surface.

29. Repeat Step 28 with the remaining cords on this side of the center.

30. Insert pushpins to secure the shirred area to the work surface.

31. Then repeat Steps 28-30 on the other side of the center markings.

32. When the two center quarters of the fabric have been shirred and secured, repeat Steps 28-30 to gather the outside quarters.

33. Remove the pushpins on the fabric one at a time and replace them with straight pins, securing the fabric to the cords but not to the work surface. Leave the pushpins at the ends of the cords.

34. Measure the distance from the machine stitching below the bottom cord to the top fold of the shirred fabric.

D MAKING THE BANDED BACKING

35A. For a curtain, cut stiffening material (drapery-weight Pellon or buckram) to the distance measured in Step 34 and wide enough to allow 1/2-inch tucks for curtain pins. To determine the width, subtract 4 inches from the finished width of shirred fabric. Divide by four and a half for sheer fabric, by five for nonsheer; count a fraction as one. Then divide by two; add this to the width of the finished shirred fabric.

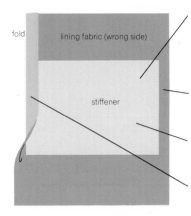

35B. If the project is not a curtain, cut a piece of stiffening material as deep as the distance measured in Step 34 and as wide as the finished shirred fabric.

36. Cut a piece of lining fabric twice as deep as the stiffener plus 1/2 inch, and as wide as the stiffener plus 2 inches.

37. To form the banded backing, first center the stiffener on the lining fabric.

38. Fold the sides of the lining fabric over the stiffener.

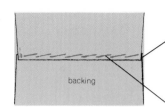

39. Fold the top and bottom of the lining over the stiffener, angling in the folded edges slightly. The top and bottom edges will overlap 1/2 inch. Press.

40. Run a line of diagonal basting stitches (*Appendix*) along the overlapped area, catching only the lining fabric, not the stiffener. If the project is not a curtain, skip to Step 45.

41. If the project is a curtain, mark the tucks and the spaces between them with pins along the top edge of the unbasted side of the banded backing. Insert the first pin 4 inches from the side seam that will be at the center of the curtain, the second pin 1/2 inch farther from the seam to indicate the first tuck. Insert pins at 4 1/2-inch and 1/2-inch intervals for sheer fabric, 5-inch and 1/2-inch intervals if the fabric is nonsheer.

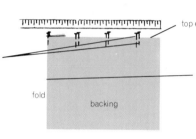

42. Fold each 1/2-inch-wide tuck area in half lengthwise. Remove the pins, and repin through the two folded layers.

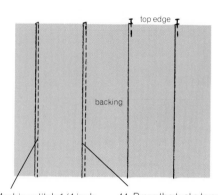

43. Machine stitch 1/4 inch from the folds of all the tucks from the top edge to the bottom of the backing.

44. Press the tucks to one side.

E ATTACHING THE BACKING TO THE SHIRRED FABRIC

45. Slide the backing, basted side up, under the shirred fabric. The top of the shirred fabric should extend 1/4 inch beyond the backing.

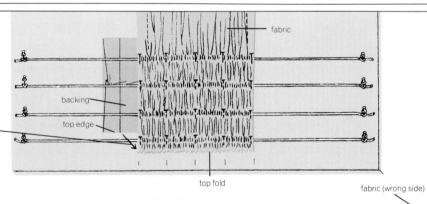

46. Pin the shirred fabric to the backing along the top and bottom cords.

47. Cut the cords, leaving 4-inch loose ends.

48. Using a zipper foot, machine stitch along the top of the cord nearest the upper edge of the project. Then stitch along the top of the bottom cord. Stitch an inch at a time, flattening the fabric as you go. Remove the pins inserted in Step 46.

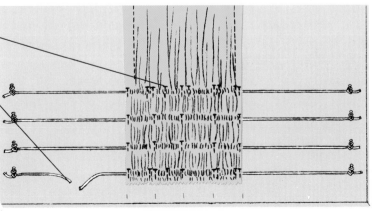

49. Cut off the ends of the cords to 1/2 inch.

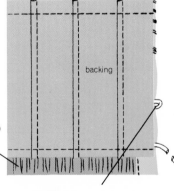

50. Tuck the end of each cord between the shirred fabric and the backing.

51. Tack (*Glossary*) the end of each cord to the shirred fabric and backing. Remove all remaining pins.

52. Slip stitch (*Appendix*) the side edges.

continued

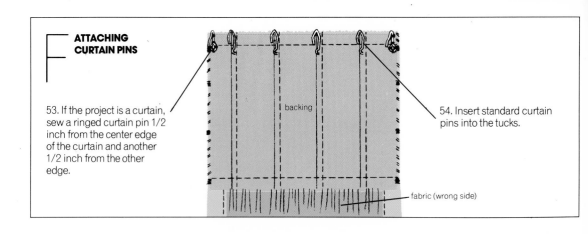

F ATTACHING CURTAIN PINS

53. If the project is a curtain, sew a ringed curtain pin 1/2 inch from the center edge of the curtain and another 1/2 inch from the other edge.

54. Insert standard curtain pins into the tucks.

backing

fabric (wrong side)

THE RUFFLE WITH A HEADING

A PREPARING THE RUFFLE FABRIC

1. To calculate the width of fabric needed for a ruffle with a heading, decide how high the ruffle and heading will be and add a total of 1/2 inch for the top and bottom double hems.

2. To calculate the length of fabric needed, multiply the desired finished length by two and a half if the fabric is lightweight, by three if the fabric is sheer. Then add a total of 2 inches for double hems at both sides if the ends of the ruffle will be finished or 1 inch for seam allowances if the ends will be inserted into seams.

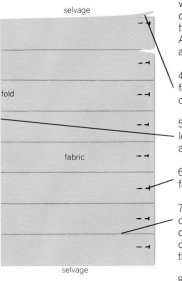

selvage

fold

fabric

selvage

3. To determine the number of strips you will need for the ruffle, divide the length calculated in Step 2 by the width of the fabric if it has a design, or by the length of the fabric if it does not. Allow 1/2 inch for seam allowances on each strip.

4. Straighten the grain of the fabric (page 88) and trim off the selvages.

5. Fold the fabric in half lengthwise if it has a design and crosswise if it does not.

6. Pin together the edges of fabric opposite the fold.

7. Mark off the strips calculated in Step 3 by drawing a series of parallel chalk lines at right angles to the fold.

8. Cut along the chalk lines. Remove the pins.

9. Join the strips with 1/8-inch French seams (Glossary) or with narrow hemmed seams. To make the hemmed seams, use a narrow-hemmer foot. Place two strips, right sides together, with the end of the bottom strip extending 1/8 inch beyond the end of the top strip. Press the seams.

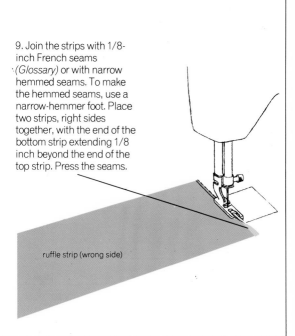

ruffle strip (wrong side)

B HEMMING THE RUFFLE STRIP

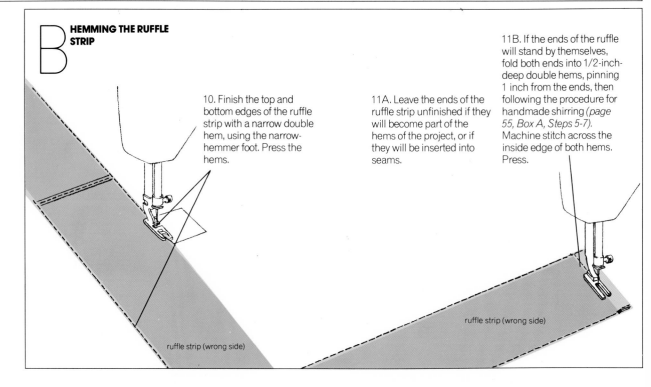

10. Finish the top and bottom edges of the ruffle strip with a narrow double hem, using the narrow-hemmer foot. Press the hems.

11A. Leave the ends of the ruffle strip unfinished if they will become part of the hems of the project, or if they will be inserted into seams.

11B. If the ends of the ruffle will stand by themselves, fold both ends into 1/2-inch-deep double hems, pinning 1 inch from the ends, then following the procedure for handmade shirring (page 55, Box A, Steps 5-7). Machine stitch across the inside edge of both hems. Press.

ruffle strip (wrong side)

ruffle strip (wrong side)

GATHERING AND ATTACHING THE RUFFLE STRIP

12A. To gather the ruffle strip with a ruffler attachment, place the strip wrong side down and stitch across the top edge at a distance equal to the desired depth of the ruffle heading.

12B. To gather the ruffle by hand, machine baste at 6 stitches to the inch with nylon thread. Stitch across the top edge at a distance equal to the desired depth of the ruffle heading, then pull the bobbin thread to create the desired fullness.

13. If the ends of the ruffle will be inserted into seams, reduce their bulkiness by pulling out 1/2 inch of the ruffling at each end. If the ends will become part of the hems of the project, pull out enough ruffling to equal the depth of the hems.

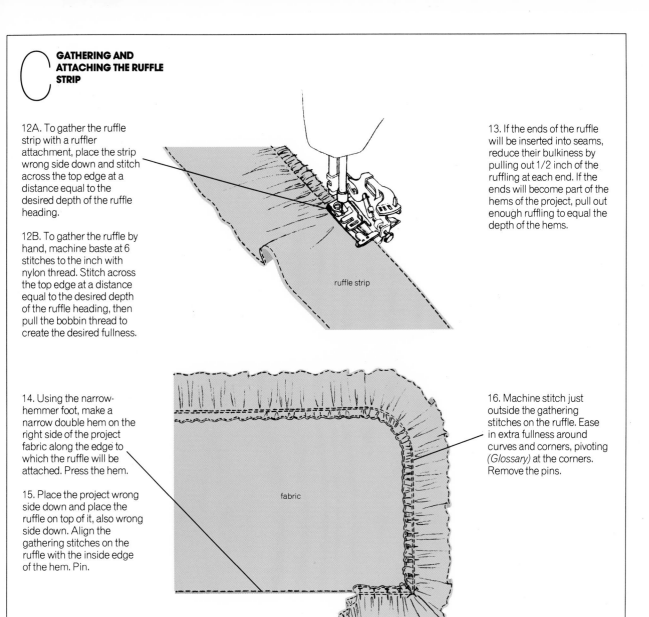

ruffle strip

14. Using the narrow-hemmer foot, make a narrow double hem on the right side of the project fabric along the edge to which the ruffle will be attached. Press the hem.

15. Place the project wrong side down and place the ruffle on top of it, also wrong side down. Align the gathering stitches on the ruffle with the inside edge of the hem. Pin.

fabric

16. Machine stitch just outside the gathering stitches on the ruffle. Ease in extra fullness around curves and corners, pivoting (*Glossary*) at the corners. Remove the pins.

THE RUFFLE WITHOUT A HEADING

1. To prepare the fabric for a ruffle without a heading, follow the instructions for a ruffle with a heading (*opposite, Box A*) with one exception: To determine the total width of the fabric needed, add 3 inches for a double hem and 1/2 inch for a seam allowance.

2. Fold the bottom edge of the ruffle into a 1 1/2-inch-deep double hem, pinning 3 inches from the bottom edge, then following the procedure for handmade shirring (*page 55, Box A, Steps 5-7*).

3. Machine stitch the bottom hem and press it.

4A. Leave the ends of the ruffle unfinished if they will become part of the hems of the project, or if they will be inserted into seams.

4B. If the ends of the ruffle will stand by themselves, fold the ends into 1/2-inch double hems. Machine stitch and press.

5. Gather the ruffle by following the procedure for a ruffle with a heading (*above, Box C*), but stitch 1/2 inch from the top edge.

6. Place the project fabric wrong side down and pin the ruffle on top of it wrong side up, aligning the raw edges.

7. Machine stitch just inside the gathering stitches on the ruffle. Remove the pins.

8. Finish the edges of the seam allowance with a zigzag stitch if the fabric is ravelly and if there is not going to be any lining.

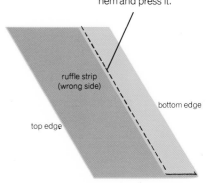

ruffle strip
(wrong side)

top edge

bottom edge

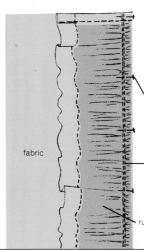

fabric

ruffle (wrong side)

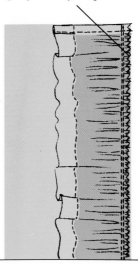

Shaping for hemlines

Although a well-made hemline for a fabric furnishing usually goes unnoticed, it can be made an eye-catching focus by curving the edge with scallops or indenting it with the toothlike pattern called dentils, shown here. The crisp dentil edge is especially attractive on valances, Roman shades and fitted bedcovers. The graceful curves of a scalloped edge are more often used for such unfitted furnishings as coverlets.

Whether scalloped or squared, shaped hemlines require careful planning. The space between each projection here, for example, falls on the line dividing the stripes.

In addition, dentils or scallops must fit evenly along the bottom of a valance or covering. Wherever there is a corner, one dentil or scallop must wrap around the turn. In fact, corner dentils and scallops should always be slightly wider to compensate for the foreshortening that occurs when they are seen on two planes at once.

THE DENTIL EDGE

A BLOCKING OUT THE PATTERN

1. To plan a dentil edge for a project such as a valance or a bedcover, measure the width of the edge where the gap-toothed pattern of dentils will be used and divide it by two. If the project fabric must go around corners, measure only the center section, not the sides.

2. On a piece of graph paper—using a scale of one square to equal 1 inch—measure off the distance determined in Step 1 and trim the graph paper to this width. The graph represents half the completed edge.

3. If the project fabric does not turn a corner, the left-hand end of the graph represents the side of the project. If the project fabric must go around corners, the left-hand end represents the point at which a corner turns.

4. The right-hand end of the graph represents the center point because the completed pattern will be flipped over in order to mark the second half of the edge identically.

5. Decide approximately how wide you wish the projections to be. Then determine how wide and how deep you wish to make the cutout spaces.

6. Place a piece of tracing paper over the graph paper. Starting at the center point, sketch half the width of a projection, following a horizontal line on the graph. Then sketch a full-width space and a full-width projection.

7. Continue marking full-width projections and spaces until you reach the left-hand end of the paper The design must end with at least a half-width projection, not a space.

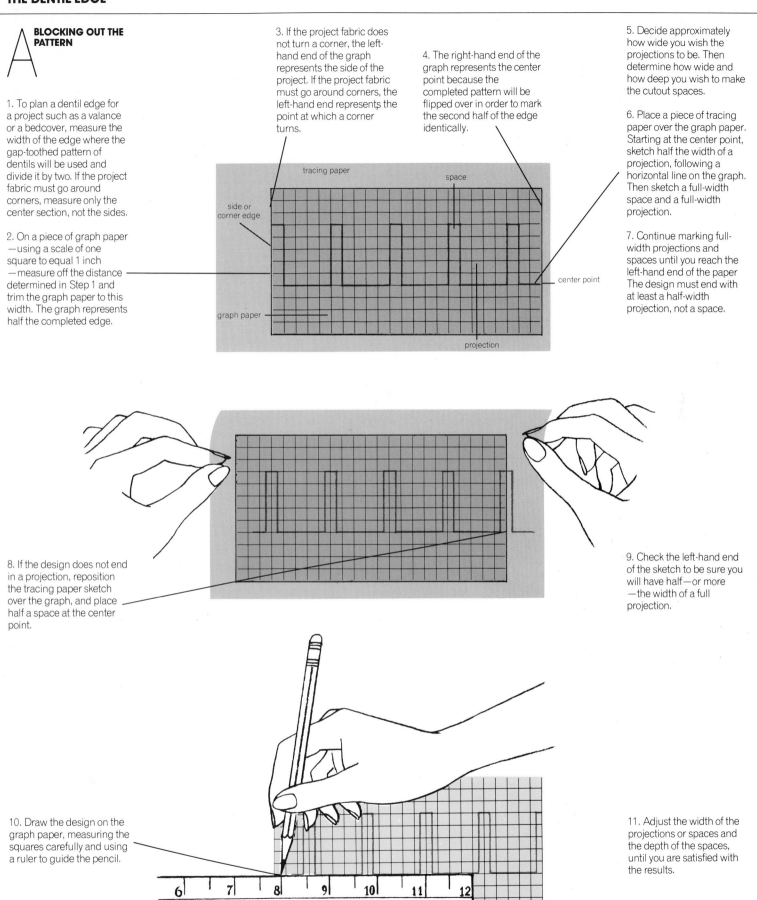

8. If the design does not end in a projection, reposition the tracing paper sketch over the graph, and place half a space at the center point.

9. Check the left-hand end of the sketch to be sure you will have half—or more—the width of a full projection.

10. Draw the design on the graph paper, measuring the squares carefully and using a ruler to guide the pencil.

11. Adjust the width of the projections or spaces and the depth of the spaces, until you are satisfied with the results.

continued

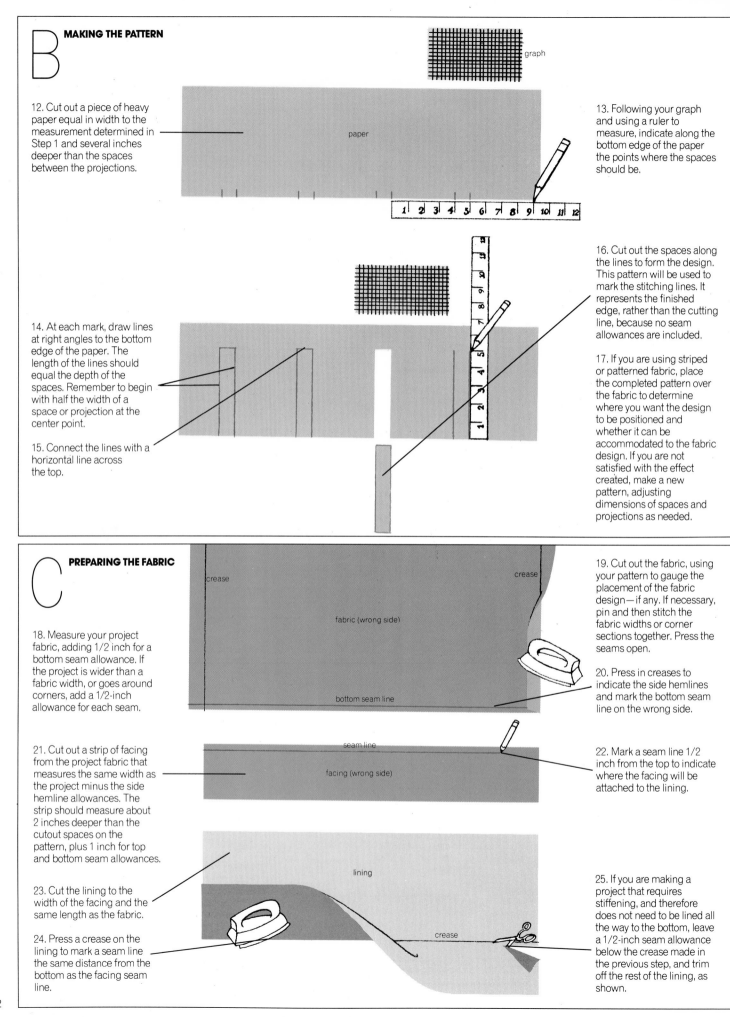

B MAKING THE PATTERN

12. Cut out a piece of heavy paper equal in width to the measurement determined in Step 1 and several inches deeper than the spaces between the projections.

13. Following your graph and using a ruler to measure, indicate along the bottom edge of the paper the points where the spaces should be.

14. At each mark, draw lines at right angles to the bottom edge of the paper. The length of the lines should equal the depth of the spaces. Remember to begin with half the width of a space or projection at the center point.

15. Connect the lines with a horizontal line across the top.

16. Cut out the spaces along the lines to form the design. This pattern will be used to mark the stitching lines. It represents the finished edge, rather than the cutting line, because no seam allowances are included.

17. If you are using striped or patterned fabric, place the completed pattern over the fabric to determine where you want the design to be positioned and whether it can be accommodated to the fabric design. If you are not satisfied with the effect created, make a new pattern, adjusting dimensions of spaces and projections as needed.

C PREPARING THE FABRIC

18. Measure your project fabric, adding 1/2 inch for a bottom seam allowance. If the project is wider than a fabric width, or goes around corners, add a 1/2-inch allowance for each seam.

19. Cut out the fabric, using your pattern to gauge the placement of the fabric design—if any. If necessary, pin and then stitch the fabric widths or corner sections together. Press the seams open.

20. Press in creases to indicate the side hemlines and mark the bottom seam line on the wrong side.

21. Cut out a strip of facing from the project fabric that measures the same width as the project minus the side hemline allowances. The strip should measure about 2 inches deeper than the cutout spaces on the pattern, plus 1 inch for top and bottom seam allowances.

22. Mark a seam line 1/2 inch from the top to indicate where the facing will be attached to the lining.

23. Cut the lining to the width of the facing and the same length as the fabric.

24. Press a crease on the lining to mark a seam line the same distance from the bottom as the facing seam line.

25. If you are making a project that requires stiffening, and therefore does not need to be lined all the way to the bottom, leave a 1/2-inch seam allowance below the crease made in the previous step, and trim off the rest of the lining, as shown.

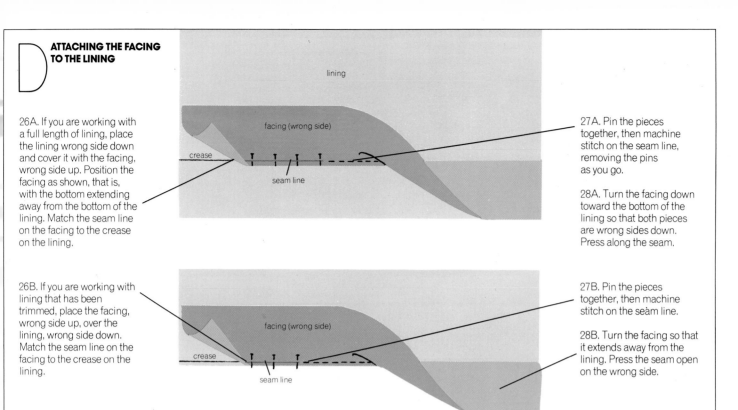

D ATTACHING THE FACING TO THE LINING

26A. If you are working with a full length of lining, place the lining wrong side down and cover it with the facing, wrong side up. Position the facing as shown, that is, with the bottom extending away from the bottom of the lining. Match the seam line on the facing to the crease on the lining.

26B. If you are working with lining that has been trimmed, place the facing, wrong side up, over the lining, wrong side down. Match the seam line on the facing to the crease on the lining.

27A. Pin the pieces together, then machine stitch on the seam line, removing the pins as you go.

28A. Turn the facing down toward the bottom of the lining so that both pieces are wrong sides down. Press along the seam.

27B. Pin the pieces together, then machine stitch on the seam line.

28B. Turn the facing so that it extends away from the lining. Press the seam open on the wrong side.

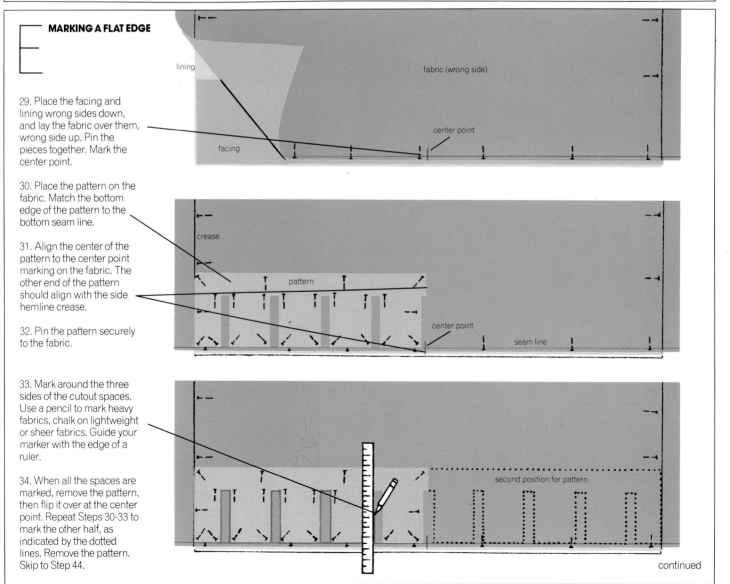

E MARKING A FLAT EDGE

29. Place the facing and lining wrong sides down, and lay the fabric over them, wrong side up. Pin the pieces together. Mark the center point.

30. Place the pattern on the fabric. Match the bottom edge of the pattern to the bottom seam line.

31. Align the center of the pattern to the center point marking on the fabric. The other end of the pattern should align with the side hemline crease.

32. Pin the pattern securely to the fabric.

33. Mark around the three sides of the cutout spaces. Use a pencil to mark heavy fabrics, chalk on lightweight or sheer fabrics. Guide your marker with the edge of a ruler.

34. When all the spaces are marked, remove the pattern, then flip it over at the center point. Repeat Steps 30-33 to mark the other half, as indicated by the dotted lines. Remove the pattern. Skip to Step 44.

continued

MARKING AN EDGE WITH CORNERS

35. Place the facing and lining wrong sides down, and lay the project fabric over them wrong side up. Pin the pieces together. Mark the center point of the center section of fabric.

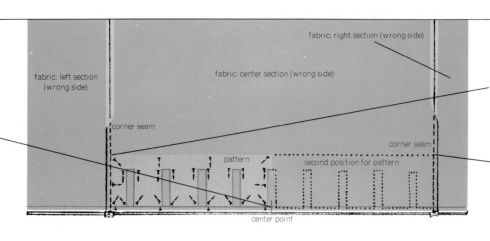

fabric: right section (wrong side)

fabric: left section (wrong side)

fabric: center section (wrong side)

corner seam

pattern

second position for pattern

corner seam

center point

36. Working on the center section only, fold back the seam allowance at the left-hand corner as shown. Align the left-hand end of your pattern to the machine stitching.

37. Repeat Steps 30-34 —folding back the right-hand seam allowance in the opposite direction—to mark the outlines of the spaces across the entire center section.

38. To go around the corner, fold back the seam allowances toward the center section as shown. Flip the pattern over once more and align the side edge to the machine stitching of this corner seam.

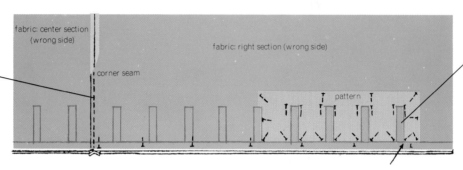

fabric: center section (wrong side)

fabric: right section (wrong side)

corner seam

pattern

39. Repeat Steps 30-34 once more to begin marking the right section of the fabric. When you have drawn the last space (arrow), remove the pattern.

40. Now slide the pattern along the edge, without flipping it over, and match the first space—or, as in this case, the half space—to the last space you drew in the previous step. Draw in the spaces as before.

41. Continue to slide the pattern along the edge, marking the spaces, as many times as necessary.

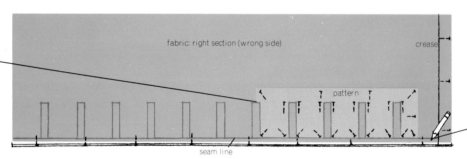

fabric: right section (wrong side)

crease

pattern

seam line

42. As you approach the crease for the side hemline, estimate how many more spaces you can accommodate without having a space or less than half a full projection at the hem. Continue the line for the last projection to the hemline crease, marking over the bottom seam line. This last projection may be up to 12 inches wide; on the finished article, it will not be easily visible.

43. Repeat Steps 38-42 on the left section of the fabric, working in the opposite direction.

FINISHING THE EDGE

44. Insert more pins, if necessary, to secure the fabric layers. Then machine stitch around the entire edge. Sew along the bottom seam line to form the bottom edge of the projections, then continue up, over and down the sides of the spaces. Pivot the fabric with the needle inserted at all bottom points of the projections and all top corners of the spaces.

45. Trim the seam allowances of all layers to 1/4 inch beyond the machine stitching.

46. Trim the bottom points of the projections diagonally, and clip into the top corners of the spaces, cutting up to —but not through—the machine stitching.

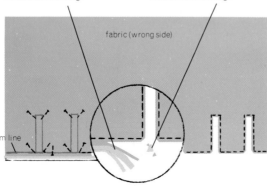

fabric (wrong side)

seam line

47. Turn the fabric right side out. The right side of the facing will be visible on the underside. Using a ruler, push out the bottom points and smooth out the top corners. Press the finished edge on the underside.

48. Finish the side edges or the end hems as instructed for your project.

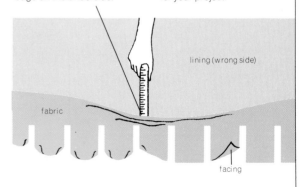

lining (wrong side)

fabric

facing

THE SCALLOPED EDGE WITH LOOSELY ROUNDED CORNERS

A | BLOCKING OUT THE PATTERN

1. To scallop around the bottom edge of a cover with loosely draped corners—for a bed or a studio couch—first measure the edge that will be most prominent when the cover is made, such as the foot of a bed or the front side of a studio couch.

2. Measure the distance—called the overhang, or drop—from the top surface to the level at which you want the finished edge.

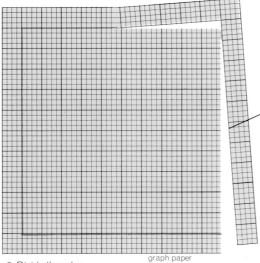

graph paper

3. Divide the edge measurement in half and add the overhang.

4. On a sheet of graph paper —using a scale of one small division of graph marking to 1 inch of measurement —draw a square with each side equal to the sum determined in Step 3. Trim the graph paper along the lines of the square. This graph represents half the pattern which will be used to mark the scallops.

5. Decide how high you wish to make the upsweeps between scallops. Measure in this distance (to scale) from the bottom edge of the trimmed graph and draw a horizontal line parallel to the trimmed edge. Make a similar line parallel to the left-hand edge of the graph.

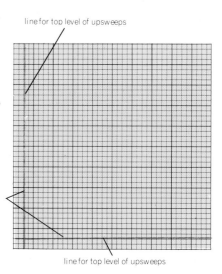

line for top level of upsweeps

line for top level of upsweeps

6. Starting at the bottom left-hand corner of the paper, measure a distance to scale equal to the overhang (Step 2) along the bottom and then along the left edge of the paper. Make marks at these points.

7. From each mark draw a line at right angles to the edge of the paper. The point at which these lines intersect indicates the top corner of the overhang on the cover.

8. Place the point of a compass at the intersection of the lines drawn in Step 7 and adjust the compass to touch the marks made in Step 6.

9. Draw the corner scallop by making an arc broad enough to intersect the two lines that indicate the top level for the upsweeps of the scallops.

10. Measure to scale from one end of the graph to the point where the corner scallop intersects a line that marks the top of the upsweeps. Double this measurement to determine how much space you have for other, smaller, scallops along the prominent edge of the cover.

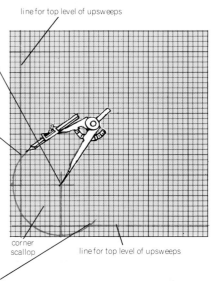

line for top level of upsweeps

corner scallop

line for top level of upsweeps

11. Decide approximately how wide you wish the smaller scallops to be —usually about half the width of the corner scallop will look right.

12. Divide the measurement determined in Step 10 by the approximate width of the scallops determined in Step 11. The result is the total number of scallops you can have along the edge. Since the division will probably not come out even, repeat it with slightly different width figures until you do get a whole result, with no fractional remainder.

line for top level of upsweeps

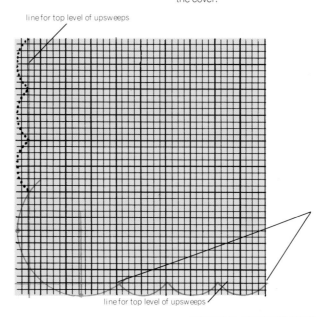

line for top level of upsweeps

13. Sketch in the scallops on the graph. If in Step 12 you found you needed an even number of small scallops, begin at the right hand of the graph at the top level line, and sketch in full scallops until you reach the upsweep for the corner scallop. For an uneven number, start at the right-hand bottom end of the graph, draw half a scallop, then full scallops. Because the graph represents half the total width, you will be drawing half the total number of small scallops.

14. Repeat Step 13 on the left-hand side of the graph.

continued

B | MAKING THE ACTUAL-SIZE PATTERN

15. Cut out of heavy paper a square with each side an inch longer than the measurement in Step 3.

16. Draw a horizontal line 1 inch—actual measurement, not scaled down—above the bottom edge of the paper to indicate where the bottom of the scallops will fall.

17. Draw a second line above the first one at a distance equal to the height of the upsweeps determined in Step 5.

18. Repeat Steps 16 and 17 on the left-hand side of the paper, drawing two vertical lines to indicate the bottoms of the scallops and the tops of the upsweeps along this edge.

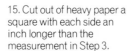

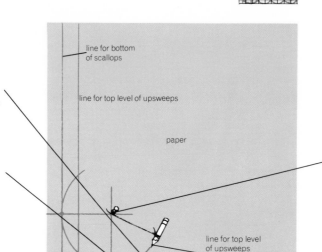

graph

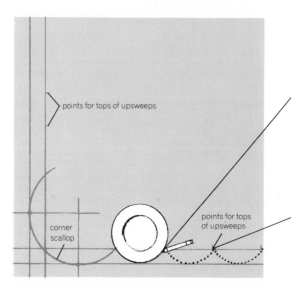

line for bottom of scallops

line for top level of upsweeps

paper

line for top level of upsweeps

line for bottom of scallops

19. Using the actual measurements, not scaled-down ones, repeat Steps 6 and 7 to mark the length of the overhang on the bottom and left-hand sides of the pattern, and to draw the intersecting lines that mark the top corner overhang, this time working along the outside lines indicating the bottoms of the scallops.

20. Tie one end of a piece of string to a thumbtack and insert it in the intersection point made in Step 19. Tie the other end to a pencil, adjusting the length of the string so that when taut it brings the pencil point to the overhang-length marks made in Step 19.

21. Holding the string taut, draw the corner scallop, making sure the ends of the arc cross the upsweep lines at both sides of the paper.

22. Taking scale measurements from your graph and converting them to full size, use a ruler to mark the points where the tops of the smaller scallops will cross the upsweep lines on the full-size pattern.

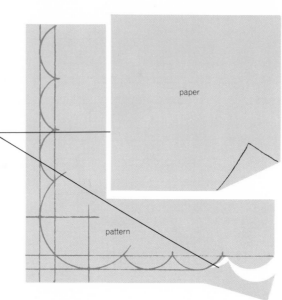

points for tops of upsweeps

corner scallop

points for tops of upsweeps

23. Sketch in the first curve freehand, starting at one edge of the corner scallop and continuing to the first upsweep mark. Find a plate with a similarly shaped curve, and use the rim of the plate to smooth the freehand curve.

24. Using the plate, draw in the rest of the scallops along this edge, beginning and ending at the upsweep marks made in Step 22.

25. Repeat Steps 23 and 24 to draw the scallops on the left-hand side of the paper.

26. Cut out around the scallops to form a full-scale paper pattern. Then trim the paper to within several inches of the upsweep line so that it will be easier to handle. The bottom edge of this pattern represents half the prominent edge of the article—measured in Step 1—and will be flipped over at the center to mark the other half. The side edge will guide the marking of the remaining edges of the cover.

paper

pattern

C MARKING THE FABRIC

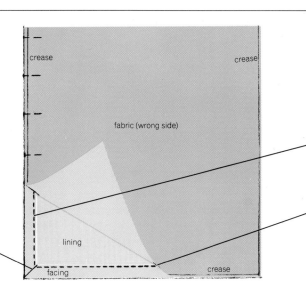

crease

crease

fabric (wrong side)

lining

facing

crease

27. Cut fabric and lining —leaving 1-inch seam allowances around the edges—to fit the object being covered. At the fabric edges press in creases to mark the seam lines.

28. To face the lining, cut out three 5-inch-wide sections of project fabric. Make two sections equal to the length of the lining plus 1/2 inch; make one section equal to the width plus 1 inch. Join the sections, following the procedure for facing the top of the bed skirt (page 144). Fold under the inside edge of the facing strip 1/2 inch and press.

29. Place the lining wrong side down and lay the facing strip over it, matching the raw outside edges. Pin the facing to the lining, then machine stitch, sewing just inside the fold.

30. Place the facing and lining wrong sides down and lay the fabric over them, wrong side up. Pin the pieces together.

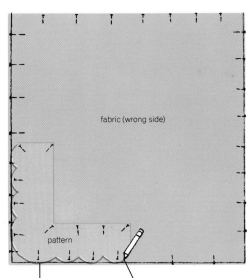

fabric (wrong side)

pattern

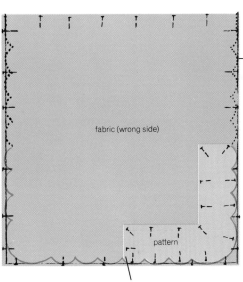

fabric (wrong side)

pattern

31. Place the pattern on the fabric so that the bottom edge of the pattern is at the most prominent edge of the cover. Align the bottom curves with the creases marking the seam lines at the edges of the fabric.

32. Pin the pattern to the fabric and draw around the scallops, using pencil to mark heavy fabrics and chalk to mark lightweight or sheer fabrics.

33. Remove the pattern, then flip it over at the center, aligning it to the seam lines and marking the scallops on this side of the fabric as in Steps 31 and 32.

34. To mark the remaining scallops, as indicated by the dotted lines, repeat Steps 40-43 for the dentil edge (page 64). Use only the small scallops on the pattern as your guide for marking, as you slide the pattern along the fabric. As you go, be sure to match the curves and upsweeps of the last scallop you drew to the first scallop on the pattern so that all the scallops are correctly positioned.

35. As you reach the corners of the edge to be left unscalloped, continue the last scallop on each side to the corner with a straight line, if necessary, to make sure there is not an upsweep at or near the corner. Remove the pattern.

D FINISHING THE EDGE

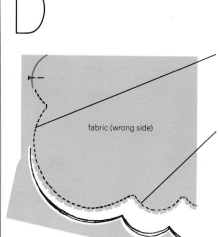

fabric (wrong side)

36. Machine stitch around the scallops, squaring off the stitches at the tops of the upsweeps by making two horizontal stitches.

37. Trim the seam allowances of all layers of fabric to 1/2 inch all around the stitching.

38. Clip into the seam allowances at the upsweeps, cutting right up to, but not through, the stitching. Notch the curves around the bottom of the scallops.

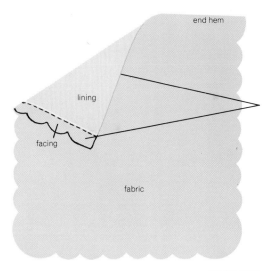

end hem

lining

facing

fabric

39. Turn the fabric right side out through the opening at the unscalloped and unstitched edge of the cover. The right side of the facing will be visible on the underside. Smooth out the curves, then press the finished edge on the underside.

40. Finish the unstitched edge—the end hem —following the procedure for hemming the bedcover (page 153).

Inconspicuous closures

The neat fit of a carefully crafted slip-cover is secured by the zipper that holds the cover in place. But to create this illusion of a second skin —one that can be removed quickly and easily for cleaning—the closure should be as inconspicuous as possible. Not only must the zipper itself be hidden by overlapping fabric but zipper and opening should be located strategically out of view—centered on the back of a box cushion (*right*), or inserted in the welted seam of a knife-edge cushion or slipcover (*page 71*).

For short closures not subjected to stress, color-matched metal dress zippers can be used, and on pillows even nylon zippers will do. But if the closure is large, and it must hold tight large expanses of heavy fabric, then only a heavy-duty upholstery zipper is suitable.

THE CENTERED ZIPPER FOR BOXED CUSHIONS

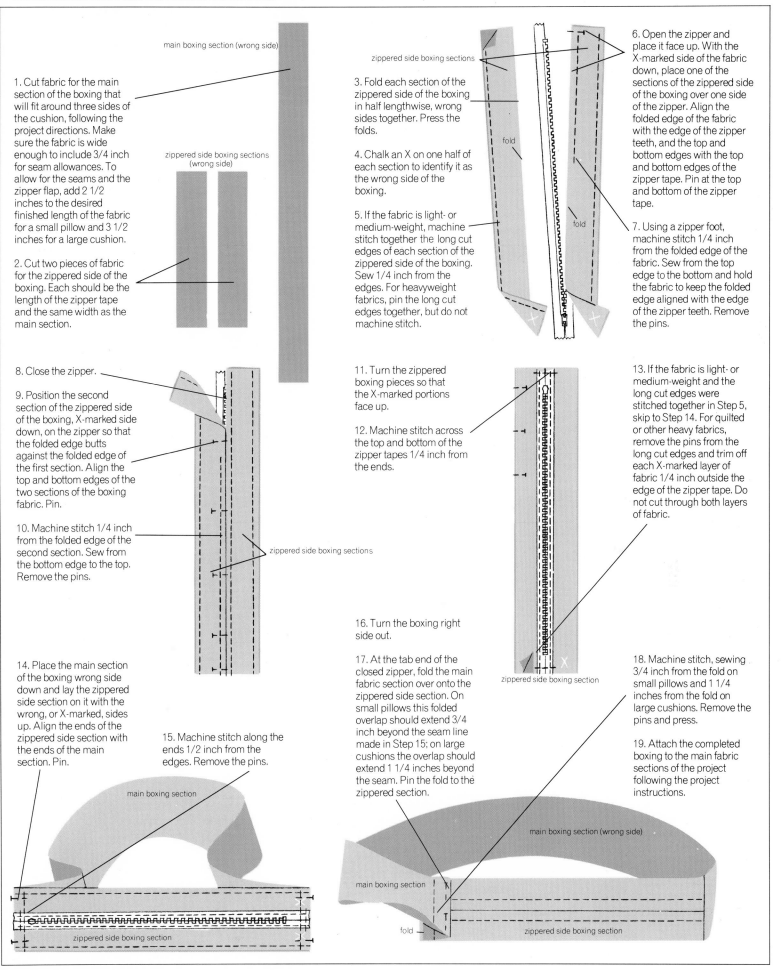

1. Cut fabric for the main section of the boxing that will fit around three sides of the cushion, following the project directions. Make sure the fabric is wide enough to include 3/4 inch for seam allowances. To allow for the seams and the zipper flap, add 2 1/2 inches to the desired finished length of the fabric for a small pillow and 3 1/2 inches for a large cushion.

2. Cut two pieces of fabric for the zippered side of the boxing. Each should be the length of the zipper tape and the same width as the main section.

3. Fold each section of the zippered side of the boxing in half lengthwise, wrong sides together. Press the folds.

4. Chalk an X on one half of each section to identify it as the wrong side of the boxing.

5. If the fabric is light- or medium-weight, machine stitch together the long cut edges of each section of the zippered side of the boxing. Sew 1/4 inch from the edges. For heavyweight fabrics, pin the long cut edges together, but do not machine stitch.

6. Open the zipper and place it face up. With the X-marked side of the fabric down, place one of the sections of the zippered side of the boxing over one side of the zipper. Align the folded edge of the fabric with the edge of the zipper teeth, and the top and bottom edges with the top and bottom edges of the zipper tape. Pin at the top and bottom of the zipper tape.

7. Using a zipper foot, machine stitch 1/4 inch from the folded edge of the fabric. Sew from the top edge to the bottom and hold the fabric to keep the folded edge aligned with the edge of the zipper teeth. Remove the pins.

8. Close the zipper.

9. Position the second section of the zippered side of the boxing, X-marked side down, on the zipper so that the folded edge butts against the folded edge of the first section. Align the top and bottom edges of the two sections of the boxing fabric. Pin.

10. Machine stitch 1/4 inch from the folded edge of the second section. Sew from the bottom edge to the top. Remove the pins.

11. Turn the zippered boxing pieces so that the X-marked portions face up.

12. Machine stitch across the top and bottom of the zipper tapes 1/4 inch from the ends.

13. If the fabric is light- or medium-weight and the long cut edges were stitched together in Step 5, skip to Step 14. For quilted or other heavy fabrics, remove the pins from the long cut edges and trim off each X-marked layer of fabric 1/4 inch outside the edge of the zipper tape. Do not cut through both layers of fabric.

14. Place the main section of the boxing wrong side down and lay the zippered side section on it with the wrong, or X-marked, sides up. Align the ends of the zippered side section with the ends of the main section. Pin.

15. Machine stitch along the ends 1/2 inch from the edges. Remove the pins.

16. Turn the boxing right side out.

17. At the tab end of the closed zipper, fold the main fabric section over onto the zippered side section. On small pillows this folded overlap should extend 3/4 inch beyond the seam line made in Step 15; on large cushions the overlap should extend 1 1/4 inches beyond the seam. Pin the fold to the zippered section.

18. Machine stitch, sewing 3/4 inch from the fold on small pillows and 1 1/4 inches from the fold on large cushions. Remove the pins and press.

19. Attach the completed boxing to the main fabric sections of the project following the project instructions.

THE LAPPED ZIPPER FOR SLIPCOVERS

1. Leaving open the back seam into which the zipper will be inserted, assemble your slipcover and complete the hem as shown for the slipcover on pages 124-139.

2. Place the slipcover, wrong side out, so that the outside back section is underneath and the outside arm section is on top.

3. To mark a guide for positioning the zipper, first turn under the 1-inch seam allowance on the unstitched outside arm section of the zipper seam. Press a crease.

4. Turn under the 1-inch seam allowance on the nonwelted bottom portion of the outside back section. Press a crease.

5. Fold the outside arm section up out of the way.

6. Open the zipper and place it face down on the welted seam of the back section, with the bottom zipper stop at the top.

7. Align the bottom zipper stop just below the stitched part of the partially finished back seam. Pin at the top of the tape.

8. Align the zipper teeth along the middle of the corded part of the welting.

9. Attach a zipper foot to the machine.

10. Holding the zipper in place as aligned in Steps 7 and 8, machine stitch partway along the left-hand strip of zipper tape 1/4 inch from the teeth. Stop stitching at the skirt seam line.

11. Reposition the zipper extending beyond the skirt seam line so that the teeth fall just inside the creased seam-line marking made in Step 4.

12. Sew at an angle to bring the stitches 1/4 inch from the zipper teeth in their new position. Then continue stitching close to the teeth to about 1 1/2 inches from the hem; stop the machine.

13. Lift up the zipper and fold under the end of the tape so that it clears the zipper teeth. Reposition the zipper and continue stitching, making sure to stitch through both layers of the folded zipper tape. Remove the pin.

14. Close the zipper and fold under the seam allowance of the outside back section to turn the zipper face up.

15. Fold down the outside arm section so that it is wrong side up on top of the outside back section.

16. Open out the outside arm section so that both the outside back and outside arm sections of the slipcover are wrong side down.

17. Lap the folded edge of the outside arm section over the zipper teeth, covering them completely. Pin, making sure to catch the unstitched strip of the zipper tape underneath. At the hem edge, fold up the end of the zipper tape to clear the zipper teeth. Pin.

18. Open the zipper.

19. Using a zipper foot, machine stitch the unattached fabric sections to the unattached side of the zipper. Sew from the finished side of the fabric 1/2 inch from the fold. Begin the stitching 1 inch above the open portion of the seam. Remove the pins and press.

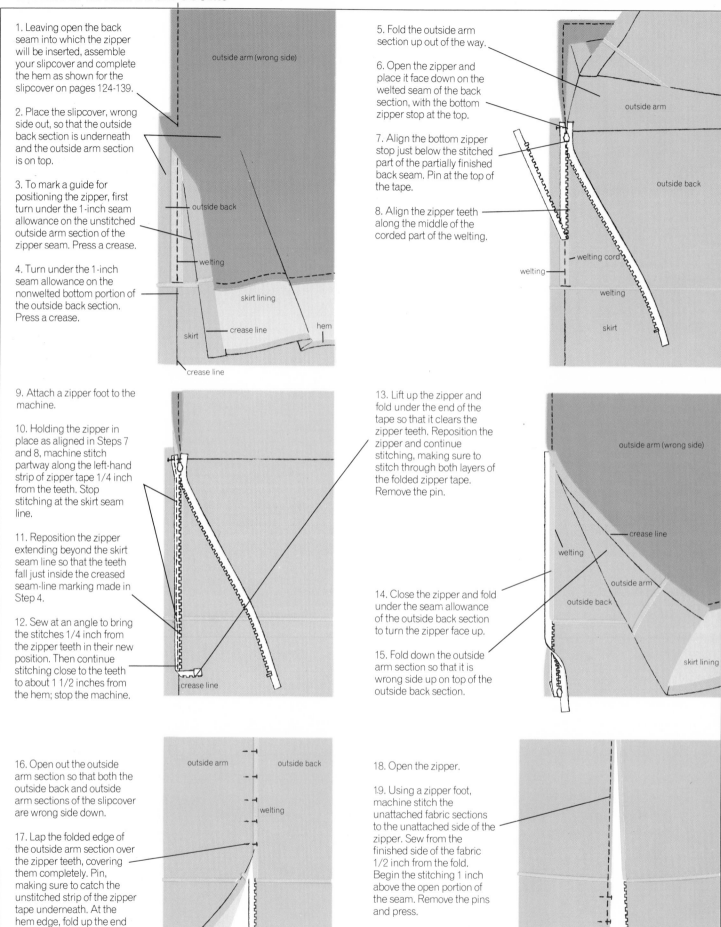

THE LAPPED ZIPPER FOR WELTED KNIFE-EDGED PILLOWS

1. Cut the fabric pieces for the pillow or cushion following the directions for the project. Make sure to leave a 1-inch seam allowance on both the front and back sections along the entire length of the side where the zipper will be inserted.

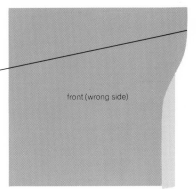

2. On each fabric section, fold the seam allowance toward the wrong side along the edge where the zipper will be attached. Press to crease in guide lines for the placement of the welting and the zipper.

3. Attach the welting to the front fabric section, aligning the machine basting on the welting with the creased guide line on the zipper edge and following the instructions for shirred welting (pages 47-49) or plain welting (pages 50-51). Then stitch together the front and back sections, wrong sides out, for 1/2 inch along each end of the seam line into which the zipper will be inserted.

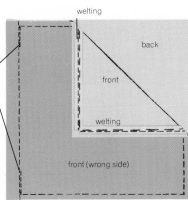

4. Place the fabric sections, wrong sides out, so that the front section is underneath.

5. Push the top layer of fabric out of the way along the seam where the zipper will be inserted.

6. Open the zipper and place one side of it face down on the welted seam with the outer edge of the zipper tape toward the fabric edge.

7. Align the top stop of the zipper just below the stitched portion of the seam and midway on the corded part of the welting. Insert a pin at the top end of the tape. Align the zipper teeth along the middle of the corded part of the welting.

8. Attach a zipper foot to the machine.

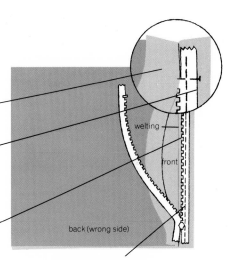

9. Machine stitch 1/4 inch from the zipper teeth. Stitch from the top edge of the zipper tape to the bottom edge, holding the zipper in place with your hand to keep the teeth lined up along the middle of the corded part of the welting. Remove the pin.

10. Open out the fabric so that both the front and back sections are wrong side down.

11. Close the zipper and fold under the seam allowance of the front section to turn the zipper face up.

12. Lap the unattached folded edge of the back section of the pillow over the zipper teeth, covering them completely. Pin, making sure to catch the zipper tape underneath.

13. Open the zipper.

14. Using a zipper foot, machine stitch the zipper to the back section of the pillow. Sew from the finished side of the fabric 1/2 inch from the fold. Remove the pins. Press.

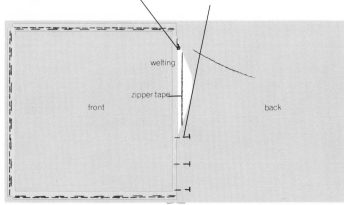

Pleats for elegant folds

Pleats have a happy faculty of adding surface interest and dimensional depth to fabrics; sometimes they do both at once. They anchor graceful folds in full draperies and give a decorative finish to slipcovers. The rollback pleat at right releases maximum fullness, while the cartridge pleat economizes on fabric and the box pleat has a full but tailored look..

How pleats are made depends partly on their use. Slipcover pleats are folded, then anchored with a line of stitching across the top; drapery pleats begin with a short vertical seam through the heading to secure the material for the pleat allowance, then are folded and tacked in place.

THE ROLLBACK PLEAT

A SEWING THE PLEAT ALLOWANCE SEAM

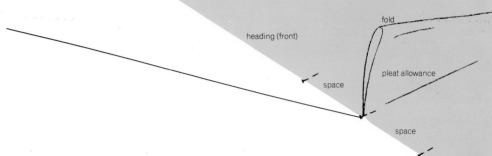

pleat allowance

space

pleat allowance

fold

heading (front)

pleat allowance

space

space

1. Plot and mark off the pleats with pins (pages 94-95), then match the pins that designate one pleat, folding the pleat allowance in half.

2. Secure the pleat allowance by eliminating one pin and inserting the other through both layers of heading.

3. Repeat Steps 1 and 2 on each of the remaining pleat allowances.

4. When all of the pleat allowances have been folded and pinned, measure the width of the heading to make sure it is the exact size you intended. Adjust the size of some or all of the pleats, if necessary, to achieve the desired heading width.

5. Measure the distance from one pleat allowance fold to the pin holding the allowance in place.

6. Measure off an equal distance at the base of the heading and insert a second pin directly below the first one.

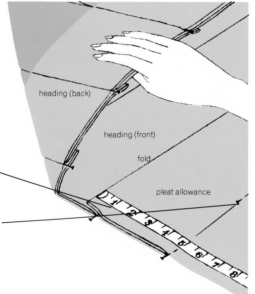

heading (back)

heading (front)

fold

pleat allowance

7. Machine stitch between the pins from about 1/4 inch above the base of the heading to the top of the drapery, backstitching at both ends.

8. Repeat Steps 5-7 on each of the remaining pleat allowances.

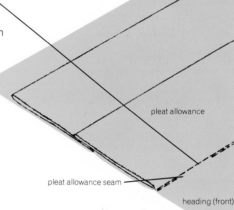

pleat allowance

pleat allowance seam

heading (front)

B FOLDING THE PLEAT

9. Thread a needle with a double strand of heavy-duty thread, and make a knot at the end.

10. Form a crease lengthwise along the fold of one pleat allowance by pressing with your fingers. Mark the top of the crease with a pin.

11. Grasp the pleat allowance with both hands approximately one fifth of the way down from the center crease.

12. Push down on the pleat allowance to form three folds. Each side fold should be twice as deep as the center fold. Be sure the inner creases align with the pleat allowance seam.

13. Pinch the folds together at their outer creases to be certain the side folds are equal. Then remove the marking pin and press in all the creases with your fingers.

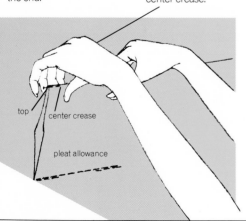

top

center crease

pleat allowance

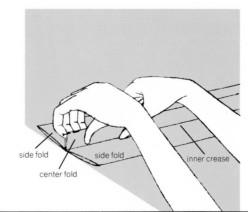

side fold

center fold

side fold

inner crease

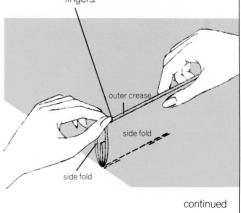

outer crease

side fold

side fold

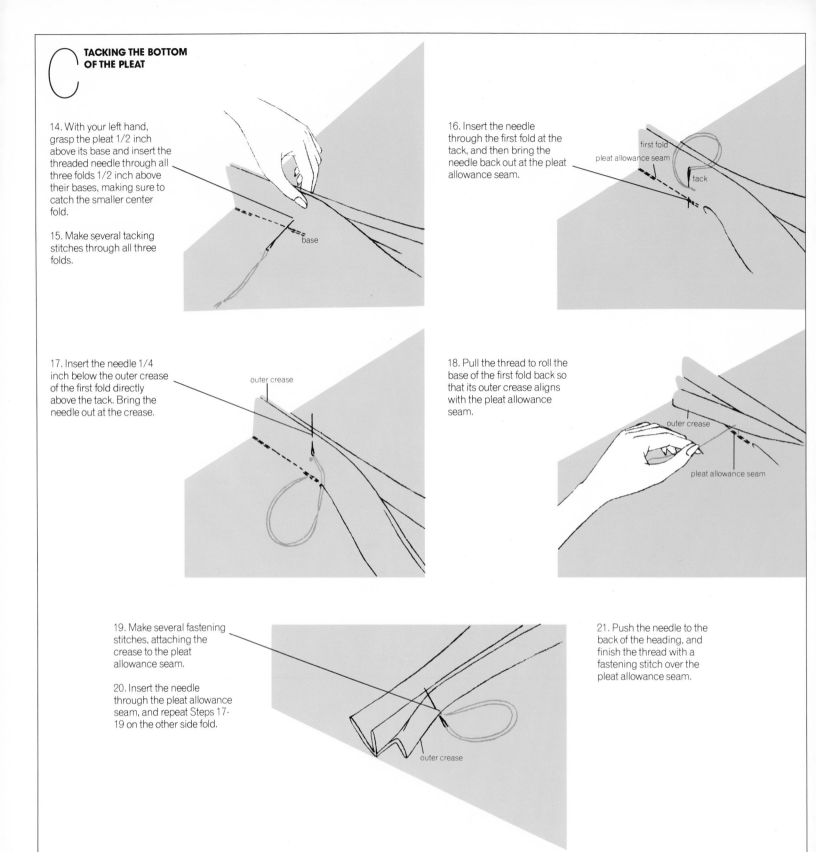

C TACKING THE BOTTOM OF THE PLEAT

14. With your left hand, grasp the pleat 1/2 inch above its base and insert the threaded needle through all three folds 1/2 inch above their bases, making sure to catch the smaller center fold.

15. Make several tacking stitches through all three folds.

16. Insert the needle through the first fold at the tack, and then bring the needle back out at the pleat allowance seam.

first fold

pleat allowance seam

tack

base

17. Insert the needle 1/4 inch below the outer crease of the first fold directly above the tack. Bring the needle out at the crease.

outer crease

18. Pull the thread to roll the base of the first fold back so that its outer crease aligns with the pleat allowance seam.

outer crease

pleat allowance seam

19. Make several fastening stitches, attaching the crease to the pleat allowance seam.

20. Insert the needle through the pleat allowance seam, and repeat Steps 17-19 on the other side fold.

21. Push the needle to the back of the heading, and finish the thread with a fastening stitch over the pleat allowance seam.

outer crease

D TACKING THE TOP OF THE PLEAT

22. Knot the thread again. Insert the needle through the back of the pleat allowance seam 1/16 inch below the top of the heading. Catch the inner crease between the center fold and one of the side folds.

23. Make several tacking stitches, allowing a 1/4-inch shank *(Glossary)* between the crease and the pleat allowance seam. Then repeat on the other inner crease.

24. Finish the thread with a fastening stitch over the back of the pleat allowance seam.

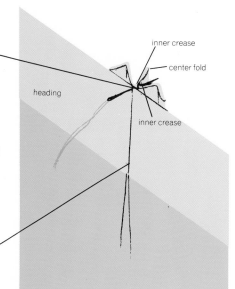

25. Knot the thread again. Insert the needle from inside the outer crease of the first fold 1/16 inch below the top edge of the heading.

26. Attach the outer crease to the heading 1/2 inch from the pleat allowance seam by making several tacking stitches over the top edge of the heading.

27. Make a fastening stitch on the back of the heading to finish the thread.

28. Repeat Steps 25-27 on the other side fold.

29. Repeat Steps 9-28 on each of the remaining pleat allowances.

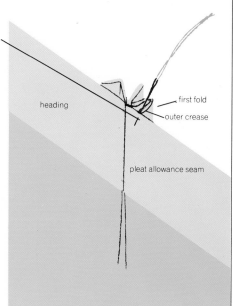

THE THREE-FOLD PINCH PLEAT

A FOLDING THE PLEAT

1. Plot and mark off the pleats with pins *(pages 94-95)* and stitch the pleat allowance seams according to the instructions in Steps 1-8 of the rollback pleat.

2. Thread a needle with a double strand of heavy-duty thread, and make a knot at the end.

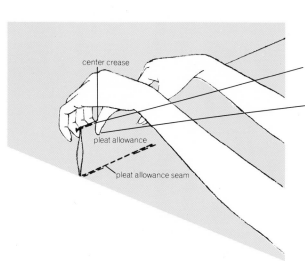

3. Form a crease lengthwise along one pleat allowance and mark the top of the crease with a pin.

4. Grasp the pleat allowance with both hands approximately one third of the way down from the center crease.

5. Push down on the pleat allowance to form three folds. Be sure the inner creases align with the pleat allowance seam.

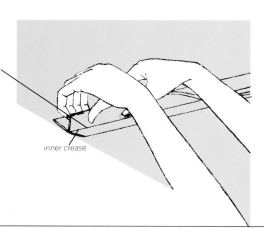

6. Pinch the folds together at their outer creases to be certain they are equal. Then remove the marking pin and press in the creases with your fingers.

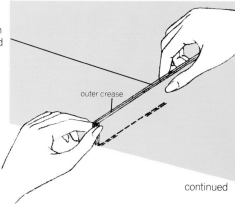

continued

7. With your left hand, grasp the pleat 1/2 inch above its base.

8. Insert the threaded needle from the inside of the pleat through the first fold 1/4 inch below its outer crease.

9. Make several tacking stitches *(Glossary)* through all three folds.

10. Insert the needle into the first fold at the tack and bring the needle out at the pleat allowance seam. Then tack again at the seam, catching both inner creases.

11. Push the needle to the back of the heading; finish with a fastening stitch over the pleat allowance seam.

12. Knot the thread again. With the back of the pleat facing you, insert the needle into the inner crease between the first and center folds 1/16 inch below the top of the heading. Bring the needle out at the seam.

13. Attach the crease to the seam with tacking stitches.

14. Tack the other inner crease in the same manner.

15. To finish the thread, make a fastening stitch over the seam at the back of the pleat.

16. Repeat Steps 2-15 on each of the remaining pleat allowances.

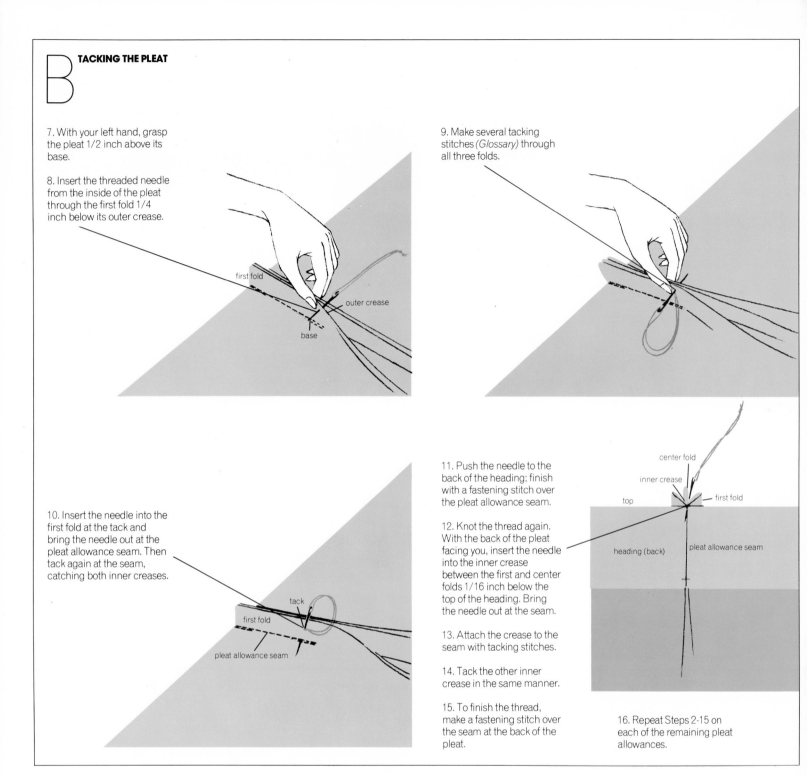

THE FOUR-FOLD PINCH PLEAT

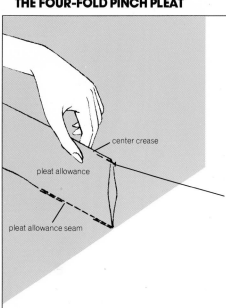

1. Plot and mark off the pleats with pins *(pages 94-95)* and stitch the pleat allowance seams according to the instructions in Steps 1-8 of the rollback pleat.

2. Thread a needle with a double strand of heavy-duty thread, and make a knot at the end.

3. Form a crease lengthwise along the center of one pleat allowance, and mark it with a pin.

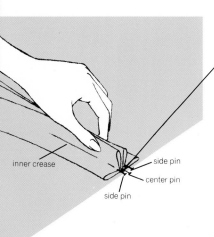

4. Flatten the pleat so that the pin inserted in Step 3 aligns with the pleat allowance seam.

5. Mark the creases formed at the sides with pins.

6. Form two pleats on each side of the center pin by aligning each of the side pins with the center one. Be sure the inner creases align with the pleat allowance seam.

7. Finish the pleat by following the procedure in Steps 6-15 of the three-fold pinch pleat.

8. Repeat Steps 2-7 on each of the remaining pleat allowances.

THE BOX PLEAT FOR DRAPERIES

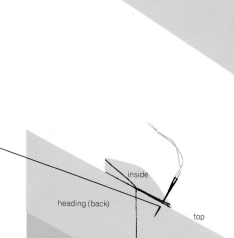

1. Plot and mark off the pleats with pins *(pages 94-95)* and stitch the pleat allowance seams according to the instructions in Steps 1-8 of the rollback pleat.

2. Thread a needle with a double strand of heavy-duty thread, and make a knot at the end.

3. Mark the top of one folded pleat allowance with a pin.

4. Flatten the pleat so that the pin aligns with the pleat allowance seam. Then, with your fingers, press in the creases formed at the sides. Remove the marking pin.

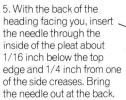
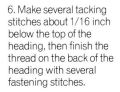
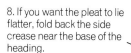

5. With the back of the heading facing you, insert the needle through the inside of the pleat about 1/16 inch below the top edge and 1/4 inch from one of the side creases. Bring the needle out at the back.

6. Make several tacking stitches about 1/16 inch below the top of the heading, then finish the thread on the back of the heading with several fastening stitches.

7. Knot the thread again and repeat Steps 5 and 6 on the other side of the pleat.

8. If you want the pleat to lie flatter, fold back the side crease near the base of the heading.

9. Make several fastening stitches through the back and inner layers of the pleat 1/4 inch above the base of the heading and 1/4 inch from the side crease. Then repeat on the other side.

10. Repeat Steps 2-9 on each of the remaining pleat allowances.

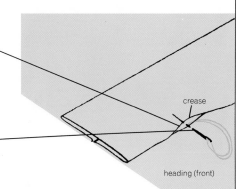

THE DOUBLE BOX PLEAT

1. Plot and mark off the pleats with pins *(pages 94-95)* and stitch the pleat allowance seams according to the instructions in Steps 1-8 of the rollback pleat.

2. Mark the top of one folded pleat allowance with a pin. Measure from this pin to the pleat allowance seam. Then divide that figure in half and add 1/4 inch.

3. Measure off the distance figured in Step 2 from the seam toward the top of the fold and insert a pin at this point.

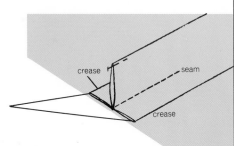

4. Machine stitch the same length as the pleat allowance seam and parallel to it at the distance marked off in Step 3. Remove the pin.

5. Thread a needle with a double strand of heavy-duty thread, and make a knot at the end.

6. Push down on the pleat allowance to form three folds, aligning the seam made in Step 4 with the pleat allowance seam. With your fingers, press the creases of the two side folds.

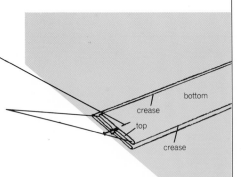

7. Flatten the remainder of the pleat allowance so that the pin inserted in Step 2 aligns with the seam made in Step 4. Again, press in creases with your fingers.

8. Tack the top of the pleats, following the procedure in Steps 5-7 of the box pleat for draperies, but tacking through both pleats at once.

9. Tack the bottom of the pleats as shown in Steps 8 and 9 of the box pleat for draperies, again tacking through both pleats at once.

10. Repeat Steps 2-9 on each of the remaining pleat allowances.

THE CARTRIDGE PLEAT

1. Plot and mark off the pleats with pins *(pages 94-95)* and stitch the pleat allowance seams according to the instructions in Steps 1-8 of the rollback pleat.

2. Cut a piece of crinoline *(Fabric Glossary)* 10 inches wide and as long as the pleat allowance seam.

3. Roll the crinoline widthwise into a tight cylinder, then insert the cylinder inside one pleat allowance. The cylinder will spring open to fill the pleat allowance snugly.

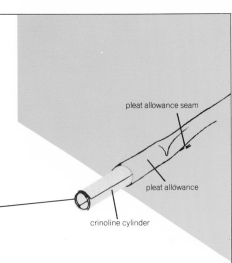

4. Thread a needle with a double strand of heavy-duty thread, and make a knot at the end.

5. Insert the threaded needle from the inside of the cylinder 1/8 inch below the top edge of the heading, catching all the layers of crinoline. Then bring the needle out 1/4 inch from the pleat allowance seam.

6. Make several tacking stitches over the top edge of the heading.

7. Make a fastening stitch at the back of the pleat to finish the thread.

8. Knot the thread again, and repeat Steps 5-7 on the other side of the pleat allowance seam.

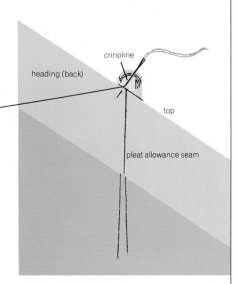

9. Repeat Steps 2-8 on each of the remaining pleat allowances.

THE ROLLBACK CARTRIDGE PLEAT

1. Plot and mark off the pleats with pins (pages 94-95) and stitch the pleat allowance seams according to the instructions in Steps 1-8 of the rollback pleat.

2. Thread a needle with a double strand of heavy-duty thread, and make a knot at the end.

3. Mark the top of one folded pleat allowance with a pin. Measure from the pin to the pleat allowance seam and insert a pin one third of the distance from the pleat allowance seam.

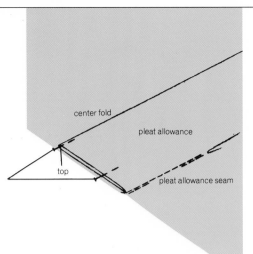

4. Grasping the top of the pleat with your left hand, push down on the center fold with the index finger of your right hand until the two marking pins meet.

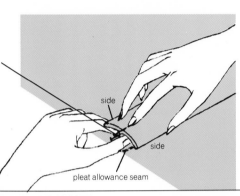

5. With the thumb and middle finger of your right hand, roll the sides of the pleat formed in Step 4 down to align with the pleat allowance seam. Pin the sides in place and remove the two center marking pins.

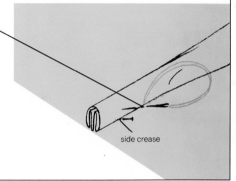

6. Slip stitch the side creases to the seam, taking care to hide the knots of the thread inside the pleat.

7. Repeat Steps 2-6 on each of the remaining pleat allowances.

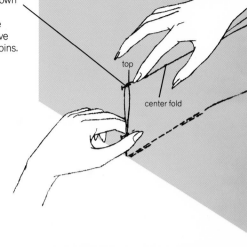

THE BOX PLEAT FOR FURNITURE SKIRTS

1. Plot and mark off the pleats with pins (pages 145-146). Then match the pins that designate one pleat, folding the pleat allowance in half.

2. Secure the pleat allowance by eliminating one pin and inserting the other through both layers of the pleat.

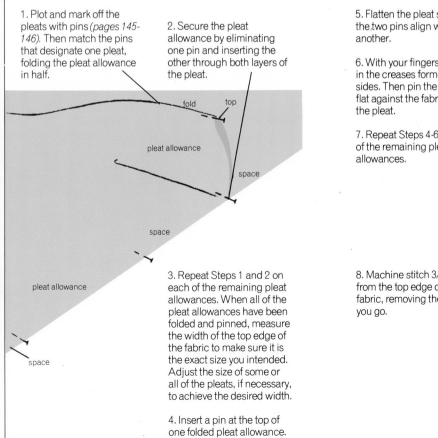

3. Repeat Steps 1 and 2 on each of the remaining pleat allowances. When all of the pleat allowances have been folded and pinned, measure the width of the top edge of the fabric to make sure it is the exact size you intended. Adjust the size of some or all of the pleats, if necessary, to achieve the desired width.

4. Insert a pin at the top of one folded pleat allowance.

5. Flatten the pleat so that the two pins align with one another.

6. With your fingers, press in the creases formed at the sides. Then pin the creases flat against the fabric behind the pleat.

7. Repeat Steps 4-6 on each of the remaining pleat allowances.

8. Machine stitch 3/8 inch from the top edge of the fabric, removing the pins as you go.

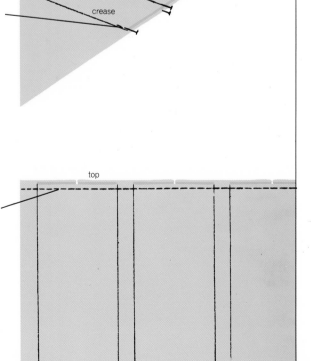

4

SCREENING THE WORLD OUTSIDE

Gleaming glass in a bare window should be as exciting to the home decorator as an empty canvas is to a painter. Imaginative window treatments can set the crowning touch of elegance or informality to a room and make it a lasting pleasure.

Draperies and curtains are particularly suited to home sewing. Long lines of straight machine stitching make the work go fast, and the detailing described in this

MORE THAN WINDOW DRESSING

chapter and throughout the book ensures the custom finish that store-bought draperies lack. In addition, the home seamstress can make exact allowances for the inconsistencies in the size of individual windows; even the pile on the carpet will make a difference in the final length.

As well as decorating a room, window treatments have to perform specific functions that may be contradictory. Windows let in light that can sometimes be too much of a good thing, they look out upon a view that can either delight or depress, and at night they turn into black holes through which the outside world can look in. To cope with these contradictories, a variety of window coverings have been invented. Draperies, curtains, blinds and shades regulate light in varying degrees and can be combined to satisfy fluctuating needs for privacy. For a living-room window with a spectacular view simple draperies alone may suffice. But if the window faces south, the midday sun may have to be diffused with an additional glass curtain of transparent material, or blocked with a shade or blind.

In a bedroom, where privacy is apt to be a major concern, transparent curtains and opaque draperies are frequently combined. An alternative to this arrangement are café curtains made of an opaque fabric; when made in tiers, they permit the top to be opened for light while the bottom remains closed for privacy. Often bedroom draperies are needed to control the light of the rising sun, which may awaken sleepers. And the daytime darkness required by people who want to sleep late calls for draperies that are lined or interlined with black fabric—a substitute for blackout curtains.

Although lining takes a little extra work, it adds durability, reduces fading and makes the draperies hang better. It helps to insulate a room against cold, especially at night, and its extra folds will soak up a lot of sound—a boon for city dwellers. When draperies in different rooms are lined with the same fabric, the exterior view of the house is unified.

Inside the house, a drapery or curtain can help the home seamstress to disguise an ill-proportioned room, or the ungainly shape of windows that are too narrow or short. The vertical line of a floor-length drapery can make a low-ceilinged room look more spacious, while draperies that are carried across adjacent windows can make the two windows read as one and unify a wall. Radiators and air conditioners that do not protrude into a room too far can sometimes be minimized by hanging draperies under a cornice or fabric valance that extends outward into the room the same distance as the heating or cooling device. Shortened draperies or permanent tieback draperies can also minimize the intruding bulk of radiators and air conditioners.

Finally, there is the role that a window treatment plays in helping to establish the character and style of a room. Café curtains are informal; full-length curtains are formal. The soft fullness of a shirred heading complements period furnishings, while the crisp line of a box-pleat heading is ideal for a room furnished in contemporary style. Austrian shades are inherently feminine in feeling; Roman shades are tailored and masculine. Furthermore, the fabrics in which these window treatments are executed will also affect the overall look of a room. Draperies can be used as a background in a neutral color, or to accent the furniture in the same or a contrasting color—perhaps with the slipcovers and draperies made from the same fabric. The choice is largely the designer's; the only essentials are careful preplanning and meticulous measurements.

Great swaths of luxury

Whether tied back in long graceful curves or falling vertically, the voluminous folds of full-length curtains and draperies do wonders to soften the angularity of windows and walls. The secret is generous amounts of fabric—two and a half times the window width for draperies and up to three times for sheer curtains.

Controlling this fullness are various kinds of pleats—rollback pleats, pinch pleats, cartridge pleats—proportioned to suit the dimensions of the window. The trickiest part—plotting the pleats and calculating yardages—becomes as straightforward as the sewing once you know the professional methods explained on the following pages.

Calculations for draperies and curtains

Whatever type of window you are curtaining —casement, double-hung sash, sliding or fixed; single or multiple; flush with a wall or set in a dormer or bay—first mount the rod that you plan to use. Then make the window measurements as described below, and, with these measurements, estimate the to-tal yardage for the materials you will need by the formulas given in the chart at right.

Separate formulas are given for drapery and curtain fabric, lining and stiffening. Insert the measurements that are called for, as identified by the letters, and then perform in sequence the necessary mathematical operations that are indicated by the stan-dard symbols.

If you are using fabric that has a pattern, you will also need the repeat measurement. To determine this dimension, measure lengthwise from the center of one promi-nent design detail in the fabric to the center of the next identical design detail.

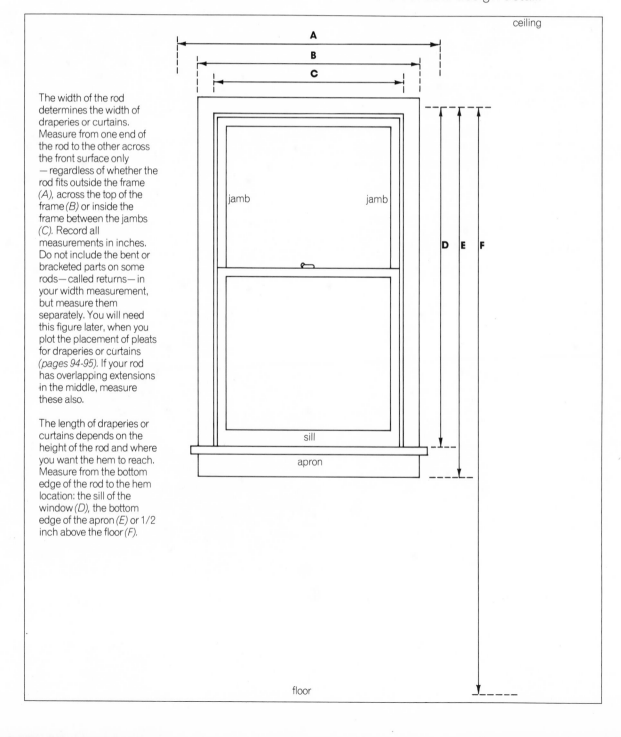

The width of the rod determines the width of draperies or curtains. Measure from one end of the rod to the other across the front surface only —regardless of whether the rod fits outside the frame (A), across the top of the frame (B) or inside the frame between the jambs (C). Record all measurements in inches. Do not include the bent or bracketed parts on some rods—called returns—in your width measurement, but measure them separately. You will need this figure later, when you plot the placement of pleats for draperies or curtains (pages 94-95). If your rod has overlapping extensions in the middle, measure these also.

The length of draperies or curtains depends on the height of the rod and where you want the hem to reach. Measure from the bottom edge of the rod to the hem location: the sill of the window (D), the bottom edge of the apron (E) or 1/2 inch above the floor (F).

ESTIMATING MATERIALS

DRAPERY AND CURTAIN FABRIC		
WIDTH	For pleats 7 inches wide or less	Number of fabric widths required for a pair of panels **= A, B OR C × 2½ ÷ FABRIC WIDTH IN INCHES***
	For hand-shirred headings	Number of fabric widths required for a pair of panels **= A, B OR C × 2½ ÷ FABRIC WIDTH IN INCHES***
	For pleats more than 7 inches wide	Number of fabric widths required for a pair of panels **= A, B OR C × 3 ÷ FABRIC WIDTH IN INCHES***
	For very light or sheer fabric	Number of fabric widths required for a pair of panels **= A, B OR C × 3 ÷ FABRIC WIDTH IN INCHES***
LENGTH	For fabrics that do not require matching a pattern	Length of each panel in inches **= D, E OR F + 18**
	For fabrics that require matching a pattern	Length of each panel in inches **= D, E OR F + 18 + LENGTH OF PATTERN REPEAT IN INCHES**
YARDAGE	Total yardage required = **NUMBER OF WIDTHS × LENGTH OF EACH PANEL IN INCHES ÷ 36**	

LINING FABRIC		
WIDTH	For pleats 7 inches wide or less	Number of fabric widths required for a pair of panels **= A, B OR C × 2½ ÷ FABRIC WIDTH IN INCHES***
	For pleats of more than 7 inches	Number of fabric widths required for a pair of panels **= A, B OR C × 2½ ÷ FABRIC WIDTH IN INCHES***
LENGTH	For all lining fabrics	Length of each panel in inches **= D, E OR F + 4**
YARDAGE	Total yardage required = **NUMBER OF FABRIC WIDTHS × LENGTH OF EACH PANEL IN INCHES ÷ 36**	

STIFFENING FOR HEADING		
WIDTH	For pleats 7 inches wide or less	Total length required in inches **= A, B OR C × 2½ + 3****
	For hand-shirred headings	Total length required in inches **= A, B OR C × 2½ + 3****
	For pleats more than 7 inches wide	Total length required in inches **= A, B OR C × 3 + 3****
	For very light or sheer fabric	Total length required in inches **= A, B OR C × 3 + 3****
DEPTH	For hand-shirred headings	Total depth required in inches equals desired depth of the hand-shirred rows, computed according to the instructions for hand shirring with a banded backing, page 55.
	For D or E length draperies and curtains	Total depth required equals 3 inches.
	For F length draperies and curtains	Total depth required equals 4 inches.

*Round off fractions to the nearest full width.

**Round off fractions to the next highest inch.

A CUTTING AND PREPARING THE FABRIC

1. Place the fabric, wrong side down, on a large table.

2A. For fabrics that are not glazed or permanently finished, straighten one edge by drawing a crosswise thread. Cut along the thread.

2B. For glazed or permanently finished fabrics, draw a chalk line at right angles to the selvages and cut along the chalk line.

3A. For fabric that does not require matching a pattern, use the panel length measurement determined by the formula on page 87 to mark and cut off as many sections as you need. Make all cuts along crosswise threads or chalk lines.

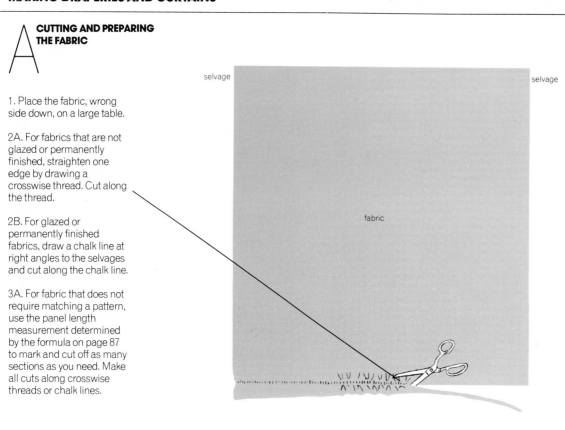

3B. For fabric with a pronounced pattern, cut off a section equal to the panel length as determined by the formula on page 87. Examine fabric and window to decide where pattern repeats should fall, then trim the section on crosswise threads or chalk lines. Cut off a total amount equal to one full repeat, but trim some from the top and some from the bottom as necessary to get the pattern positioned suitably. Match each subsequent section to the first by aligning the pattern along the selvages before cutting the fabric.

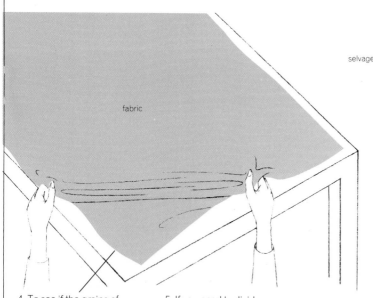

4. To see if the grains of fabrics that are not glazed or permanently finished need straightening, align two adjacent sides of a section to a right-angled corner of a table. If the edges do not align properly, gently pull on the true bias of the fabric until its sides are at right angles, then steam-press. Repeat on the other sections.

5. If you need to divide one fabric section into two half widths, fold the section lengthwise down the center and cut it along the fold.

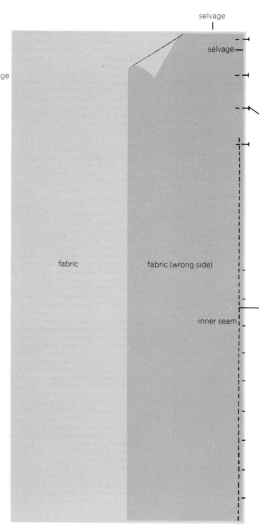

6. To make a panel out of more than one section of fabric, place one piece on top of the other wrong sides out if the fabric is opaque, but wrong sides together if the fabric is sheer. Match the pattern at the selvage, if necessary, then pin. If the selvages are very wide, trim them to 1 inch. If half widths are required, position them so that they will hang at the outside edge of the window in each of the panels of the draperies or curtains and pin them to the full widths along the selvage edges. Repeat for each additional section of fabric required.

7. Machine stitch along the inner edge of the selvages. Make a plain seam for lined draperies, an interlocking fell seam *(Appendix)* for unlined draperies and opaque curtains, a French seam *(Appendix)* for sheer curtains. Clip into untrimmed selvages at regular intervals to prevent the seams from puckering.

8. Join the second panel of the pair similarly.

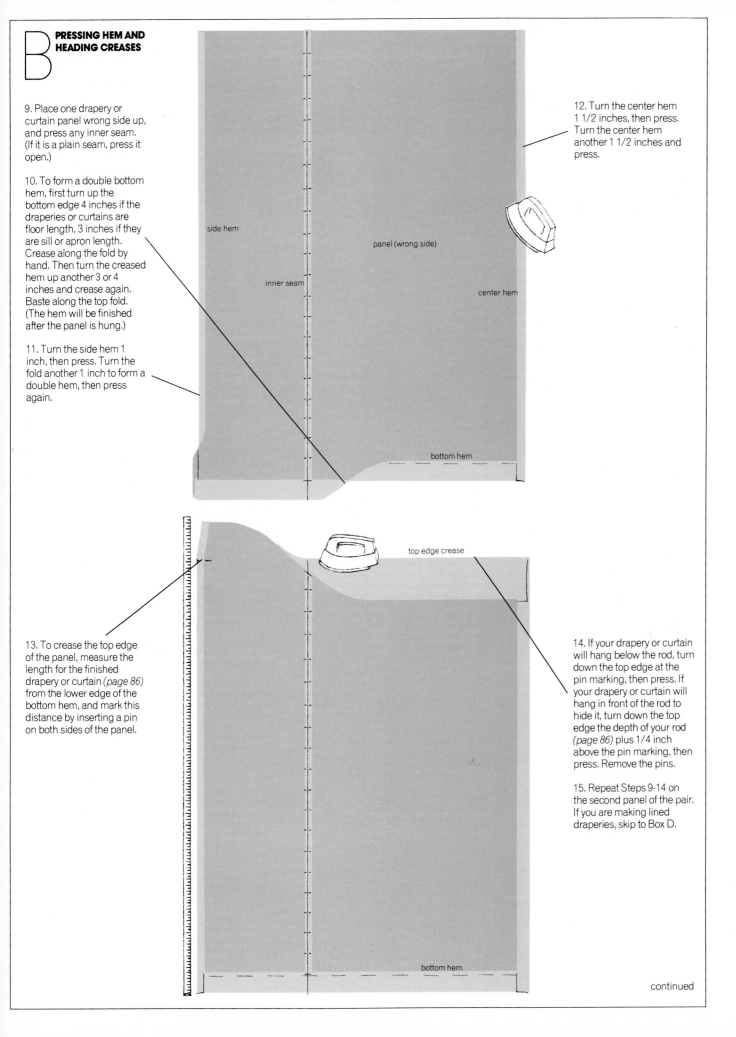

9. Place one drapery or curtain panel wrong side up, and press any inner seam. (If it is a plain seam, press it open.)

10. To form a double bottom hem, first turn up the bottom edge 4 inches if the draperies or curtains are floor length, 3 inches if they are sill or apron length. Crease along the fold by hand. Then turn the creased hem up another 3 or 4 inches and crease again. Baste along the top fold. (The hem will be finished after the panel is hung.)

11. Turn the side hem 1 inch, then press. Turn the fold another 1 inch to form a double hem, then press again.

side hem

inner seam

panel (wrong side)

center hem

bottom hem

12. Turn the center hem 1 1/2 inches, then press. Turn the center hem another 1 1/2 inches and press.

top edge crease

13. To crease the top edge of the panel, measure the length for the finished drapery or curtain (page 86) from the lower edge of the bottom hem, and mark this distance by inserting a pin on both sides of the panel.

bottom hem

14. If your drapery or curtain will hang below the rod, turn down the top edge at the pin marking, then press. If your drapery or curtain will hang in front of the rod to hide it, turn down the top edge the depth of your rod (page 86) plus 1/4 inch above the pin marking, then press. Remove the pins.

15. Repeat Steps 9-14 on the second panel of the pair. If you are making lined draperies, skip to Box D.

continued

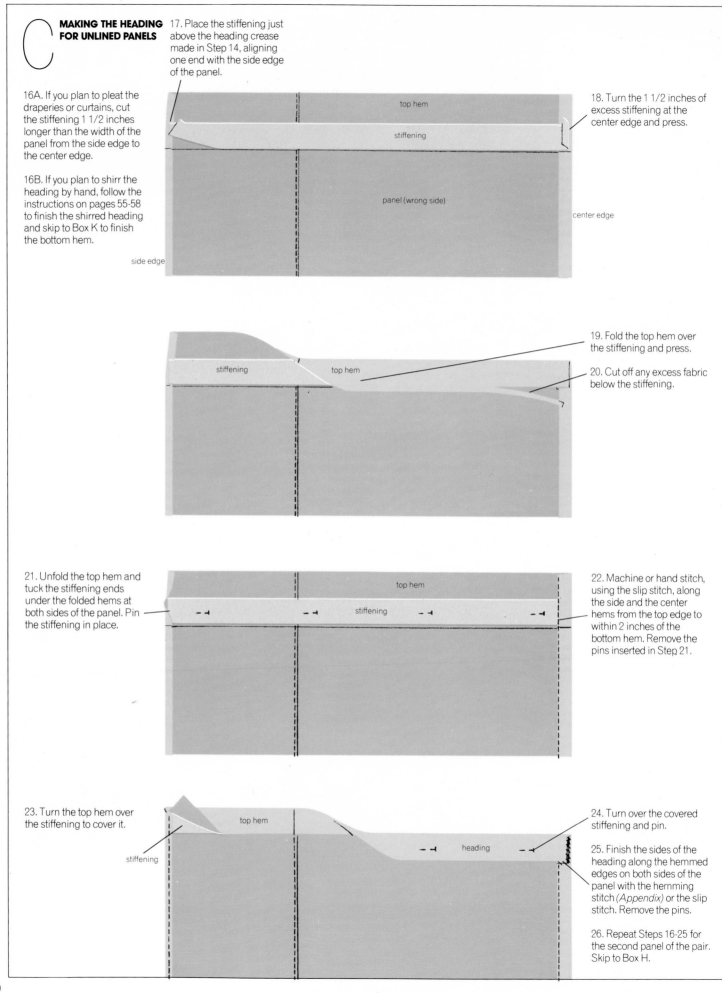

C **MAKING THE HEADING FOR UNLINED PANELS**

16A. If you plan to pleat the draperies or curtains, cut the stiffening 1 1/2 inches longer than the width of the panel from the side edge to the center edge.

16B. If you plan to shirr the heading by hand, follow the instructions on pages 55-58 to finish the shirred heading and skip to Box K to finish the bottom hem.

17. Place the stiffening just above the heading crease made in Step 14, aligning one end with the side edge of the panel.

18. Turn the 1 1/2 inches of excess stiffening at the center edge and press.

19. Fold the top hem over the stiffening and press.

20. Cut off any excess fabric below the stiffening.

21. Unfold the top hem and tuck the stiffening ends under the folded hems at both sides of the panel. Pin the stiffening in place.

22. Machine or hand stitch, using the slip stitch, along the side and the center hems from the top edge to within 2 inches of the bottom hem. Remove the pins inserted in Step 21.

23. Turn the top hem over the stiffening to cover it.

24. Turn over the covered stiffening and pin.

25. Finish the sides of the heading along the hemmed edges on both sides of the panel with the hemming stitch (*Appendix*) or the slip stitch. Remove the pins.

26. Repeat Steps 16-25 for the second panel of the pair. Skip to Box H.

Labels within the diagrams: top hem, stiffening, panel (wrong side), center edge, side edge, heading

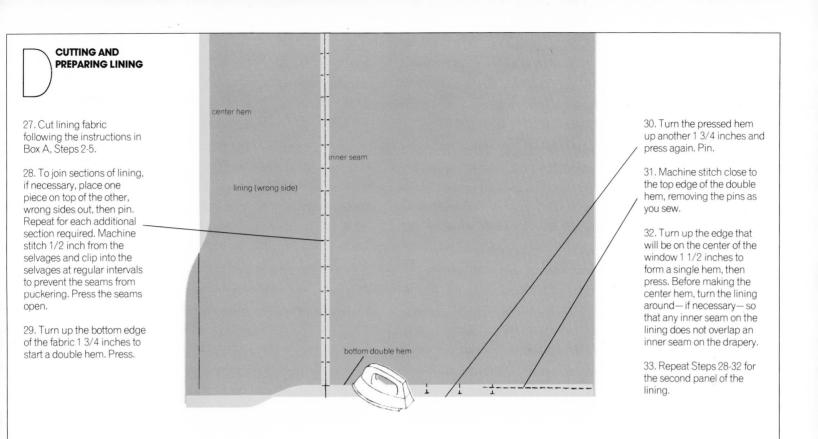

D CUTTING AND PREPARING LINING

center hem

inner seam

lining (wrong side)

bottom double hem

27. Cut lining fabric following the instructions in Box A, Steps 2-5.

28. To join sections of lining, if necessary, place one piece on top of the other, wrong sides out, then pin. Repeat for each additional section required. Machine stitch 1/2 inch from the selvages and clip into the selvages at regular intervals to prevent the seams from puckering. Press the seams open.

29. Turn up the bottom edge of the fabric 1 3/4 inches to start a double hem. Press.

30. Turn the pressed hem up another 1 3/4 inches and press again. Pin.

31. Machine stitch close to the top edge of the double hem, removing the pins as you sew.

32. Turn up the edge that will be on the center of the window 1 1/2 inches to form a single hem, then press. Before making the center hem, turn the lining around—if necessary—so that any inner seam on the lining does not overlap an inner seam on the drapery.

33. Repeat Steps 28-32 for the second panel of the lining.

E ATTACHING THE LINING TO THE CENTER EDGE SEAM

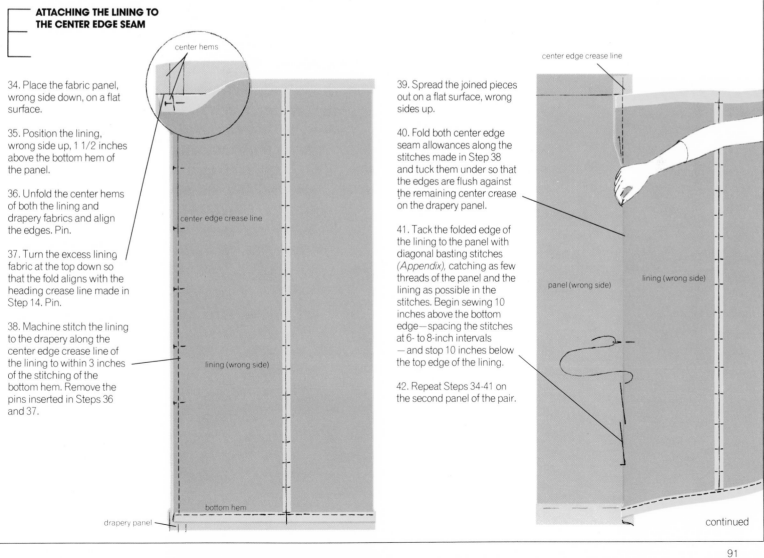

center hems

center edge crease line

lining (wrong side)

bottom hem

drapery panel

center edge crease line

panel (wrong side)

lining (wrong side)

34. Place the fabric panel, wrong side down, on a flat surface.

35. Position the lining, wrong side up, 1 1/2 inches above the bottom hem of the panel.

36. Unfold the center hems of both the lining and drapery fabrics and align the edges. Pin.

37. Turn the excess lining fabric at the top down so that the fold aligns with the heading crease line made in Step 14. Pin.

38. Machine stitch the lining to the drapery along the center edge crease line of the lining to within 3 inches of the stitching of the bottom hem. Remove the pins inserted in Steps 36 and 37.

39. Spread the joined pieces out on a flat surface, wrong sides up.

40. Fold both center edge seam allowances along the stitches made in Step 38 and tuck them under so that the edges are flush against the remaining center crease on the drapery panel.

41. Tack the folded edge of the lining to the panel with diagonal basting stitches (Appendix), catching as few threads of the panel and the lining as possible in the stitches. Begin sewing 10 inches above the bottom edge—spacing the stitches at 6- to 8-inch intervals —and stop 10 inches below the top edge of the lining.

42. Repeat Steps 34-41 on the second panel of the pair.

continued

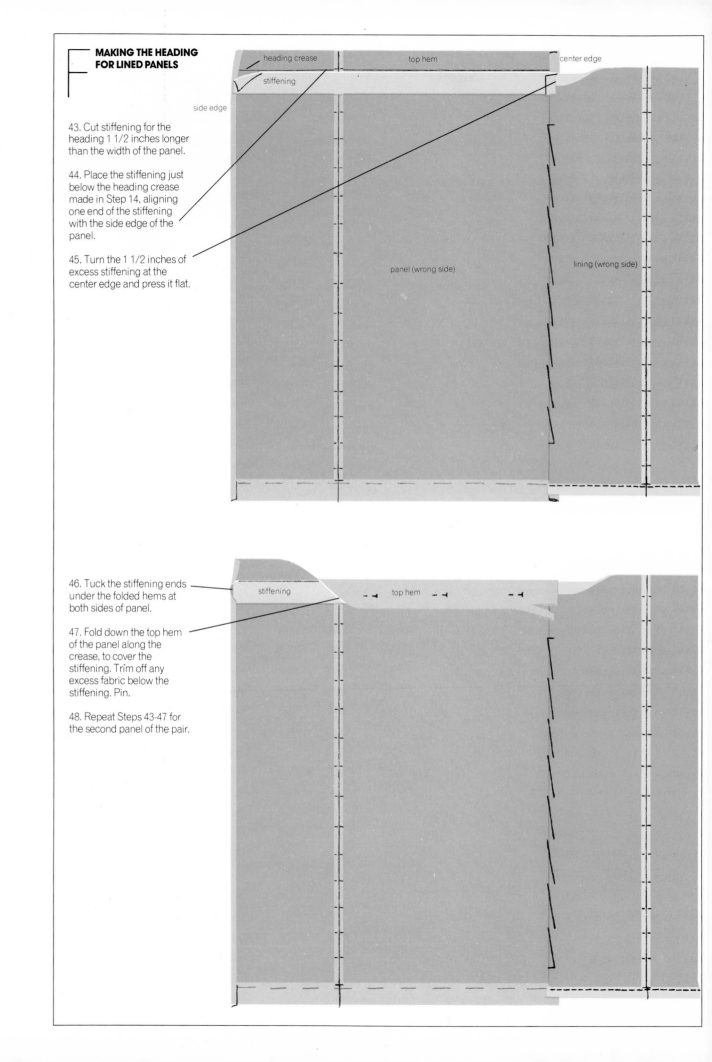

MAKING THE HEADING FOR LINED PANELS

43. Cut stiffening for the heading 1 1/2 inches longer than the width of the panel.

44. Place the stiffening just below the heading crease made in Step 14, aligning one end of the stiffening with the side edge of the panel.

45. Turn the 1 1/2 inches of excess stiffening at the center edge and press it flat.

46. Tuck the stiffening ends under the folded hems at both sides of panel.

47. Fold down the top hem of the panel along the crease, to cover the stiffening. Trim off any excess fabric below the stiffening. Pin.

48. Repeat Steps 43-47 for the second panel of the pair.

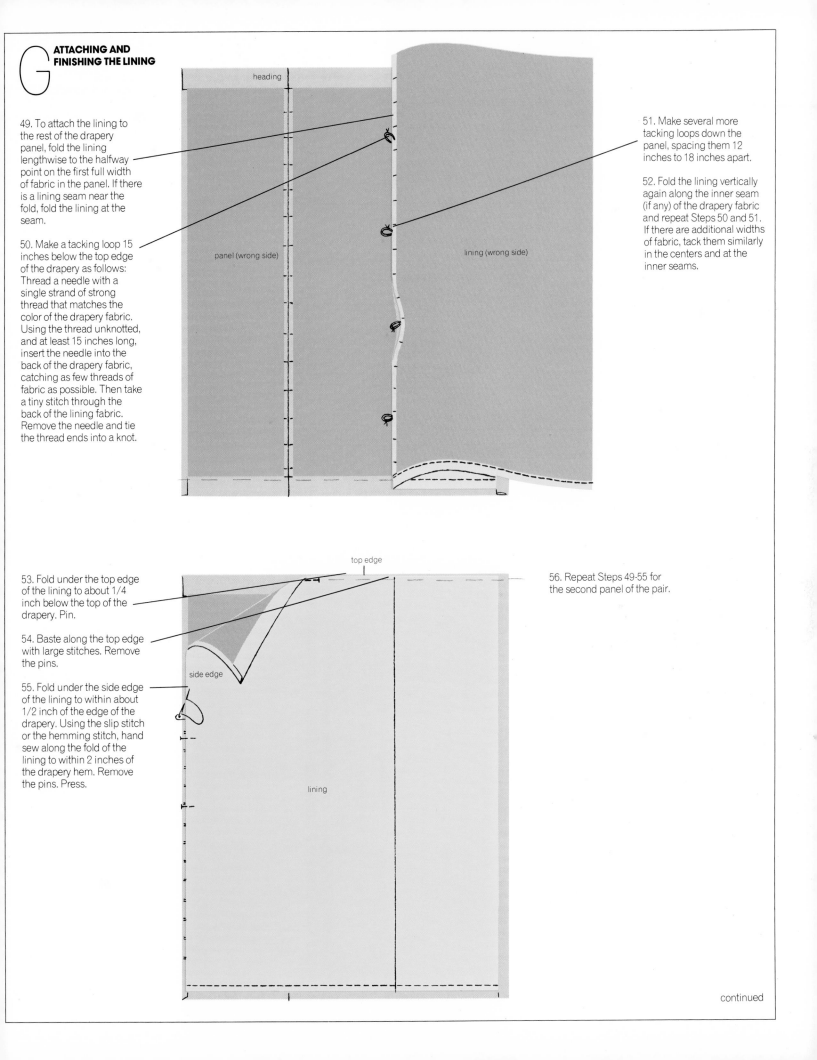

heading

panel (wrong side)

lining (wrong side)

49. To attach the lining to the rest of the drapery panel, fold the lining lengthwise to the halfway point on the first full width of fabric in the panel. If there is a lining seam near the fold, fold the lining at the seam.

50. Make a tacking loop 15 inches below the top edge of the drapery as follows: Thread a needle with a single strand of strong thread that matches the color of the drapery fabric. Using the thread unknotted, and at least 15 inches long, insert the needle into the back of the drapery fabric, catching as few threads of fabric as possible. Then take a tiny stitch through the back of the lining fabric. Remove the needle and tie the thread ends into a knot.

51. Make several more tacking loops down the panel, spacing them 12 inches to 18 inches apart.

52. Fold the lining vertically again along the inner seam (if any) of the drapery fabric and repeat Steps 50 and 51. If there are additional widths of fabric, tack them similarly in the centers and at the inner seams.

top edge

side edge

lining

53. Fold under the top edge of the lining to about 1/4 inch below the top of the drapery. Pin.

54. Baste along the top edge with large stitches. Remove the pins.

55. Fold under the side edge of the lining to within about 1/2 inch of the edge of the drapery. Using the slip stitch or the hemming stitch, hand sew along the fold of the lining to within 2 inches of the drapery hem. Remove the pins. Press.

56. Repeat Steps 49-55 for the second panel of the pair.

continued

PLEAT SELECTION GUIDE

STYLE OF PLEAT		PLEAT ALLOWANCE	SPACE BETWEEN PLEATS	DECORATIVE USES
THREE-FOLD PINCH PLEAT		5-7 inches	4-5 inches	The most popular style of drapery and curtain pleating, these pinch pleats can be made of any fabric.
FOUR-FOLD PINCH PLEAT		7-9 inches	4-5 inches	This style produces a maximum number of vertical folds and is also suitable for any fabric.
ROLLBACK PLEAT		8-10 inches	5-6 inches	Providing the maximum fullness, this style is especially effective on plain fabrics.
CARTRIDGE PLEAT		3-4 inches	3-4 inches	This style produces small, columnar folds and is most suitable for lightweight fabrics.
ROLLBACK CARTRIDGE PLEAT		7-8 inches	4-5 inches	Large, columnar folds are created in any fabric by this style.
BOX PLEAT		6-7 inches	6-7 inches	Crisply tailored vertical folds can be made in any fabric with this pleat.
DOUBLE BOX PLEAT		10-12 inches	6-7 inches	More luxurious tailored folds than the box pleat are made in any fabric by this style.

ESTIMATING PLEAT ALLOWANCES

57. To determine how much fabric you can use for all of the pleats, divide the width of the rod by two. If the rod has side returns that carry the fabric back to the wall, measure from the front of the rod to the wall bracket along one return, if you have not already done so, and add this figure to half the width measurement.

58. If your draperies or curtains will overlap at the center, measure the length of one of the overlapping extensions on the rod, if you have not already done so.

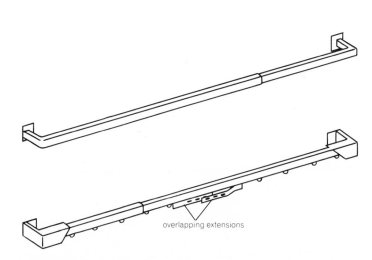

overlapping extensions

59. Subtract the figure determined in Step 57 from the width of one panel of the drapery or curtain to find the overall pleat allowance.

60. Divide the overall pleat allowance by the approximate number of inches required for the style of pleat you plan to use (chart, above) to determine how many pleats you can have in one panel and what the exact dimensions of the individual pleat allowance for each of them will be.

PLOTTING PLEATS

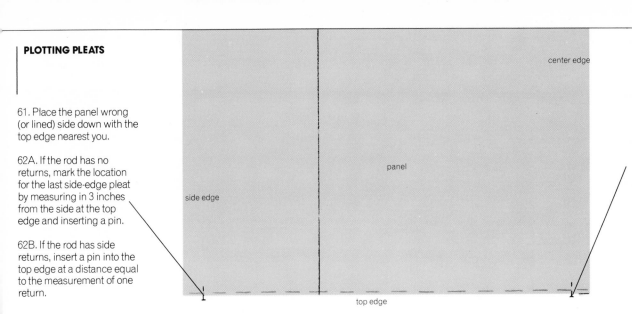

center edge

panel

side edge

top edge

61. Place the panel wrong (or lined) side down with the top edge nearest you.

62A. If the rod has no returns, mark the location for the last side-edge pleat by measuring in 3 inches from the side at the top edge and inserting a pin.

62B. If the rod has side returns, insert a pin into the top edge at a distance equal to the measurement of one return.

63A. If your curtains or draperies will not overlap at the center, mark the location for the first pleat beside the center hem by measuring in 2 inches from the center edge and inserting a pin on the top edge.

63B. If your draperies or curtains will overlap at the center, divide the measurement made in Step 58 by two, add 2 inches and insert a pin into the top edge at this distance from the center edge.

inner seam

64. To find the space allowance between each pleat, measure the distance between the pins and subtract the overall pleat allowance determined in Step 59. Divide this result by one less than the total number of pleats (Step 60).

65. Insert pins into the panel between the side-edge and center-edge pin marks to mark off pleat allowances (Step 60) and space allowances (Step 64) alternately. Begin by measuring off one pleat allowance inside the center-edge pin mark and end with one pleat allowance inside the side-edge pin mark.

66. Check the results to see if the panel is divided properly, noting how pleats relate to inner seams. The inner seams should fall on or close to one of the pin markings so they will be hidden by the folds of the finished pleats. You may want to rearrange the pins or change the sizes of the pleats or spaces. Slight differences between pleats or spaces will be barely noticeable on the finished draperies or curtains.

67. Repeat Steps 61-66 for the second panel. To stitch and shape the pleats, follow the instructions on pages 73-79.

FINISHING THE HEADING

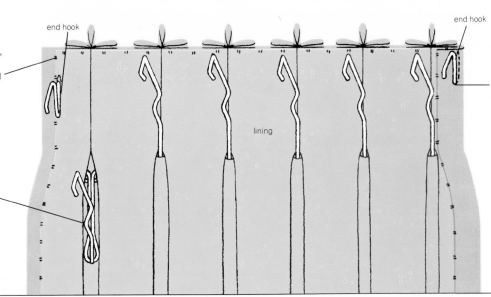

end hook

end hook

lining

68. If the draperies are lined, use the hemming or slip stitch to hand sew the lining to each panel along the top edge between pleats. Remove the basting made in Step 54.

69. If the draperies or curtains are pleated, insert slip-in hooks into the backs of the pleats. On unlined draperies or curtains, slide the prongs of the hook under the top hem with one prong on each side of the pleat allowance seam. On lined draperies, slide the prongs into the folds at the center of the pleat.

70. Attach or insert end hooks at both sides of each panel, making sure that the top bend of each end hook aligns with the top bend on the adjacent slip-in hook.

71. If the draperies or curtains are shirred, attach the hooks according to the instructions on page 58.

continued

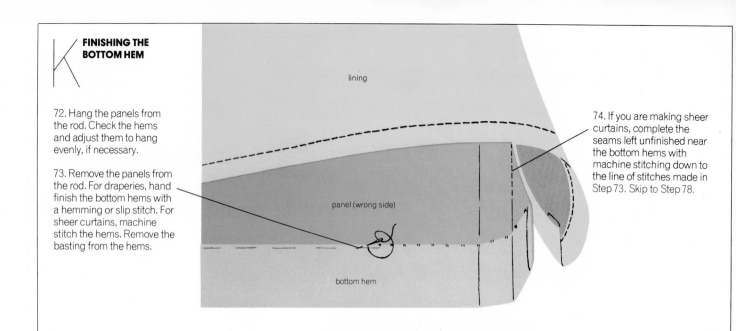

K | FINISHING THE BOTTOM HEM

72. Hang the panels from the rod. Check the hems and adjust them to hang evenly, if necessary.

73. Remove the panels from the rod. For draperies, hand finish the bottom hems with a hemming or slip stitch. For sheer curtains, machine stitch the hems. Remove the basting from the hems.

lining

panel (wrong side)

bottom hem

74. If you are making sheer curtains, complete the seams left unfinished near the bottom hems with machine stitching down to the line of stitches made in Step 73. Skip to Step 78.

L | FINISHING THE PANELS

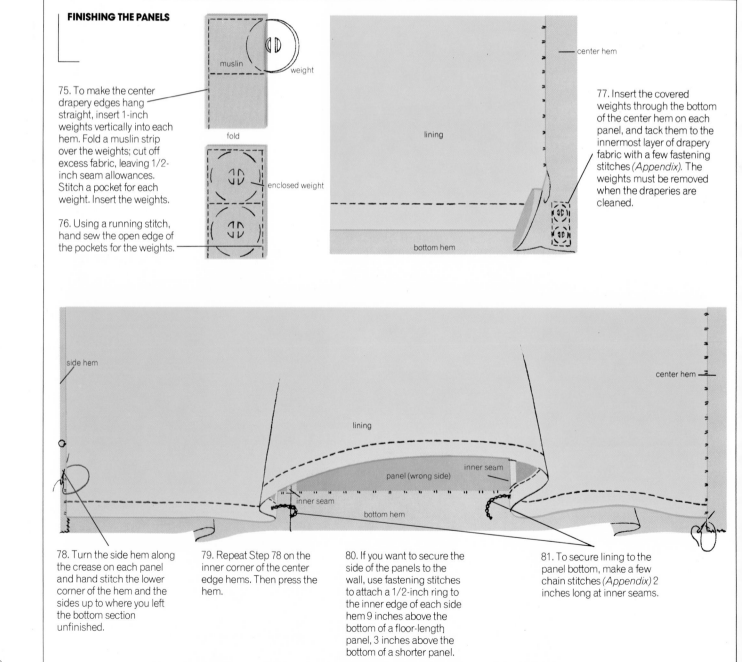

muslin

weight

fold

enclosed weight

center hem

lining

bottom hem

75. To make the center drapery edges hang straight, insert 1-inch weights vertically into each hem. Fold a muslin strip over the weights; cut off excess fabric, leaving 1/2-inch seam allowances. Stitch a pocket for each weight. Insert the weights.

76. Using a running stitch, hand sew the open edge of the pockets for the weights.

77. Insert the covered weights through the bottom of the center hem on each panel, and tack them to the innermost layer of drapery fabric with a few fastening stitches (Appendix). The weights must be removed when the draperies are cleaned.

side hem

lining

inner seam

panel (wrong side)

inner seam

bottom hem

center hem

78. Turn the side hem along the crease on each panel and hand stitch the lower corner of the hem and the sides up to where you left the bottom section unfinished.

79. Repeat Step 78 on the inner corner of the center edge hems. Then press the hem.

80. If you want to secure the side of the panels to the wall, use fastening stitches to attach a 1/2-inch ring to the inner edge of each side hem 9 inches above the bottom of a floor-length panel, 3 inches above the bottom of a shorter panel.

81. To secure lining to the panel bottom, make a few chain stitches (Appendix) 2 inches long at inner seams.

M SETTING THE FOLDS

82. Hang the panels on the rod. Screw a small hook in the wall behind the ring attached in Step 80. Do not hook the ring until after the folds are set in.

83. To set the folds, pull each panel to the outsides of the rod. Starting at the top, shape each pleat by hand downward to the hem. Tie each panel with a series of ribbons or tapes spaced along it at regular intervals. Leave the panels tied for several days.

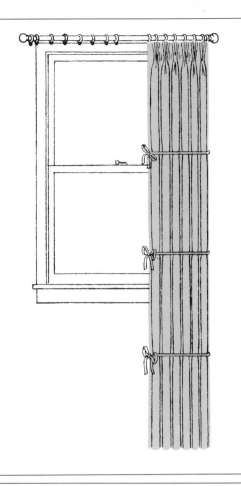

N MAKING THE TIEBACKS

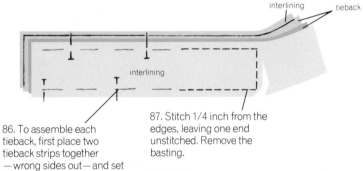

84. Wrap a tape measure around one panel to decide where to place the tieback and to determine how long and wide it should be.

85. Cut out four strips of fabric this size, leaving 1/4-inch seam allowances. Using muslin, cut interlining strips the same size.

86. To assemble each tieback, first place two tieback strips together —wrong sides out—and set two interlining strips over them. Pin and baste. Remove the pins.

87. Stitch 1/4 inch from the edges, leaving one end unstitched. Remove the basting.

88. Cut the corners diagonally and grade (Appendix) the seams.

89. Using a ruler, turn the tieback right side out through the opening, and pull the corners out with a needle. Press.

90. Turn in the raw edges 1/4 inch and hand sew the seam using a hemming or slip stitch. Press.

91. Sew on the attachments appropriate for your tieback holders to the end of each tieback.

92. Wrap the tiebacks around the panels, and hook on the ends to the holders.

93. Drape the panels along the center edges, and arrange the folds to make them look neat at the tieback and hemlines.

Crisp and delicate shades

An Austrian shade *(above and far right)* and a Roman shade *(center)* represent two extremes in window coverings: from lush formality to no-nonsense crispness. The Austrian shade is best made of a lightweight fabric that will shirr gracefully and fall in puffy folds. The Roman shade should be of a sturdy fabric rein-forced by lining; the combination has sufficient body to fold evenly and to hang plumb. Carefully placed un-derpinnings of tapes and the rings that guide the draw cords make both types behave as they should, as shown on the following pages.

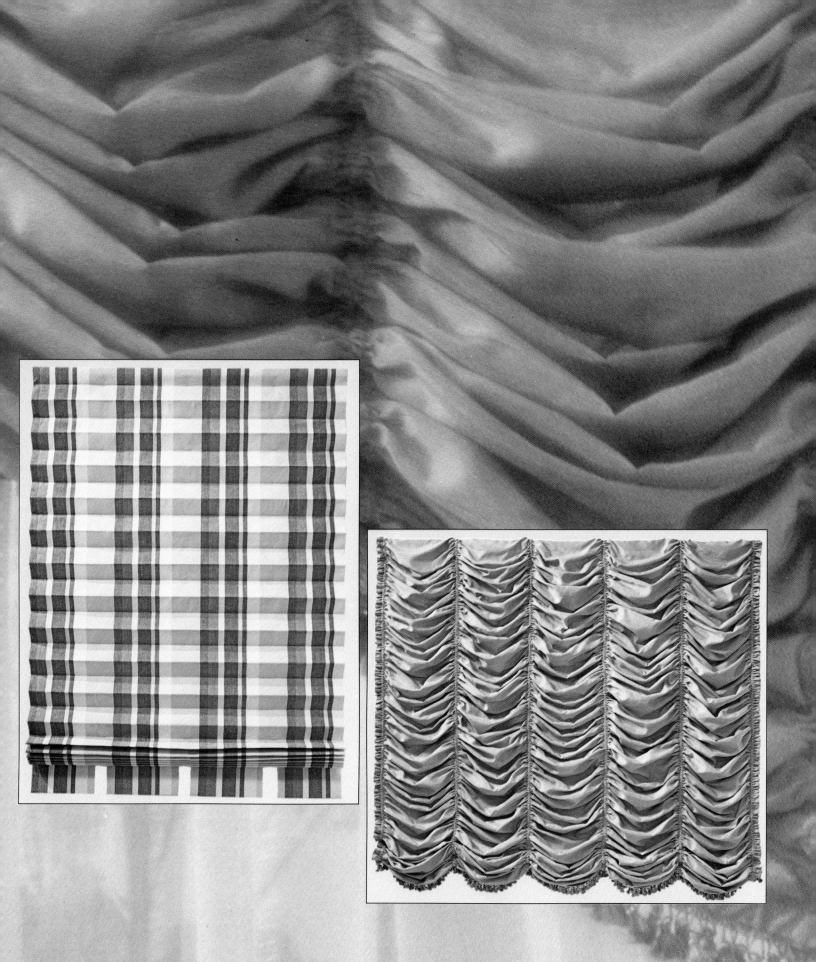

THE AUSTRIAN SHADE

A PREPARING THE FABRIC

1. To determine the finished shade length, measure from inside the top of the window frame to the sill. To calculate the fabric length, multiply by two and one half and add 3 inches.

2. To determine the finished shade width, measure between the jambs and subtract 1/2 inch. Decide how many shirred sections of 8 to 14 inches each you want. To calculate the fabric width, add 3 inches for side hems and 3 inches for each section to the finished shade width; to calculate the spacing for the shirring tapes, subtract 6 inches and divide this figure by the number of sections.

3. Cut the fabric to the length determined in Step 1.

4. With chalk, mark the fold line for one side hem 1 1/2 inches inside one selvage edge.

5. Mark a guide line for the first strip of shirring tape 1 1/2 inches inside the side hem fold line.

6. Mark the next guide line for the shirring tape parallel to the previous one and at the interval determined in Step 2.

7. Continue to mark shirring tape guide lines at the same interval until you have the number of shirred spaces you need or until you cannot fit any more lines on the fabric.

8. If pieces of fabric must be joined, cut the new piece to the same length. Trim the first piece 3/8 inch outside the last guide line marked. Pin both pieces along the guide line, machine stitch and remove the pins. Press open the seams and continue marking.

9. Mark another side hem fold line 1 1/2 inches outside of, and parallel to, the last shirring tape guide line.

10. Draw a cutting line 1 1/2 inches outside the hem fold line. Trim off the excess fabric along the cutting line.

side hem fold line

shirring tape guide line

shade fabric (wrong side)

selvage

shirring tape guide line

side hem fold line

selvage

B SHAPING THE TOP OF THE SHADE

11. To taper the top edge of the shade to the finished width (Step 2), mark darts at the top end of each shirring tape guide line. For each dart, first mark the dart point on the tape guide line 5 inches below the top edge of the fabric.

12. Mark the top edge on each side of the tape guide lines, 3/4 inch from the two outermost lines and 1 1/2 inches from the others.

13. Draw the seam lines of each dart by connecting the marks made in Step 11 with the mark made in Step 12.

14. Pin each dart along the seam lines and machine stitch. Remove the pins.

15. Press the darts open without cutting the fabric.

side hem fold line

shade (wrong side)

shirring tape guide line

side hem fold line

shirring tape guide line

C HEMMING THE SHADE

16. Fold down the top edge of the fabric 1/2 inch and press. Then fold it down again 1/2 inch and press.

17. Machine stitch the top hem close to the inner folded edge.

18. To reinforce the top edge of the shade where it will be attached to a wood strip, cut a piece of 1-inch-wide twill tape 3 inches shorter than the finished width of the shade (Step 2).

19. Place the twill tape over the top hem of the fabric. Align the top edge of the tape just below the fabric edge and the ends along the side hemline markings. Pin.

20. Machine stitch the twill tape to the fabric just inside the top and bottom edges of the tape. Remove the pins.

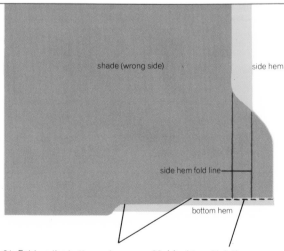

shade (wrong side)

side hem

side hem fold line

bottom hem

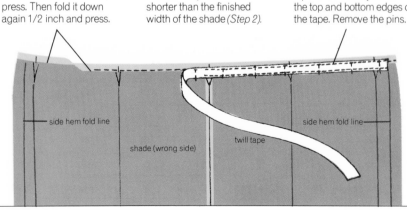

side hem fold line

shade (wrong side)

twill tape

side hem fold line

21. Fold up the bottom edge of the fabric 1/4 inch and press. Then fold it up again 1/4 inch and press.

22. Machine stitch the bottom hem close to the inner folded edge.

23. Fold under the side edges of the shade along the hem fold lines. Press.

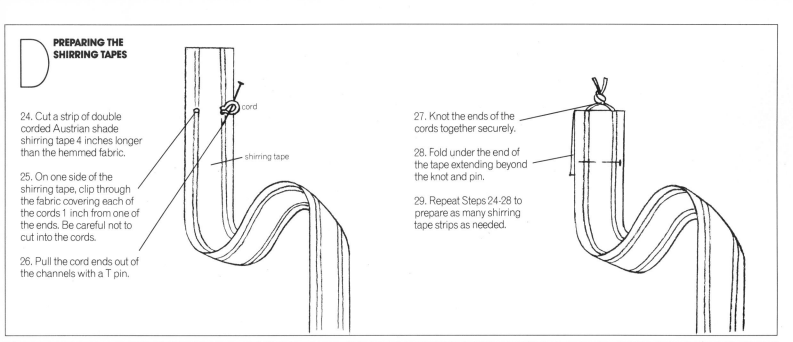

D PREPARING THE SHIRRING TAPES

24. Cut a strip of double corded Austrian shade shirring tape 4 inches longer than the hemmed fabric.

25. On one side of the shirring tape, clip through the fabric covering each of the cords 1 inch from one of the ends. Be careful not to cut into the cords.

26. Pull the cord ends out of the channels with a T pin.

cord

shirring tape

27. Knot the ends of the cords together securely.

28. Fold under the end of the tape extending beyond the knot and pin.

29. Repeat Steps 24-28 to prepare as many shirring tape strips as needed.

E ATTACHING THE SHIRRING TAPES

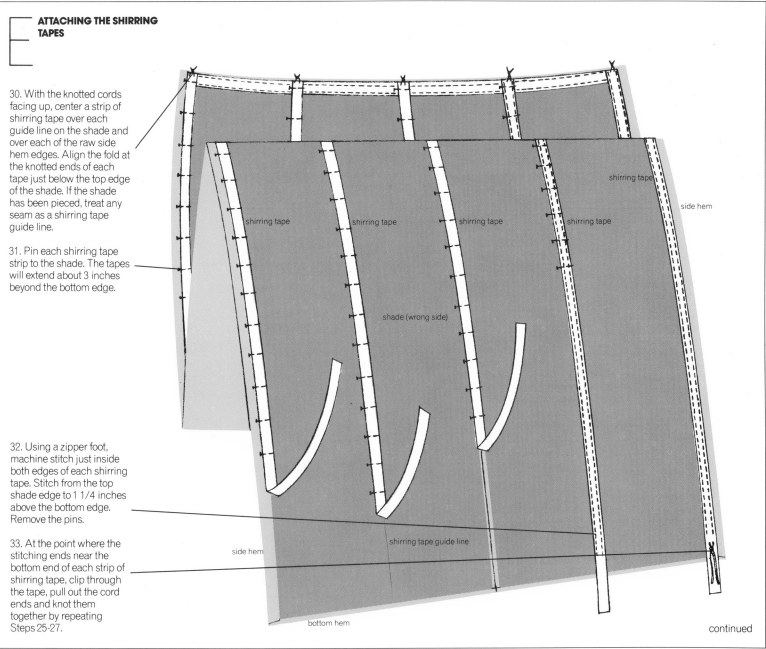

30. With the knotted cords facing up, center a strip of shirring tape over each guide line on the shade and over each of the raw side hem edges. Align the fold at the knotted ends of each tape just below the top edge of the shade. If the shade has been pieced, treat any seam as a shirring tape guide line.

31. Pin each shirring tape strip to the shade. The tapes will extend about 3 inches beyond the bottom edge.

32. Using a zipper foot, machine stitch just inside both edges of each shirring tape. Stitch from the top shade edge to 1 1/4 inches above the bottom edge. Remove the pins.

33. At the point where the stitching ends near the bottom end of each strip of shirring tape, clip through the tape, pull out the cord ends and knot them together by repeating Steps 25-27.

shirring tape

side hem

shade (wrong side)

side hem

shirring tape guide line

bottom hem

continued

F SHIRRING THE SHADE

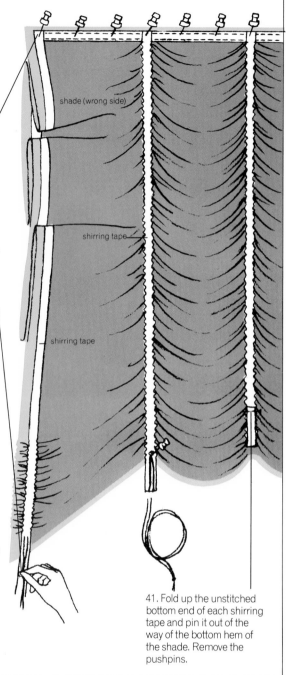

34. Spread out the shade, wrong side up, on a large surface—such as a cutting board—into which you can insert pins.

35. Pull the fabric taut along the top edge, and anchor it securely to the work surface by inserting pushpins through each shirring tape below the knotted cords. Add pushpins at 5-inch intervals along the top hem.

36. Start at one side hem and, working across the shade toward the other side, shirr the tapes one at a time. To shirr each tape, pull the knotted cords at the bottom end with one hand while pushing the fabric and shirring tape toward the top edge with the other hand.

37. Stop shirring the tape when the fabric measures 3 inches less—from the top hem edge to the bottom hem edge—than the finished length of the shade (Step 1).

38. Reknot the ends of the cords close to the openings in the shirring tape. Then trim the cords even with the bottom edge of the tape.

39. Pull the shirring tape until the fabric is taut lengthwise. Then anchor the tape and the bottom hem of the shade to the work surface with a pushpin.

40. Repeat Steps 36-39 to shirr the remaining tapes. Then adjust the shirring so that it is even across the shade.

shade (wrong side)

shirring tape

shirring tape

41. Fold up the unstitched bottom end of each shirring tape and pin it out of the way of the bottom hem of the shade. Remove the pushpins.

G ATTACHING THE FRINGED TRIM

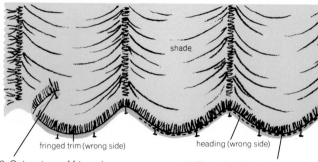

shade

fringed trim (wrong side)   heading (wrong side)

42. Cut a piece of fringed trim 1 inch longer than the bottom edge of the shade. Fold each end to the wrong side 1/2 inch and pin.

43. Place the shade wrong side down. Attach the trim to the bottom edge of the shade as shown for fringed trim (page 53, Steps 1-6).

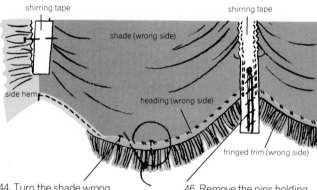

shirring tape

shade (wrong side)

shirring tape

side hem

heading (wrong side)

fringed trim (wrong side)

44. Turn the shade wrong side up. Fold up the bottom edge 3/8 inch; if the stitches holding the trim are more than 3/8 inch from the edge, fold on the stitching line. Pin.

45. Attach the hem with slip stitches (Appendix). Remove the pins from the hem.

46. Remove the pins holding the tape ends. Fold down the ends and center the cords on each tape. Sew the cords to the tapes with overcast stitches (Appendix).

47. Repin each tape to the shade and machine stitch, sewing through all layers. Sew forward to the hem edge, back and forward again. Remove the pins.

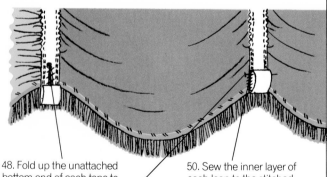

48. Fold up the unattached bottom end of each tape to meet the hem edge.

49. Fold each tape end up again at the hem edge to form a loop. At the top fold, pin the inner layer of the loop to the stitched tape.

50. Sew the inner layer of each loop to the stitched tape along the side edges with overcast stitches.

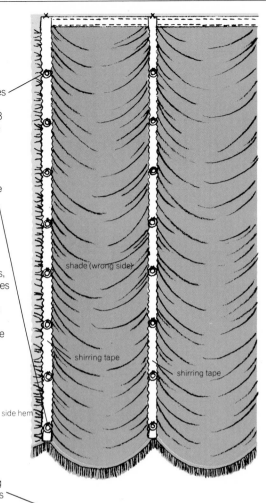

51. Using fastening stitches (*Appendix*), sew a curtain ring to each shirring tape 8 inches below the top edge of the shade.

52. Sew a curtain ring to each shirring tape just above the tape loops at the bottom of the shade.

53. Sew rings along each shirring tape at evenly spaced intervals between the top and bottom rings. On medium-weight fabrics, space the rings 5 to 6 inches apart; on sheer fabrics, 3 1/2 to 4 inches apart. Be sure to attach the rings at the same location on all the tapes.

shade (wrong side)

shirring tape

shirring tape

side hem

54. Cut a 1-by-2-inch strip of wood to the measurement determined in Step 3. Paint the board or cover it with fabric if desired.

55. Place the top edge of the shade, wrong side down, on the board as shown, and attach it with upholstery or carpet tacks. Tack on both sides of each shirring tape strip and at 2- to 3-inch intervals in between.

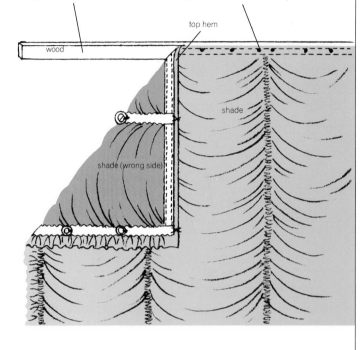

wood

top hem

shade

shade (wrong side)

56. Place the shade wrong side up. Attach screw eyes to the underside of the board, centering one above each shirring tape.

57. For each shirring tape, cut a piece of No. 2 traverse cord the width plus one and one half the length of the finished shade.

58. Knot one end of a traverse cord around the bottom ring of the tape nearest the left-hand edge of the shade. Thread the cord through all rings on the tape and, from right to left, through the screw eye on the board above the tape.

59. Working to the right, repeat Step 58 to attach and thread a cord through the rings on each remaining tape. Thread each ensuing cord through all rings on the tape, from right to left through the screw eye above the tape and through all the screw eyes to the left of it.

60. Cut a heavyweight 3/8-inch metal rod to the finished shade width and insert it through the tape loops at the bottom of the shade.

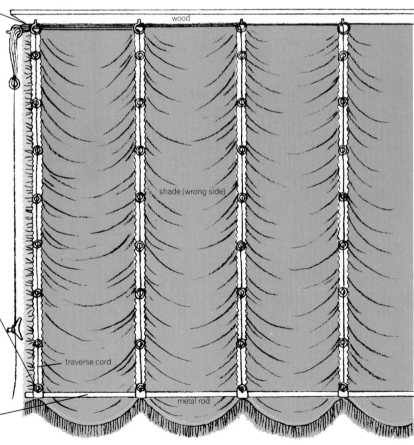

wood

shade (wrong side)

traverse cord

metal rod

61. Attach the shade to the window frame, wrong side against the window, with angle brackets or nails.

62. Attach a screw eye to the inside of the right-hand jamb just below the level of the screw eyes on the board. Thread the ends of the traverse cords through the screw eye on the jamb and adjust the cords until the shade pulls up and down evenly.

63. Knot the cords around a curtain ring about 12 inches below the screw eye on the jamb. Trim off the excess from all but the longest cord.

64. Fasten a cleat to the inside of the jamb at a comfortable height. Loop the cord around the cleat to hold the shade in position.

A ☐ PREPARING THE FABRIC

1. To determine the finished shade length, measure from inside the top of the window frame to the sill. To find the number of pleats, divide the window length by four and a half—rounding off fractions to the next full number—and add two and a half. To find the fabric length, multiply the number of pleats by 5 inches and add 16 1/2 inches.

2. To determine the finished shade width, measure between the jambs and subtract 1/2 inch. To calculate the fabric width required, add 4 inches.

3. To determine the length for the lining subtract 6 1/2 inches from the shade fabric length (Step 1). To determine the length of the heavyweight nonwoven interfacing, subtract 1/2 inch from the fabric length (Step 1). The width of both lining and interfacing will be the same as the finished shade width (Step 2).

4. Make a paper pattern for the dentil edge of the bottom flap of the shade as shown on pages 61-62, Boxes A and B. Make the pattern 6 inches deep, the projections at least 6 inches wide and the cutout spaces 1 1/2 inches wide and 4 1/2 inches deep.

5. Using the fabric length and width measurements calculated in Steps 1 and 2, cut the shade fabric. To make a shade that is wider than one fabric width, cut two equal strips for the added width required and attach one strip to each side of the center panel. Match at the selvages and stitch the strips to the center panel just inside the selvages. Press open the seams.

6. Place the fabric wrong side down and fold up the bottom edge 6 1/2 inches to form a facing for the bottom flap. Pin.

7. Mark the center point on the fold with chalk.

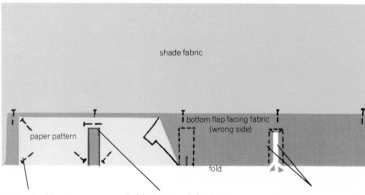

8. Place the dentil pattern on the facing, matching the bottom edge with the fabric fold and the inner edge with the center point mark on the fabric. Pin.

9. Mark around the three sides of the cutout spaces, then unpin the pattern and flip it over at the center point to mark the other half of the fabric. Set the pattern aside.

10. Inserting more pins if necessary, machine stitch along the markings around each cutout space. Then trim the seam allowances to 3/8 inch; clip into the inside corners and trim the outside corners diagonally.

B ☐ PREPARING THE LINING AND THE INTERFACING

11. Cut the lining and interfacing, using the measurements in Step 3. If needed, repeat Step 5 to join widths of lining. To join interfacing, cut an extra panel and a strip of 1/2-inch twill tape of the same length. Butt the two panels over the tape. Pin and sew with a machine zigzag stitch. Remove the pins.

12. Place the interfacing with the tape up and fold up the bottom edge 6 inches. Press.

13. Place the lining, wrong side down, on the interfacing and align all the edges. Pin.

14. Mark the center on the bottom edge of the lining.

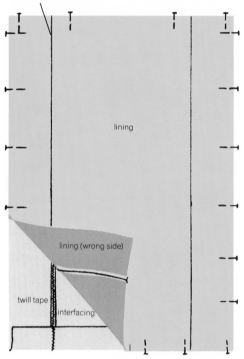

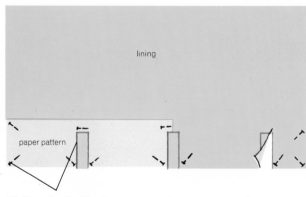

15. Place the dentil pattern on the lining and match the bottom edges. Align the side edges of the pattern with the center mark and side edge of the lining. Pin. Then repeat Step 9 to mark the cutout spaces.

16. Insert more pins, if needed, to secure the layers of lining and interfacing. Then cut out the spaces 1/8 inch inside the markings.

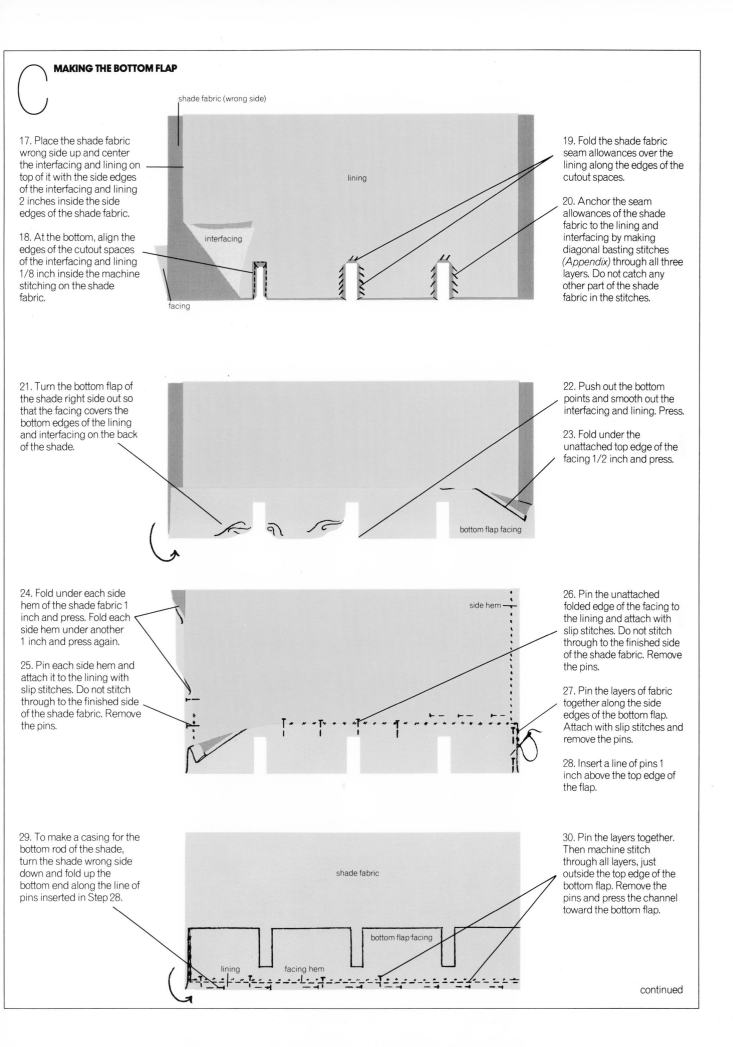

C **MAKING THE BOTTOM FLAP**

shade fabric (wrong side)

lining

interfacing

facing

17. Place the shade fabric wrong side up and center the interfacing and lining on top of it with the side edges of the interfacing and lining 2 inches inside the side edges of the shade fabric.

18. At the bottom, align the edges of the cutout spaces of the interfacing and lining 1/8 inch inside the machine stitching on the shade fabric.

19. Fold the shade fabric seam allowances over the lining along the edges of the cutout spaces.

20. Anchor the seam allowances of the shade fabric to the lining and interfacing by making diagonal basting stitches (*Appendix*) through all three layers. Do not catch any other part of the shade fabric in the stitches.

21. Turn the bottom flap of the shade right side out so that the facing covers the bottom edges of the lining and interfacing on the back of the shade.

bottom flap facing

22. Push out the bottom points and smooth out the interfacing and lining. Press.

23. Fold under the unattached top edge of the facing 1/2 inch and press.

24. Fold under each side hem of the shade fabric 1 inch and press. Fold each side hem under another 1 inch and press again.

25. Pin each side hem and attach it to the lining with slip stitches. Do not stitch through to the finished side of the shade fabric. Remove the pins.

side hem

26. Pin the unattached folded edge of the facing to the lining and attach with slip stitches. Do not stitch through to the finished side of the shade fabric. Remove the pins.

27. Pin the layers of fabric together along the side edges of the bottom flap. Attach with slip stitches and remove the pins.

28. Insert a line of pins 1 inch above the top edge of the flap.

29. To make a casing for the bottom rod of the shade, turn the shade wrong side down and fold up the bottom end along the line of pins inserted in Step 28.

shade fabric

bottom flap facing

lining   facing hem

30. Pin the layers together. Then machine stitch through all layers, just outside the top edge of the bottom flap. Remove the pins and press the channel toward the bottom flap.

continued

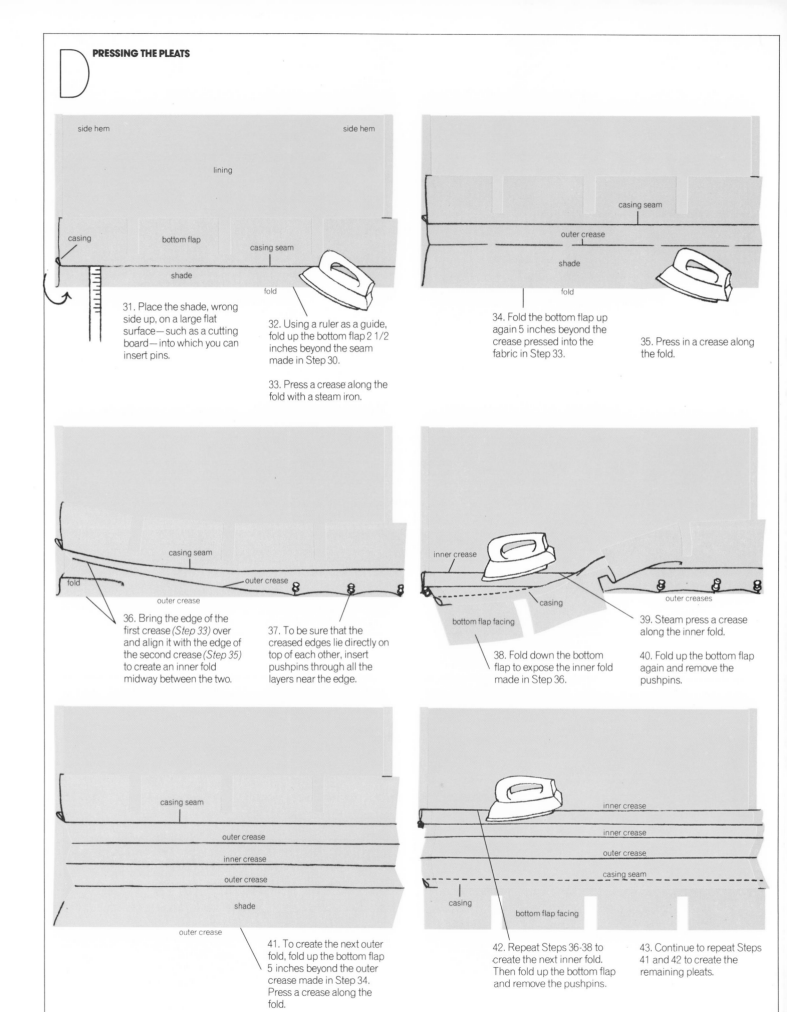

side hem   lining   side hem

casing   bottom flap   casing seam

shade

fold

31. Place the shade, wrong side up, on a large flat surface—such as a cutting board—into which you can insert pins.

32. Using a ruler as a guide, fold up the bottom flap 2 1/2 inches beyond the seam made in Step 30.

33. Press a crease along the fold with a steam iron.

casing seam

outer crease

shade

fold

34. Fold the bottom flap up again 5 inches beyond the crease pressed into the fabric in Step 33.

35. Press in a crease along the fold.

casing seam

fold   outer crease

outer crease

36. Bring the edge of the first crease (Step 33) over and align it with the edge of the second crease (Step 35) to create an inner fold midway between the two.

37. To be sure that the creased edges lie directly on top of each other, insert pushpins through all the layers near the edge.

inner crease

casing   outer creases

bottom flap facing

38. Fold down the bottom flap to expose the inner fold made in Step 36.

39. Steam press a crease along the inner fold.

40. Fold up the bottom flap again and remove the pushpins.

casing seam

outer crease

inner crease

outer crease

shade

outer crease

41. To create the next outer fold, fold up the bottom flap 5 inches beyond the outer crease made in Step 34. Press a crease along the fold.

inner crease

inner crease

outer crease

casing seam

casing   bottom flap facing

42. Repeat Steps 36-38 to create the next inner fold. Then fold up the bottom flap and remove the pushpins.

43. Continue to repeat Steps 41 and 42 to create the remaining pleats.

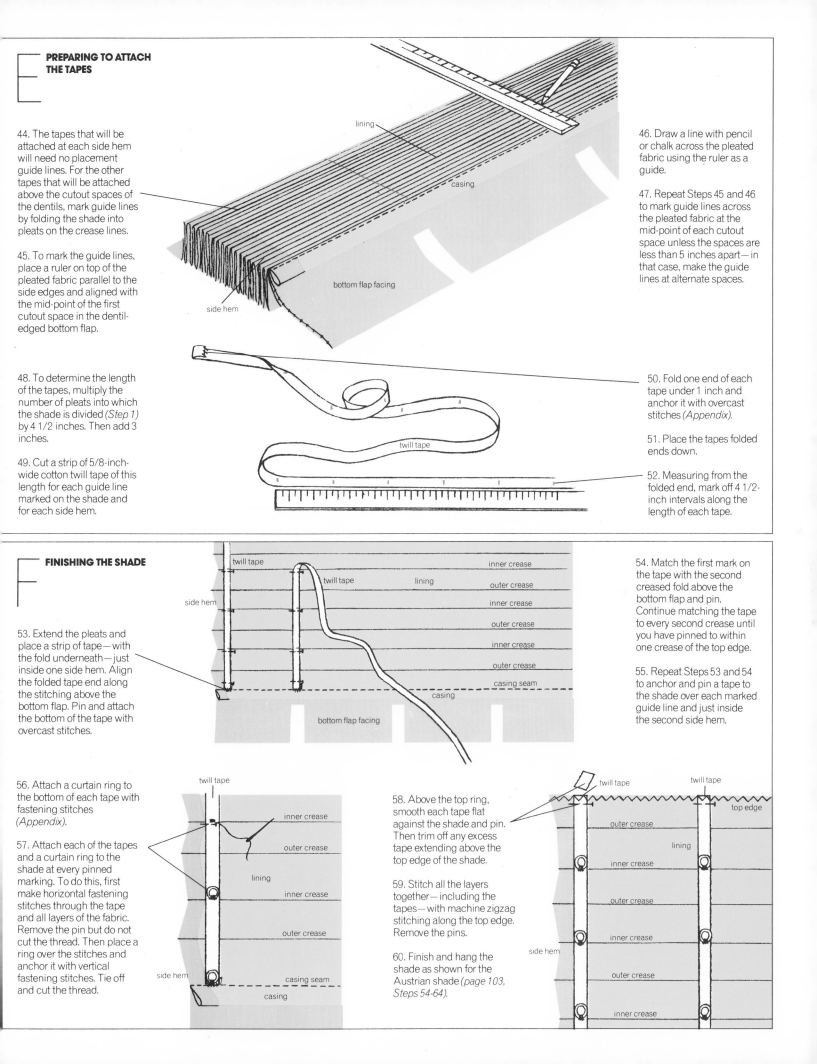

PREPARING TO ATTACH THE TAPES

44. The tapes that will be attached at each side hem will need no placement guide lines. For the other tapes that will be attached above the cutout spaces of the dentils, mark guide lines by folding the shade into pleats on the crease lines.

45. To mark the guide lines, place a ruler on top of the pleated fabric parallel to the side edges and aligned with the mid-point of the first cutout space in the dentil-edged bottom flap.

lining

casing

bottom flap facing

side hem

twill tape

46. Draw a line with pencil or chalk across the pleated fabric using the ruler as a guide.

47. Repeat Steps 45 and 46 to mark guide lines across the pleated fabric at the mid-point of each cutout space unless the spaces are less than 5 inches apart — in that case, make the guide lines at alternate spaces.

48. To determine the length of the tapes, multiply the number of pleats into which the shade is divided *(Step 1)* by 4 1/2 inches. Then add 3 inches.

49. Cut a strip of 5/8-inch-wide cotton twill tape of this length for each guide line marked on the shade and for each side hem.

50. Fold one end of each tape under 1 inch and anchor it with overcast stitches *(Appendix)*.

51. Place the tapes folded ends down.

52. Measuring from the folded end, mark off 4 1/2-inch intervals along the length of each tape.

FINISHING THE SHADE

53. Extend the pleats and place a strip of tape — with the fold underneath — just inside one side hem. Align the folded tape end along the stitching above the bottom flap. Pin and attach the bottom of the tape with overcast stitches.

twill tape

twill tape

lining

side hem

inner crease

outer crease

inner crease

outer crease

inner crease

outer crease

casing seam

casing

bottom flap facing

54. Match the first mark on the tape with the second creased fold above the bottom flap and pin. Continue matching the tape to every second crease until you have pinned to within one crease of the top edge.

55. Repeat Steps 53 and 54 to anchor and pin a tape to the shade over each marked guide line and just inside the second side hem.

56. Attach a curtain ring to the bottom of each tape with fastening stitches *(Appendix)*.

57. Attach each of the tapes and a curtain ring to the shade at every pinned marking. To do this, first make horizontal fastening stitches through the tape and all layers of the fabric. Remove the pin but do not cut the thread. Then place a ring over the stitches and anchor it with vertical fastening stitches. Tie off and cut the thread.

twill tape

inner crease

outer crease

lining

inner crease

outer crease

side hem

casing seam

casing

58. Above the top ring, smooth each tape flat against the shade and pin. Then trim off any excess tape extending above the top edge of the shade.

59. Stitch all the layers together — including the tapes — with machine zigzag stitching along the top edge. Remove the pins.

60. Finish and hang the shade as shown for the Austrian shade *(page 103, Steps 54-64)*.

twill tape

twill tape

top edge

outer crease

lining

inner crease

outer crease

inner crease

side hem

outer crease

inner crease

The casual charm of café curtains

Most versatile of all window coverings, café curtains can be made in multiple tiers of varying depths, any of which can be opened or closed independently. They lend themselves to almost any heading that suits the mood of the room—scalloped *(near right),* saw-toothed *(far right)* or gathered. Sometimes they are gathered top and bottom, as in the variation at center right.

Diagrams overleaf explain how to measure for café curtains, and directions follow for making the three curtain styles shown here as well as other designs.

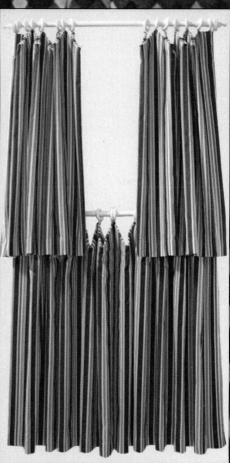

Calculations for making café curtains

Before measuring your windows for café curtains, mount the rod or rods you expect to use. Whatever heading one-tier café curtains may have—shaped, pleated, hand shirred or gathered through a tunnel of fabric called a casing—the rod can be attached anywhere on the window frame.

Two-tier café curtains, as well as one-tier curtains that are gathered through casings at both ends of each panel, will generally hang from rods attached to the top and middle of the frame.

When the rod or rods have been mounted, make the measurements indicated below, then apply them to the formulas on the chart at right to estimate how much fabric you will require.

Separate formulas are given for each curtain style. Insert the measurements called for, as identified by the letters on the drawing below, and perform in sequence the mathematical operations indicated by the standard symbols.

For fabric with a repeated pattern that needs matching, determine the length of one repeat by measuring along a selvage from one design detail to the next identical design detail.

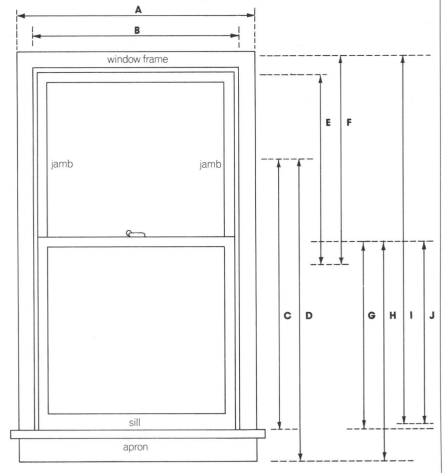

The width of the rod or rods dictates the number of fabric widths you will need for curtains. Whether a rod is mounted across the front of the window frame (A) or between the jambs (B), measure the width from one end to the other—including the bent or bracketed return sections, if any. Record all measurements in inches.

The length of curtains varies with the style as well as with the measurement from the rods to the hems. For one-tier café curtains and the bottom panels of two-tier curtains, measure (in inches) from the lower edge of the rod to the sill or the lower edge of the apron (C or D and G or H). For the top panels of two-tier curtains, measure from the lower edge of the higher rod to 2 inches below the lower rod (E or F); for shaped top headings add 2 inches. For curtains with both top and bottom casings, measure from the lower edge of the top rod to the upper edge of the bottom rod (I or J).

ESTIMATING MATERIALS

ONE-TIER CAFÉ CURTAINS		
WIDTH	For medium- to heavyweight fabrics	Number of fabric widths required for a pair of curtains **= A OR B × 2½ ÷ FABRIC WIDTH IN INCHES ✱**
	For lightweight or sheer fabrics	Number of fabric widths required for a pair of curtains **= A OR B × 3 ÷ FABRIC WIDTH IN INCHES ✱**
LENGTH	For fabrics that do not require matching a pattern	Total length required for one curtain in inches **= C OR D + 15**
	For fabrics that require matching a pattern	Total length required for one curtain in inches **= C OR D + 15 + LENGTH OF PATTERN REPEAT IN INCHES**
YARDAGE	Total yardage required = **NUMBER OF WIDTHS × TOTAL LENGTH OF ONE CURTAIN IN INCHES ÷ 36**	

TWO-TIER CAFÉ CURTAINS		
WIDTH	For medium- to heavyweight fabrics	Number of fabric widths required for a pair of curtains **= A OR B × 2½ ÷ FABRIC WIDTH IN INCHES ✱**
	For lightweight or sheer fabrics	Number of fabric widths required for a pair of curtains **= A OR B × 3 ÷ FABRIC WIDTH IN INCHES ✱**
LENGTH	For fabrics that do not require matching a pattern	Total length in inches required **= LENGTH FOR ONE TOP CURTAIN (E OR F) + LENGTH REQUIRED FOR ONE BOTTOM CURTAIN (G OR H) + 30**
	For fabrics that require matching a pattern	Total length in inches required **= LENGTH FOR ONE TOP CURTAIN (E OR F) + LENGTH REQUIRED FOR ONE BOTTOM CURTAIN (G OR H) + 30 + TWO TIMES LENGTH OF PATTERN REPEAT IN INCHES**
YARDAGE	Total yardage required = **NUMBER OF WIDTHS × TOTAL LENGTH REQUIRED IN INCHES ÷ 36**	

CAFÉ CURTAINS WITH TOP AND BOTTOM CASINGS		
WIDTH	For medium- to heavyweight fabrics	Number of fabric widths required for a pair of curtains **= A OR B × 2½ ÷ FABRIC WIDTH IN INCHES ✱**
	For lightweight or sheer fabrics	Number of fabric widths required for a pair of curtains **= A OR B × 3 ÷ FABRIC WIDTH IN INCHES ✱**
LENGTH	For fabrics that do not require matching a pattern	Total length required for one curtain in inches **= I OR J + 24**
	For fabrics that require matching a pattern	Total length required for one curtain in inches **= I OR J + 24 + LENGTH OF PATTERN REPEAT IN INCHES**
YARDAGE	Total yardage required = **NUMBER OF WIDTHS × TOTAL LENGTH REQUIRED FOR ONE CURTAIN IN INCHES ÷ 36**	

✱Round off fractions to the nearest full width.

A CUTTING AND PREPARING THE FABRIC

1. Place the fabric, wrong side down, on a large table. Straighten one edge by drawing a crosswise thread and cutting along the drawn thread or by drawing and cutting along a chalk line, following the instructions for draperies and curtains (Step 2, page 88).

2A. For fabric that does not require matching a pattern, use the desired panel length measurement (page 111) to mark and cut off as many sections as you need for the width of your window. Make all cuts along crosswise threads or chalk lines.

2B. For fabric with a pronounced pattern, cut off a section equal to the panel length as determined by the formula on page 111. Examine fabric and window to decide where pattern repeats should fall, then trim the section. Cut off a total amount equal to one full pattern repeat, but trim some from the top and some from the bottom as necessary to get the pattern positioned suitably. Match each subsequent section to the first by aligning the pattern along the selvages before cutting the fabric.

3. If you need to straighten the fabric grains, follow the instructions for draperies and curtains (Step 4, page 88).

4. To divide a fabric section into two half-widths, or to make a panel from two or more fabric sections, follow the instructions for draperies and curtains (Steps 5-8, page 88). Make the joining seams narrow —especially if the fabric is sheer.

B HEMMING THE SIDES OF THE PANELS

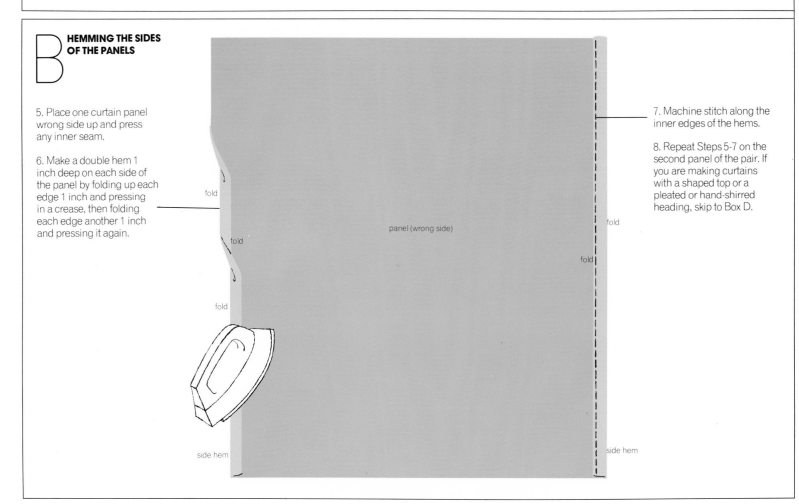

5. Place one curtain panel wrong side up and press any inner seam.

6. Make a double hem 1 inch deep on each side of the panel by folding up each edge 1 inch and pressing in a crease, then folding each edge another 1 inch and pressing it again.

7. Machine stitch along the inner edges of the hems.

8. Repeat Steps 5-7 on the second panel of the pair. If you are making curtains with a shaped top or a pleated or hand-shirred heading, skip to Box D.

C ▸ MAKING CASING TOPS

9. To find the depth necessary for casing tops, measure the diameter of your round rod by placing a ruler in front of it; then double the figure. If you have a flat rod, measure its depth and add 3/8 inch.

10. To determine the number of inches of fabric you need to make a double hem for the casing and heading—i.e., the top section that will extend above the casing—multiply the figure calculated in the previous step by four.

11. Measure this distance from the top edge on both sides of the panel and pin.

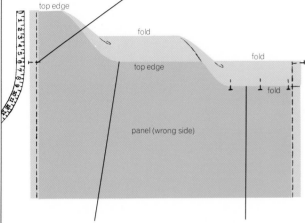

12. Make a double hem for the casing and heading by folding the top of the panel down to the pin markings and pressing in a crease.

13. Fold the panel down again, aligning the crease made in the preceding step with the pins. Press in another crease along the fold and remove the pin markings. Then pin along the double hem.

14. Stitch as close to the inner edge of the hem as possible. Make sure to backstitch at each end. Remove the pins.

15. To make the casing, insert pins at 2-inch intervals midway between the panel top and the line of stitching.

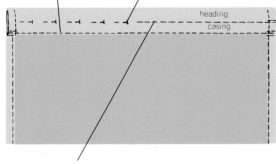

16. Stitch along the row of pins, removing the pins as you sew. Make sure to backstitch at each end.

17. Repeat Steps 11-16 on the second panel of the pair. Skip to Box H.

D ▸ MAKING BACKED AND STIFFENED TOPS

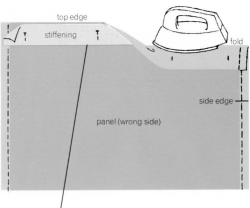

18. For hand-shirred headings, make the shirred rows and attach the backing by following the instructions on pages 55-58. Skip to Box H to finish the hem.

19. For pleated headings and shaped tops, place one panel, wrong side up, on a flat surface and measure the finished width.

20. Cut a strip of stiffening 1/4 inch shorter than the width of the panel, using a 4-inch-deep stiffening for the shaped tops, a 3-inch one for the pleated headings.

21. Align one edge of the stiffening with the top edge of the panel, and center the stiffening so that the ends fall just inside the side edges. Pin. Fold down the top of the panel along the bottom edge of the stiffening, then press on the fold.

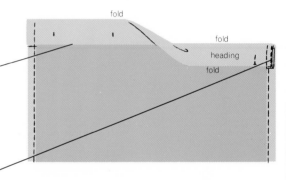

22A. To make the headings for pleats, fold down the covered stiffening again and press. Remove the pins inserted in Step 21, then insert pins near the sides of the heading.

23A. Machine or hand stitch down each side edge and along the bottom of the heading only as far as the inner edge of the hem on the side of the panel. Use the slip stitch or a hemming stitch (Appendix) if you hand sew. Remove the pins.

24A. Repeat Steps 19-21 and 22A and 23A on the second panel of the pair. To plot the pleats, follow the instructions in draperies and curtains (Boxes H and I, pages 94-95); instructions for making the pleats appear on pages 73-79. To finish the hem, skip to Box H.

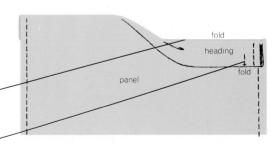

22B. To make the headings for shaped tops, first turn the panel wrong side down. Then fold over the covered stiffening along the bottom edge of the heading and press on the fold, avoiding pins.

23B. Remove the pins inserted in Step 21. Pin the heading and stiffening together at the sides.

24B. Repeat Steps 19-21 and 22B and 23B on the second panel of the pair.

continued

25. To make shaped tops with evenly spaced identical designs but no pleats, cut out a strip of tissue paper the length and width of the panel heading (*Steps 19 and 20*).

tissue paper

26. If your rod has side returns and you want the top of the curtains to be unshaped along the returns, measure the length of one return and cut this distance off the paper strip.

27. Fold the paper strip in half across its width.

fold

28. Fold the strip into quarters.

fold

fold

29. Finally fold the strip again into eighths.

fold

fold

fold

30. Unfold the strip to examine the spacing. If you want more divisions, fold the paper again as many times as necessary.

31. Draw a line across the bottom of the strip 3/4 inch from the edge to determine the bottom point for your design.

32. Starting at the top corner of one end and finishing at the top corner of the other end, draw the design you want between the folded segments and above the pencil line made in Step 31.

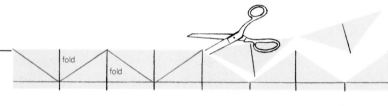

fold

fold

33. Cut out the design to create a paper pattern.

34. With the panel wrong side down, position the paper pattern on the heading 1/4 inch below the top edge, aligning the ends with the side edges of the panel. If you provided for a return in Step 26, align the right-hand end of the pattern with the right-hand side edge of the panel that you plan to hang at the left of the window. Pin.

35. Trace the outline of the design onto the heading with dressmaker's chalk. Remove the pattern.

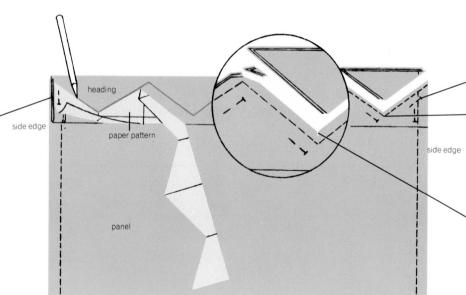

heading

side edge

paper pattern

panel

side edge

36. Pin the layers of heading together, avoiding the chalk lines.

37. Machine stitch on the chalk lines. Remove all the pins.

38. Cut out the design 1/4 inch above the stitching.

39A. For straight-edged designs, cut off outside corners diagonally and clip into the seam allowance at the bottom of inside corners.

39B. For curved designs, notch the outside curves and clip along inside curves.

40. Turn the stitched top edge inside out by lifting up the heading from the front of the panel and turning it over onto the back. Push out the shaped tops with your fingers. Bring out corners by gently pulling them with the tip of a needle. Press.

41. Pin along each side of the heading, and finish the sides, following Step 23A.

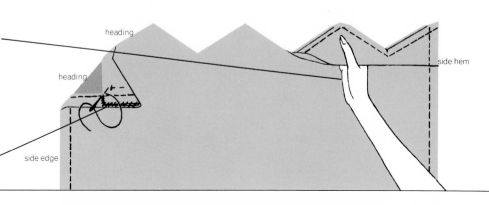

heading

heading

side edge

side hem

42. Repeat Steps 34-41 on the second panel of the pair. If you provided for a return in Step 26, however, align the left-hand end of the pattern with the left-hand side edge of the panel. Skip to Box H.

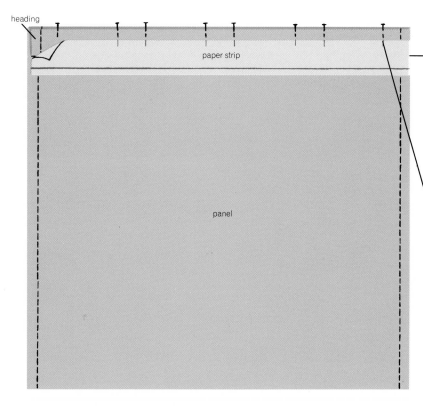

43. To make curtains with headings that combine pleats with cutout shapes, first plot the pleats with pins —following the directions on pages 94-95. If you want the first and last pleat on the panel directly at the edges, do not subtract for the side and center margins as indicated in those directions.

44. Before stitching the pleat allowance seams, cut a strip of tissue paper to make a pattern for the shaped cutouts and draw a line across the bottom by repeating Steps 25 and 31.

45. Place the paper strip over the heading of the pinned panel and align the top edges.

46. Draw a vertical pencil line over each pin inserted in Step 43, then remove the paper strip from the panel. Remove the pins.

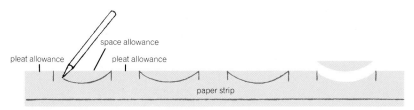

47. Using a ruler or a compass or saucer, draw the shape of the cutout design you want within each of the individual space allowances between the pencil-marked pleat allowances. Make sure to keep the bottom point of each shape above the bottom pencil line.

48. Cut out the paper pattern along the drawn designs.

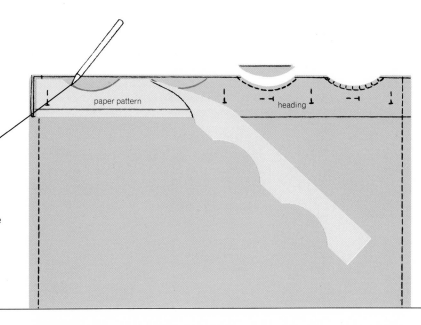

49. Pin the paper pattern to the heading of the panel, aligning the top and side edges. Then trace the outlines for the cutout shapes onto the fabric with dressmaker's chalk. Remove the pattern.

50. Repeat Steps 35-40 to finish and stitch the cutout shapes. Using the paper pattern as a guide, reinsert the pin markings for the pleats. Then follow the directions on pages 73-79 to stitch and shape the pleats.

51. Repeat Steps 49 and 50 on the second panel of the pair. Skip to Box H.

continued

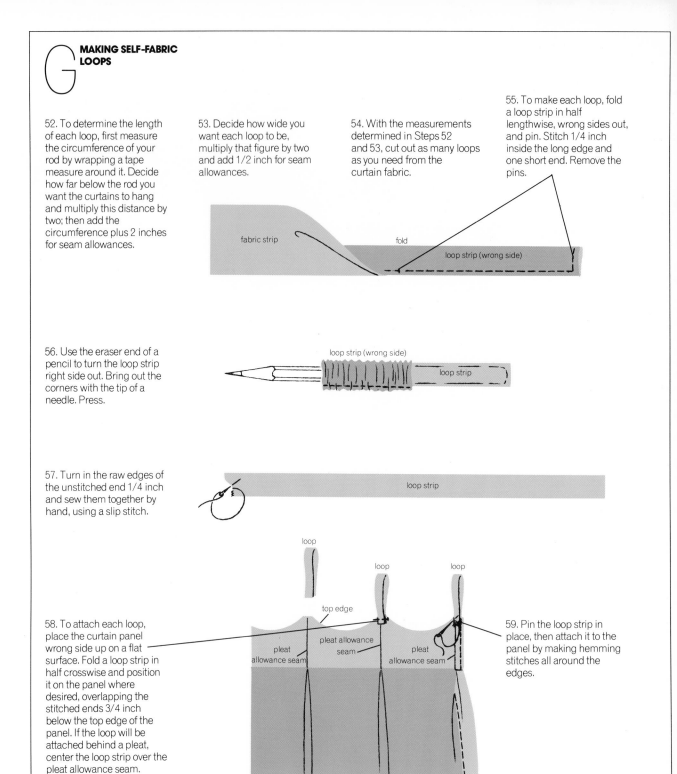

G MAKING SELF-FABRIC LOOPS

52. To determine the length of each loop, first measure the circumference of your rod by wrapping a tape measure around it. Decide how far below the rod you want the curtains to hang and multiply this distance by two; then add the circumference plus 2 inches for seam allowances.

53. Decide how wide you want each loop to be, multiply that figure by two and add 1/2 inch for seam allowances.

54. With the measurements determined in Steps 52 and 53, cut out as many loops as you need from the curtain fabric.

55. To make each loop, fold a loop strip in half lengthwise, wrong sides out, and pin. Stitch 1/4 inch inside the long edge and one short end. Remove the pins.

fabric strip

fold

loop strip (wrong side)

56. Use the eraser end of a pencil to turn the loop strip right side out. Bring out the corners with the tip of a needle. Press.

loop strip (wrong side)

loop strip

57. Turn in the raw edges of the unstitched end 1/4 inch and sew them together by hand, using a slip stitch.

loop strip

loop

loop

loop

top edge

pleat allowance seam

pleat allowance seam

pleat allowance seam

58. To attach each loop, place the curtain panel wrong side up on a flat surface. Fold a loop strip in half crosswise and position it on the panel where desired, overlapping the stitched ends 3/4 inch below the top edge of the panel. If the loop will be attached behind a pleat, center the loop strip over the pleat allowance seam.

59. Pin the loop strip in place, then attach it to the panel by making hemming stitches all around the edges.

panel (wrong side)

60. Before finishing the hems for any style of curtain, hang the panels in place on the rod or rods.

61A. For curtains with continuous shaped tops, sew a ring at the uppermost point of each design segment or insert a pin hook so that the top bend is 1/4 inch below the uppermost point. Insert the rod through the rings or hang the hooks from the rod.

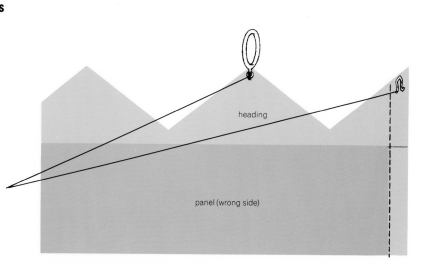

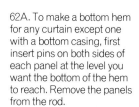

61B. For curtains with a casing at the top, insert the rod so that two layers of the hem are in front of it when the rod is hung.

61C. For curtains with self-fabric loops, simply insert the rod through the loops.

61D. For curtains with fully pleated or shaped pleated headings, attach or insert hooks, following the directions on page 95, then attach the hooks to the rod.

61E. For curtains with hand-shirred headings, attach or insert hooks, following the directions on page 58, then attach the hooks to the rod.

62A. To make a bottom hem for any curtain except one with a bottom casing, first insert pins on both sides of each panel at the level you want the bottom of the hem to reach. Remove the panels from the rod.

63A. Trim off each panel 4 inches below the pin marks.

64A. Turn each panel top side down, then make a 2-inch-wide double hem, following the instructions in Steps 12 and 13. Press.

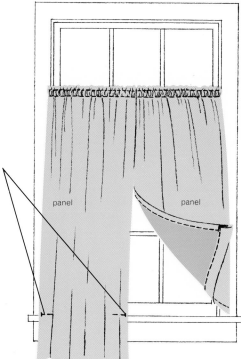

62B. To make bottom casings on curtains, first insert pins on both sides of each panel just above the bottom rod. Remove the panels from the rod.

63B. Turn each panel top side down, then multiply the casing depth (Step 9) by six and measure this distance from the pins to the unfinished edge. Trim off excess fabric.

64B. Divide the figure determined in Step 63B by three and use chalk to mark off this distance from the pins toward the unfinished edge. Turn the edge up to the chalk marks and press in a crease. Then turn up the crease, aligning it with the chalk marks. Repeat Steps 14-16 to stitch the double hem for the bottom heading and casing.

5

A WARDROBE TO DRESS UP FURNITURE

aced with a sudden visit from the Lord Lieutenant of Ireland in 1745, a certain Mrs. Delany, housekeeper to an aristocratic English household, later wrote, "To work went all my maids, stripping covers off the chairs." The record does not indicate whether she replaced the everyday covers with fancier ones for His Lordship's eyes. But she may well have done so, for the great 18th Century furniture makers supplied assorted sets

A PERFECT FIT FOR COVERS AND SPREADS

of slipcovers for the furniture they designed — some in gilded leather, some in elegant crimson damask with gold and silver fringe, some in simple checked gingham. They even provided chamois "stockings" for their delicately wrought chair legs.

From the very beginning (the oldest known slipcover dates from about 1670) slipcovers have served a number of purposes: to protect fine furniture from everyday wear and tear; to dress it up for special occasions; and to give new life to an old piece. In Victorian times slipcovers were ill-fitting, makeshift affairs, thrown on to keep off summer dust or perhaps to hide the scars of hand-me-down furniture.

Today, some 300 years after their first appearance, slipcovers are still going strong; indeed they are enjoying something of a renaissance as fashion worthy of attention in their own right. "If a slipcover is properly made it is indistinguishable from a permanent cover," says New York decorator Billy Baldwin. Most contemporary decorators generally take the same view—but not all. "I don't like slipcovers to look like upholstery," counters San Francisco's Michael Taylor. "They should be loose, airy, baggy; that way they relax the room."

Either way, slipcovers are eminently practical; a removable slipcover is more easily cleaned than upholstery. And they are infinitely versatile; the homemaker restless for change can switch covers with the seasons (replacing a warm, wintry corduroy with an airy cotton for summer, for instance) or with her moods (moving from tailored to frilly, for example). Slipcovers are not necessarily cheap, for they can be made in the finest and most expensive of fabrics, but they are more economical than upholstery because it takes less time and money to switch slipcovers than to reupholster a piece of furniture.

What fabric to use for the slipcover? It should be strong enough to hold its shape but pliant enough to curve over arms and backs and—if the slipcover is to have a ruffled or pleated skirt—to hang in folds. Linen, chintz and damask lend themselves to slip-

covering very well; so do corduroy, cretonne, various other silks and cottons, and many man-made fabrics—except for those that stretch.

Figuring importantly in the final effect, too, is the type of fabric *under* the slipcover. If the furniture upholstery itself is slippery, like satin, it will not hold an overlying fabric in place. Nubby upholstery will show through a slipcover that is lighter in weight than itself. And velvet abrades easily under a slipcover—something to bear in mind if the velvet upholstery has not already had its day and will be wanted for future use. For that matter, some decorators even urge their clients to have new furniture upholstered in plain muslin or, better yet, neutral twill or ticking, and then to use a custom-made slipcover for the furniture's regular attire. The advantage of these never-to-be-seen upholstery fabrics is that any of them serves well under any slipcover, and survives any number of redecorations. And they are not so ugly that they cannot be lived with for the duration of an incumbent slipcover's trip to the cleaners.

Making a slipcover, like any sewing for the home, requires patience, forethought and care. Particularly crucial to success are the blocking and cutting of the fabric *(pages 125-129)*. But even those important operations are not so formidable as might be imagined. "I think it's easier to make a slipcover than a dress," says New York upholsterer Henrietta Blau. "Your chair won't move. It won't breathe while you're measuring, pinning and cutting. And it doesn't need a coffee break."

As snug
as upholstery

The slipcover at right, with its snug fit, illustrates the basic problems in making any slipcover. Because the fabric has a large repeated pattern, its major feature—an exotic bird perched on a limb—has to be carefully and smoothly centered on the major focal points of the sofa: the three cushions along the back, and the upper planes of the three cushions that form the seat.

Making slipcovers so that the fabric pattern suits and hugs the contours of the furniture requires proper measuring and blocking out of the fabric as well as the furniture. The following pages tell how to achieve an effect as professional as the one shown here, whether you use a print, plaid, stripe or plain color.

Calculations for making slipcovers

The chart below gives rough estimates of the number of yards of fabric a sofa or chair slipcover will require. To use the chart, add the estimate for body and cushion fabric to the estimated yardage for welting and the desired style of skirt.

These figures are based on requirements for standard pieces of furniture covered in solid-colored or small-patterned fabrics. For special sizes and shapes of furniture and for more precise fabric estimating—particularly with stripes or large pattern repeats—you should measure your own furniture by the system that professionals call blocking. Blocking also serves as a guide to cutting fabric into rectangular sections—blocks—to pin and shape on the furniture.

In blocking, furniture is measured and slipcovers are cut as rectangles—whatever the finished shapes of the sections will be.

The entire center section of a sofa or chair forms a single block. This block extends up from the bottom of the outside back over and down the inside back, across the platform with the cushions removed to the bottom of the front base, which is known as the drop. Each arm is treated as three blocks—an inside, an outside, and a top and front surface. On a wing chair, each wing is covered by two blocks—an inside and an outside. On an armless sofa or chair, each side section forms a block.

Each cushion is figured in two blocks—the front boxing together with the top section and the bottom section. The other three sides of the boxing are picked up from leftover fabric. If there is a separate pleated or ruffled skirt, it constitutes another block.

With the techniques shown at right and on the next page, you can block furniture of any size or shape by measuring it in sections as outlined by the seams in the upholstery. Be sure, though, to leave a tuck-in allowance twice the depth of any groove or indentation between sections, and to provide 3/8-inch seam allowances all around every block after you fit it to the sofa or chair (pages 130-136).

APPROXIMATE YARDAGE REQUIRED FOR SLIPCOVERS

FURNITURE	NUMBER OF CUSHIONS	BODY AND CUSHION FABRIC		STRAIGHT SKIRT OR LINING FABRIC		RUFFLED SKIRT OR LINING FABRIC		PLEATED SKIRT OR LINING FABRIC		WELTING FABRIC		WELTING CORD
		Width		Width		Width		Width		Width		Length
		48"	36"	48"	36"	48"	36"	48"	36"	48"	36"	Yards
SOFA	SIX	20½	25½	1½	2	3	4½	4	6	2¾	3⅔	64
	FOUR	18	29	1½	2	3	4½	4	6	2¼	2¾	50
	THREE	16	21	1½	2	3	4½	4	6	2	2⅔	46
	TWO	14	23	1½	2	3	4½	4	6	1⅔	2¼	38
	ONE	14	21	1½	2	3	4½	4	6	1½	2	34
	NONE	10	15	1½	2	3	4½	4	6	1	1¼	20
LOVE SEAT	FOUR	15½	17	1½	2	2	3	3	4½	2	2⅔	46½
	TWO	12½	14	1½	2	2	3	3	4½	1½	2	34½
	ONE	12½	14	1½	2	2	3	3	4½	1⅓	1¾	30½
	NONE	8½	10	1½	2	2	3	3	4½	1	1¼	18½
ARMCHAIR	TWO	9½	10½	1	1½	1½	2½	2½	3½	1¼	1½	27
	ONE	8	9	1	1½	1½	2½	2½	3½	1	1¼	21
	NONE	6	6	1	1½	1½	2½	2½	3½	¾	1	15

BLOCKING THE SLIPCOVER

A MARKING THE SKIRT ATTACHMENT LINE

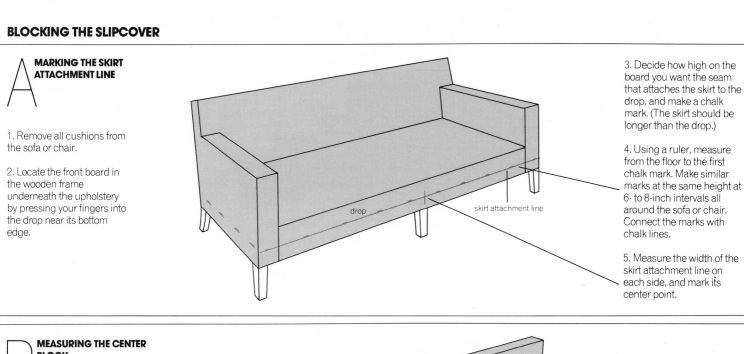

1. Remove all cushions from the sofa or chair.

2. Locate the front board in the wooden frame underneath the upholstery by pressing your fingers into the drop near its bottom edge.

3. Decide how high on the board you want the seam that attaches the skirt to the drop, and make a chalk mark. (The skirt should be longer than the drop.)

4. Using a ruler, measure from the floor to the first chalk mark. Make similar marks at the same height at 6- to 8-inch intervals all around the sofa or chair. Connect the marks with chalk lines.

5. Measure the width of the skirt attachment line on each side, and mark its center point.

B MEASURING THE CENTER BLOCK

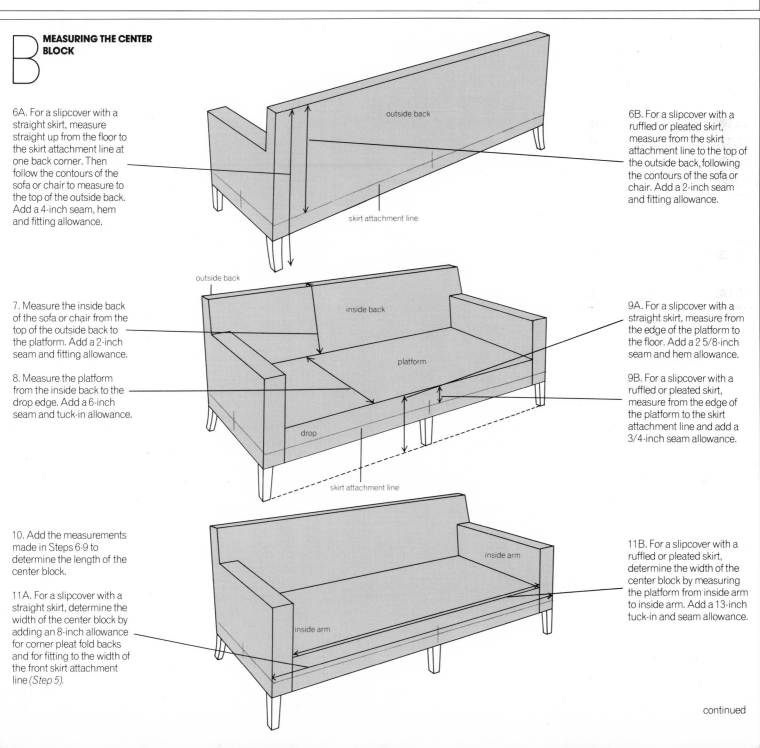

6A. For a slipcover with a straight skirt, measure straight up from the floor to the skirt attachment line at one back corner. Then follow the contours of the sofa or chair to measure to the top of the outside back. Add a 4-inch seam, hem and fitting allowance.

6B. For a slipcover with a ruffled or pleated skirt, measure from the skirt attachment line to the top of the outside back, following the contours of the sofa or chair. Add a 2-inch seam and fitting allowance.

7. Measure the inside back of the sofa or chair from the top of the outside back to the platform. Add a 2-inch seam and fitting allowance.

8. Measure the platform from the inside back to the drop edge. Add a 6-inch seam and tuck-in allowance.

9A. For a slipcover with a straight skirt, measure from the edge of the platform to the floor. Add a 2 5/8-inch seam and hem allowance.

9B. For a slipcover with a ruffled or pleated skirt, measure from the edge of the platform to the skirt attachment line and add a 3/4-inch seam allowance.

10. Add the measurements made in Steps 6-9 to determine the length of the center block.

11A. For a slipcover with a straight skirt, determine the width of the center block by adding an 8-inch allowance for corner pleat fold backs and for fitting to the width of the front skirt attachment line *(Step 5)*.

11B. For a slipcover with a ruffled or pleated skirt, determine the width of the center block by measuring the platform from inside arm to inside arm. Add a 13-inch tuck-in and seam allowance.

continued

C MEASURING THE ARM BLOCKS

12A. To make a slipcover for a square-armed sofa or chair using a ruffled or pleated skirt, determine the outside arm block length by measuring from the top edge to the skirt attachment line. Add a 2-inch seam and fitting allowance.

13A. For a straight-skirted slipcover, determine the length of the outside arm block by measuring from the top edge of the arm to the floor. Add a 4-inch hem, seam and fitting allowance.

14A. For a straight-skirted slipcover, determine the width of the outside arm block by adding an 8-inch pleat and fitting allowance to the skirt attachment line width *(Step 5)*.

12B. To make a slipcover for a curved-arm sofa or chair, first draw a horizontal chalk line on the arm at the outermost point on the curve to represent the top edge for the outside arm and the inside arm.

13B-17B. Follow Steps 12A-17A, using the chalk line whenever you need to make a measurement from the top edge of the arm.

15A. For a ruffled or pleated slipcover, determine the width of the outside arm block by measuring the outside arm at its widest point and adding a 2-inch seam and fitting allowance.

16A. To determine the length of the inside arm block, measure from the top edge of the arm to the platform. Add a 2-inch seam allowance.

17A. To determine the width of the inside arm, measure its widest point and add a 4-inch seam and fitting allowance.

18A. To determine the length of the block covering the top and front of the arm, measure from the back edge of the arm forward and down to the skirt attachment line. Add a 4-inch seam and fitting allowance.

19A. To determine the width of the arm top and front block, measure the arm at its widest point and add a 3/4-inch seam allowance.

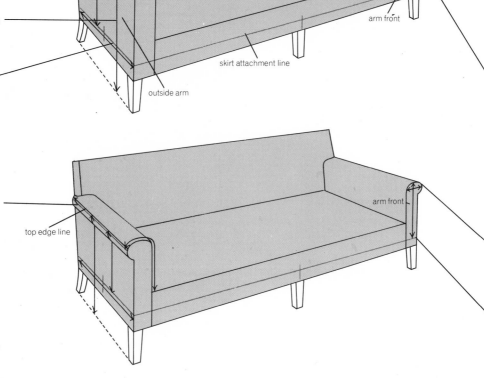

top edge — back edge — arm top — top edge — inside arm — platform — arm front — skirt attachment line — outside arm

top edge line — arm front

18B. To determine the width of the arm front block, measure the arm at its widest point and add a 3/4-inch seam allowance.

19B. To determine the length of the block covering the front of the arm, measure from the top of the arm to the skirt attachment line. Add a 2-inch seam and fitting allowance.

D MEASURING CUSHION BLOCKS

20A. To determine the length of each rectangular cushion top block, measure the top of the cushion at its longest point. Add the depth of the boxing and a 2-inch seam and fitting allowance.

21A. To determine the width of each rectangular cushion top block, measure the cushion at its widest point and add a 4-inch allowance for seams and for boxing turn-ins.

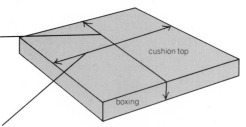

cushion top — boxing

22A. To determine the length and width of each rectangular cushion bottom block, measure the bottom of the cushion at its longest and widest points. Add a 4-inch seam and fitting allowance to each dimension. Do not block the boxing of the cushion at this stage; it will be cut later from fabric scraps.

20B. To determine the length of each T-shaped or semi T-shaped cushion top block, follow Step 20A.

21B. To determine the width of each T-shaped or semi T-shaped cushion top block, measure the cushion top at its widest point. Add a 2-inch seam and fitting allowance.

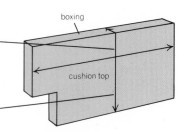

boxing — cushion top

22B. To determine the length and width of each T-shaped or semi T-shaped cushion bottom block, follow Step 22A.

MEASURING RUFFLED AND PLEATED SKIRT BLOCKS

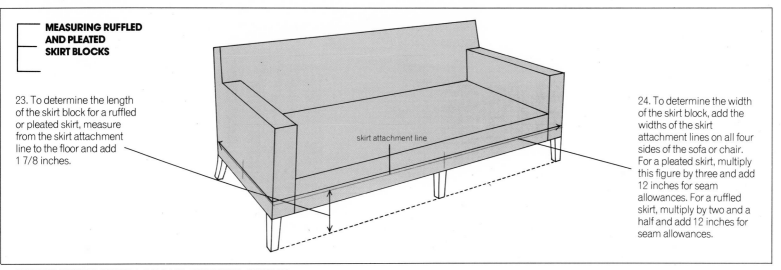

skirt attachment line

23. To determine the length of the skirt block for a ruffled or pleated skirt, measure from the skirt attachment line to the floor and add 1 7/8 inches.

24. To determine the width of the skirt block, add the widths of the skirt attachment lines on all four sides of the sofa or chair. For a pleated skirt, multiply this figure by three and add 12 inches for seam allowances. For a ruffled skirt, multiply by two and a half and add 12 inches for seam allowances.

DETERMINING YARDAGE AND CUTTING GUIDES

A PLANNING FOR PLAIN FABRICS AND SMALL PATTERNS

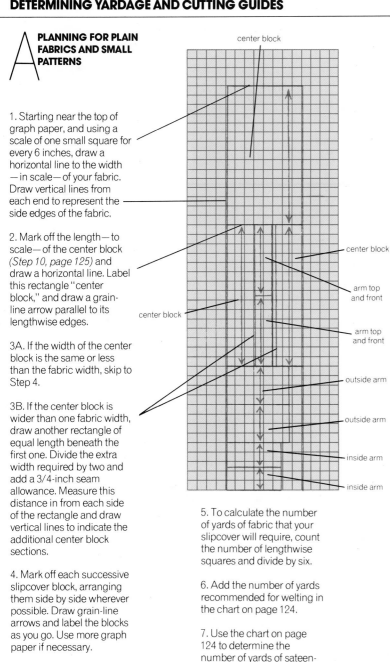

center block

center block

center block

arm top and front

arm top and front

outside arm

outside arm

inside arm

inside arm

1. Starting near the top of graph paper, and using a scale of one small square for every 6 inches, draw a horizontal line to the width —in scale—of your fabric. Draw vertical lines from each end to represent the side edges of the fabric.

2. Mark off the length—to scale—of the center block (Step 10, page 125) and draw a horizontal line. Label this rectangle "center block," and draw a grain-line arrow parallel to its lengthwise edges.

3A. If the width of the center block is the same or less than the fabric width, skip to Step 4.

3B. If the center block is wider than one fabric width, draw another rectangle of equal length beneath the first one. Divide the extra width required by two and add a 3/4-inch seam allowance. Measure this distance in from each side of the rectangle and draw vertical lines to indicate the additional center block sections.

4. Mark off each successive slipcover block, arranging them side by side wherever possible. Draw grain-line arrows and label the blocks as you go. Use more graph paper if necessary.

5. To calculate the number of yards of fabric that your slipcover will require, count the number of lengthwise squares and divide by six.

6. Add the number of yards recommended for welting in the chart on page 124.

7. Use the chart on page 124 to determine the number of yards of sateen-type skirt-lining fabric you need.

B INDICATING STRIPES AND LARGE PATTERN REPEATS

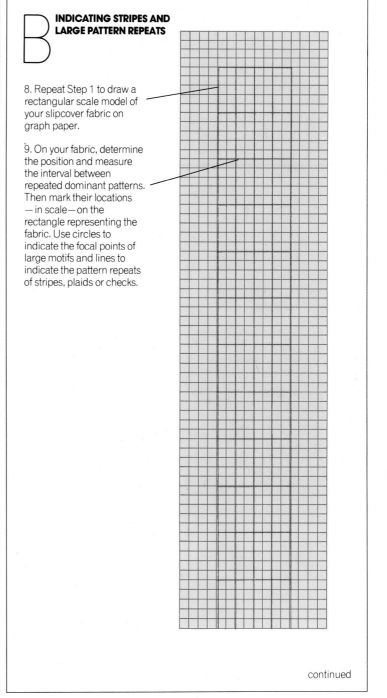

8. Repeat Step 1 to draw a rectangular scale model of your slipcover fabric on graph paper.

9. On your fabric, determine the position and measure the interval between repeated dominant patterns. Then mark their locations —in scale—on the rectangle representing the fabric. Use circles to indicate the focal points of large motifs and lines to indicate the pattern repeats of stripes, plaids or checks.

continued

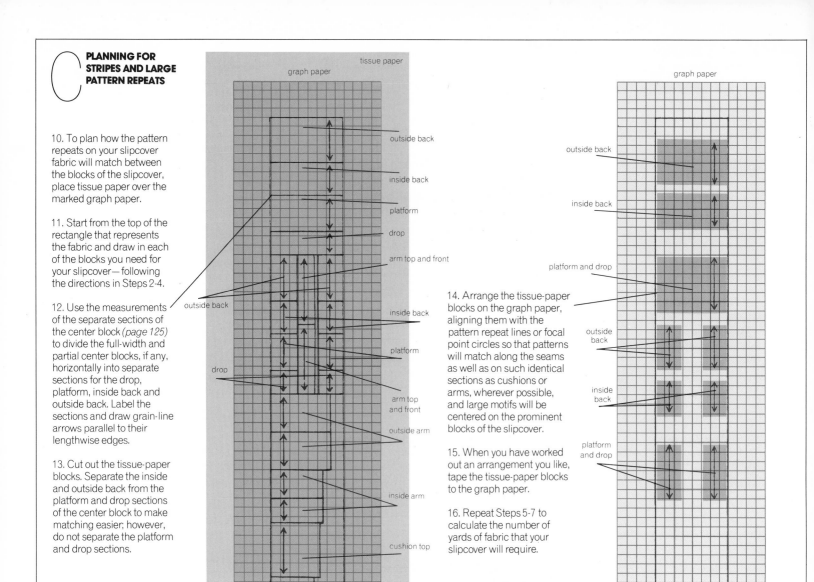

graph paper

tissue paper

outside back

inside back

platform

drop

arm top and front

outside back

inside back

platform

drop

arm top and front

outside arm

inside arm

cushion top

graph paper

outside back

inside back

platform and drop

outside back

inside back

platform and drop

10. To plan how the pattern repeats on your slipcover fabric will match between the blocks of the slipcover, place tissue paper over the marked graph paper.

11. Start from the top of the rectangle that represents the fabric and draw in each of the blocks you need for your slipcover—following the directions in Steps 2-4.

12. Use the measurements of the separate sections of the center block (page 125) to divide the full-width and partial center blocks, if any, horizontally into separate sections for the drop, platform, inside back and outside back. Label the sections and draw grain-line arrows parallel to their lengthwise edges.

13. Cut out the tissue-paper blocks. Separate the inside and outside back from the platform and drop sections of the center block to make matching easier; however, do not separate the platform and drop sections.

14. Arrange the tissue-paper blocks on the graph paper, aligning them with the pattern repeat lines or focal point circles so that patterns will match along the seams as well as on such identical sections as cushions or arms, wherever possible, and large motifs will be centered on the prominent blocks of the slipcover.

15. When you have worked out an arrangement you like, tape the tissue-paper blocks to the graph paper.

16. Repeat Steps 5-7 to calculate the number of yards of fabric that your slipcover will require.

CUTTING THE SLIPCOVER

A **PREPARING THE FABRIC BLOCKS**

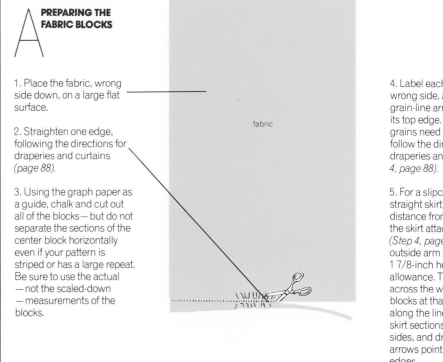

fabric

1. Place the fabric, wrong side down, on a large flat surface.

2. Straighten one edge, following the directions for draperies and curtains (page 88).

3. Using the graph paper as a guide, chalk and cut out all of the blocks—but do not separate the sections of the center block horizontally even if your pattern is striped or has a large repeat. Be sure to use the actual —not the scaled-down —measurements of the blocks.

4. Label each block on its wrong side, and draw a grain-line arrow pointing to its top edge. If the fabric grains need straightening, follow the directions for draperies and curtains (Step 4, page 88).

5. For a slipcover with a straight skirt, mark off the distance from the floor to the skirt attachment line (Step 4, page 125) on each outside arm block. Add a 1 7/8-inch hem and seam allowance. Then draw lines across the width of the blocks at that point, and cut along the lines. Label the skirt sections on their wrong sides, and draw grain-line arrows pointing to their top edges.

B JOINING CENTER BLOCK WIDTHS

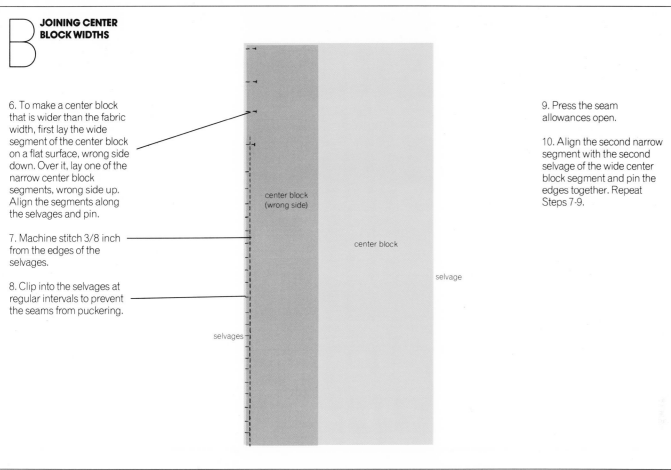

6. To make a center block that is wider than the fabric width, first lay the wide segment of the center block on a flat surface, wrong side down. Over it, lay one of the narrow center block segments, wrong side up. Align the segments along the selvages and pin.

7. Machine stitch 3/8 inch from the edges of the selvages.

8. Clip into the selvages at regular intervals to prevent the seams from puckering.

9. Press the seam allowances open.

10. Align the second narrow segment with the second selvage of the wide center block segment and pin the edges together. Repeat Steps 7-9.

C SEPARATING CENTER BLOCK LENGTHS

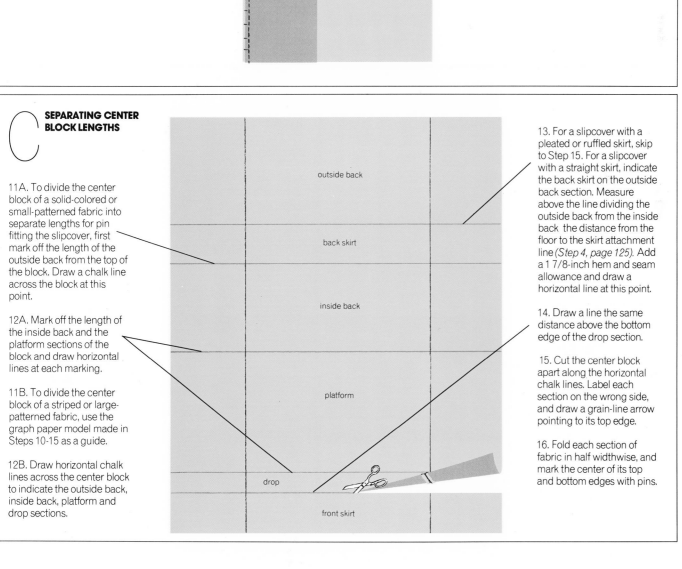

11A. To divide the center block of a solid-colored or small-patterned fabric into separate lengths for pin fitting the slipcover, first mark off the length of the outside back from the top of the block. Draw a chalk line across the block at this point.

12A. Mark off the length of the inside back and the platform sections of the block and draw horizontal lines at each marking.

11B. To divide the center block of a striped or large-patterned fabric, use the graph paper model made in Steps 10-15 as a guide.

12B. Draw horizontal chalk lines across the center block to indicate the outside back, inside back, platform and drop sections.

13. For a slipcover with a pleated or ruffled skirt, skip to Step 15. For a slipcover with a straight skirt, indicate the back skirt on the outside back section. Measure above the line dividing the outside back from the inside back the distance from the floor to the skirt attachment line *(Step 4, page 125)*. Add a 1 7/8-inch hem and seam allowance and draw a horizontal line at this point.

14. Draw a line the same distance above the bottom edge of the drop section.

15. Cut the center block apart along the horizontal chalk lines. Label each section on the wrong side, and draw a grain-line arrow pointing to its top edge.

16. Fold each section of fabric in half widthwise, and mark the center of its top and bottom edges with pins.

A POSITIONING THE SECTIONS

1. With the wrong side of the drop section fabric facing in, match the center pin on the section to the center mark on the front skirt attachment line.

2. Align the drop section to extend 3/8 inch below the skirt attachment line and 3/8 inch above the platform edge.

3. Smooth the fabric over the upholstery, and pin it in position.

4. Lay the platform section wrong side down on the platform of the sofa or chair, aligning the center pin on the section with the center pin on the drop.

5. Align the front edge of the platform section with the top edge of the drop section. Then pin the sections together 3/8 inch inside their raw edges.

6. Smooth the platform section toward the arms and back of the sofa or chair and fold up the excess fabric at the back and side edges. Then, using the end of a ruler, tuck 2 or 3 inches of the folded fabric at the back of the platform section into the crease between the inside back and the platform of the sofa or chair.

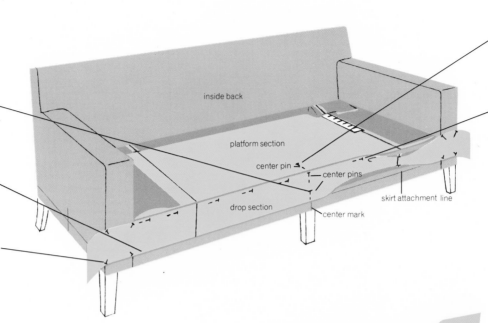

7. With the wrong side of one outside arm section of the fabric facing in, match the center pin on the section to the center mark on one side skirt attachment line.

8. Align the outside arm section to extend 3/8 inch below the skirt attachment line.

9. Smooth the fabric over the upholstery, and pin it in position. Then trim away any fitting allowance that extends more than 1 inch beyond the side edges of the outside arm of the sofa or chair.

10. Repeat Steps 7-9 on the other outside arm.

11. With the wrong side of the outside back section of the fabric facing in, match the center pin on the section to the center mark on the back skirt attachment line.

12. Align the outside back section to extend 3/8 inch below the skirt attachment line.

13. Smooth the fabric over the upholstery, and pin it in position. Then trim away any fitting allowance that extends more than 1 inch beyond the side edges of the outside back of the sofa or chair.

14. Still working from the back, place the inside back section on the sofa or chair with the fabric wrong side in. Align the center pin on the section with the center pin on the outside back section.

15. Align the top edge of the inside back section to extend 3/8 inch above the upper edge of the outside back of the sofa or chair. Then pin the inside back and outside back sections together, pinning as closely as possible to the upper edge of the outside back of the sofa or chair.

16. Smooth the inside back section toward the arms and platform.

17. Fold the platform section fabric so that the raw back edge aligns with the bottom edge of the inside back section. Then pin the two sections together 3/8 inch inside their raw edges. Stop pinning several inches from the inside arm on each side.

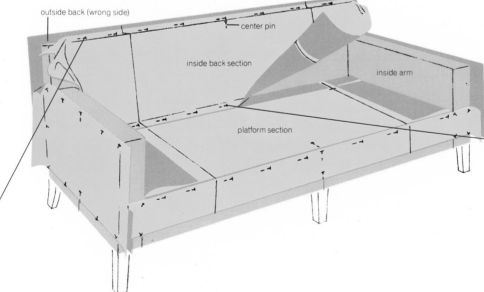

B FITTING THE INSIDE BACK OVER THE ARM

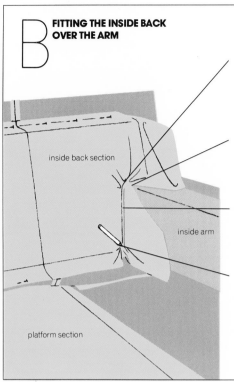

inside back section

inside arm

platform section

18. At the top of the inside arm, tuck the inside back section into the indentation between the inside arm and the inside back of the sofa or chair.

19. Slash the inside back section to within 3/4 inch of the indentation as shown. The cut should align approximately with the top edge of the inside arm.

20. Continue to tuck the inside back section into the indentation from the slash to the platform.

21. With dressmaker's chalk, trace along the indentation from the slash to the platform.

22. Pull the fabric out of the indentation, and trim away the excess 3/4 inch outside the chalk line.

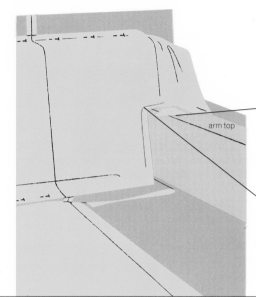

arm top

23. Tuck the trimmed fabric back into the indentation, and then tuck the inside back section into the indentation over the top of the arm.

24. Trace along the indentation at the top of the arm with chalk.

25. Pull the fabric out of the indentation, and trim away the excess 3/4 inch outside the chalk line.

26. Slash the inside back section at the corner of the inside back and the top of the arm to within 1/4 inch of the chalk line.

27. Repeat Steps 18-26 on the other side of the inside back.

C FITTING THE INSIDE ARM

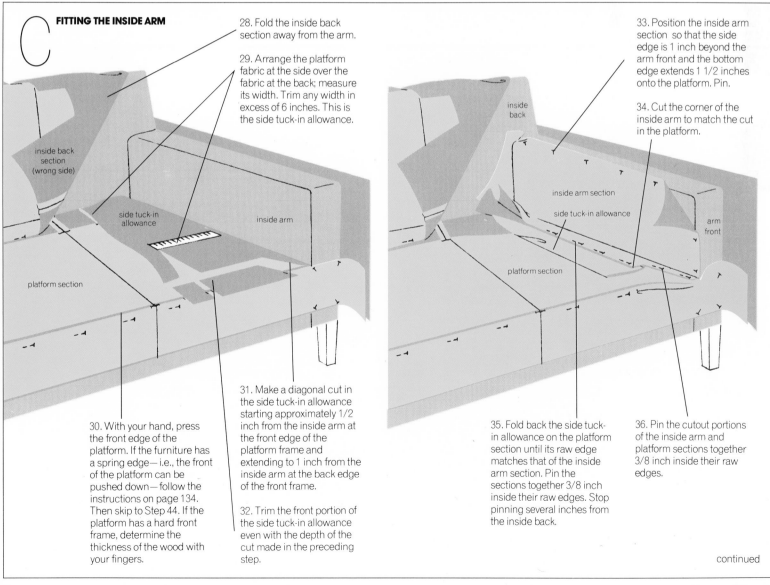

inside back section (wrong side)

side tuck-in allowance

inside arm

platform section

inside back

inside arm section

side tuck-in allowance

platform section

arm front

28. Fold the inside back section away from the arm.

29. Arrange the platform fabric at the side over the fabric at the back; measure its width. Trim any width in excess of 6 inches. This is the side tuck-in allowance.

30. With your hand, press the front edge of the platform. If the furniture has a spring edge—i.e., the front of the platform can be pushed down—follow the instructions on page 134. Then skip to Step 44. If the platform has a hard front frame, determine the thickness of the wood with your fingers.

31. Make a diagonal cut in the side tuck-in allowance starting approximately 1/2 inch from the inside arm at the front edge of the platform frame and extending to 1 inch from the inside arm at the back edge of the front frame.

32. Trim the front portion of the side tuck-in allowance even with the depth of the cut made in the preceding step.

33. Position the inside arm section so that the side edge is 1 inch beyond the arm front and the bottom edge extends 1 1/2 inches onto the platform. Pin.

34. Cut the corner of the inside arm to match the cut in the platform.

35. Fold back the side tuck-in allowance on the platform section until its raw edge matches that of the inside arm section. Pin the sections together 3/8 inch inside their raw edges. Stop pinning several inches from the inside back.

36. Pin the cutout portions of the inside arm and platform sections together 3/8 inch inside their raw edges.

continued

D | PIN FITTING THE ARM TOP AND FRONT SECTION

37. Remove the pins from the end of the drop section and pin back the fabric to expose the arm front.

38A. For a sofa or chair with curved arms, follow the instructions on page 134, then skip to Step 44.

41. Pin the inside arm and the outside arm to the arm top 3/8 inch inside its long raw edges.

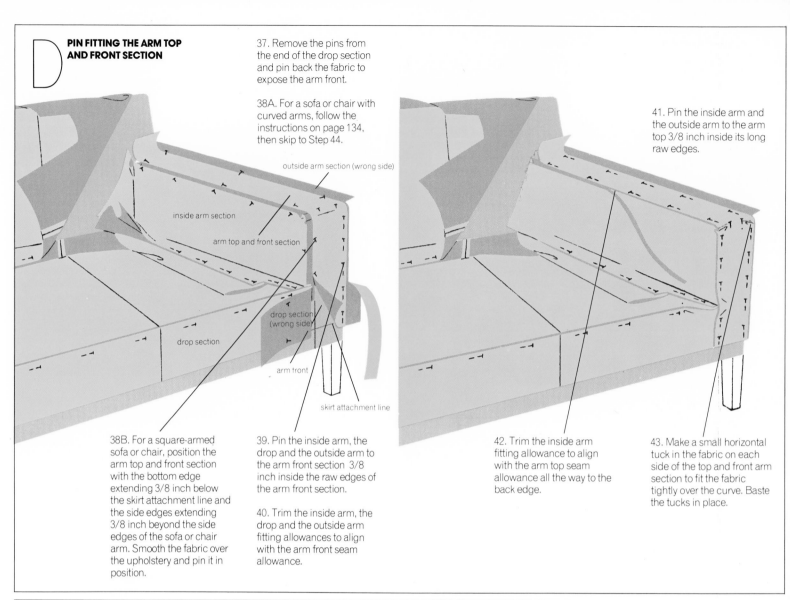

outside arm section (wrong side)

inside arm section

arm top and front section

drop section (wrong side)

arm front

drop section

skirt attachment line

38B. For a square-armed sofa or chair, position the arm top and front section with the bottom edge extending 3/8 inch below the skirt attachment line and the side edges extending 3/8 inch beyond the side edges of the sofa or chair arm. Smooth the fabric over the upholstery and pin it in position.

39. Pin the inside arm, the drop and the outside arm to the arm front section 3/8 inch inside the raw edges of the arm front section.

40. Trim the inside arm, the drop and the outside arm fitting allowances to align with the arm front seam allowance.

42. Trim the inside arm fitting allowance to align with the arm top seam allowance all the way to the back edge.

43. Make a small horizontal tuck in the fabric on each side of the top and front arm section to fit the fabric tightly over the curve. Baste the tucks in place.

E | FITTING THE ARM AT THE INSIDE BACK

44. With the end of the ruler, tuck the back of the inside arm section into the indentation between the inside arm and the inside back.

45. With chalk, mark the wrong side of the fabric at the edge of the indentation.

46. Pull the fabric out of the indentation and cut 3/4 inch outside the chalk line.

47. Finish pinning the arm top to the inside arm.

48. Trim the back edge of the arm top section even with the back edge of the inside arm.

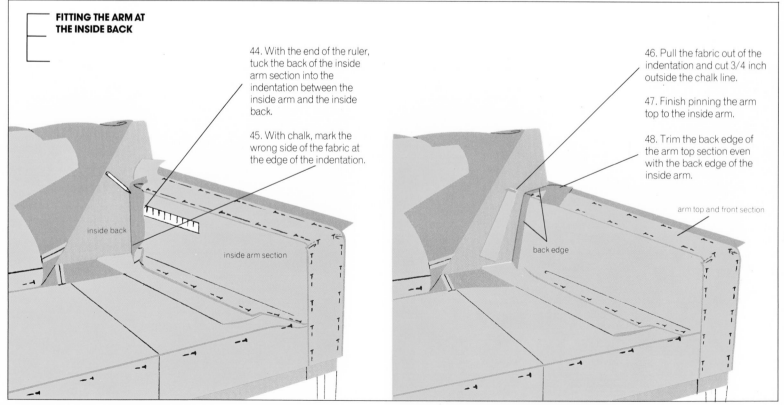

inside back

inside arm section

back edge

arm top and front section

F JOINING THE INSIDE BACK AND ARM

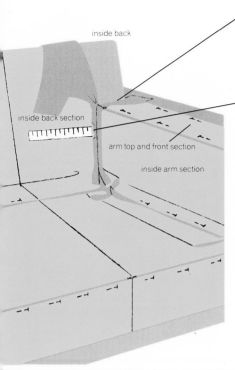

inside back

inside back section

arm top and front section

inside arm section

49. Using the ruler, tuck the inside arm and top and front arm sections into the indentation between the arm and the inside back of the sofa or chair.

50. Tuck the inside back section into the indentation at the inside arm and top arm of the sofa or chair.

51. Make a horizontal clip in the inside back section at the junction between the inside arm and top arm sections to fit the fabric smoothly over the arm.

52. Pin the inside back section to the arm top and inside arm sections as closely as possible to the indentation in the sofa or chair.

53. Trim away any excess fitting allowance on the top arm section even with the inside back seam allowance.

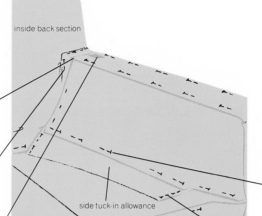

inside back section

side tuck-in allowance

platform section

54. Pull the pinned sections out of the indentation at the bottom corner of the inside back and inside arm.

55. Finish pinning the bottom edge of the inside back section to the back edge of the platform section 3/8 inch from their raw edges.

56. Finish pinning the inside arm section to the side tuck-in allowance of the platform section 3/8 inch from their raw edges.

57. Pin together the layers of the folded side tuck-in allowance 3/8 inch inside their raw edges at both the back and front ends.

G FITTING THE OUTSIDE ARM AND OUTSIDE BACK

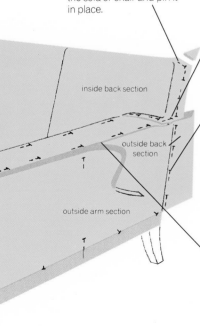

inside back section

outside back section

outside arm section

58. Smooth the unpinned edge of the inside back section around the side of the sofa or chair and pin it in place.

59. Make a dart in the inside back section at the junction between the top and the side edges of the sofa or chair.

60. Pin the outside arm and the inside back sections together on a line with the top of the arm.

61. Starting at the top of the sofa or chair, pin the inside back and the outside arm sections to the outside back section. Insert the pins close to the back edge of the sofa or chair. Be careful not to catch the horizontal seam allowances of the inside back and outside arm sections with the pins.

62. Trim the seam allowance for the dart made in Step 59 to 3/8 inch.

63. Trim the outside arm and the inside back seam allowances to 3/8 inch. Continue trimming the outside arm seam allowance up to the front arm edge.

64. Repeat Steps 28-63 on the other side of the sofa or chair.

65. Decide on which back seam the zipper will be. On the other side, trim the seam allowances of the outside back, inside back and outside arm sections to 3/8 inch.

66. On the zipper side, measure 24 1/2 inches from the floor, following the contour of the outside back edge. Mark with chalk.

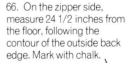

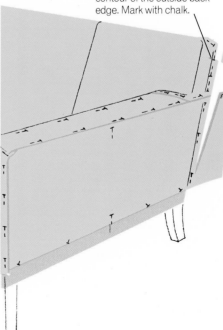

67. Above the chalk mark, trim the outside back and inside back seam allowances to 3/8 inch.

68. Below the chalk mark, trim the seam allowances to 1 inch.

69. On the side that will have a zipper, spread apart the outside back seam allowance and mark the zipper opening seam line with chalk.

70. Make cross marks on the seam allowance near the top and center of the outside arm.

71. Examine the seam allowances on the slipcover to be sure that all of them have been trimmed to 3/8 inch, except the one for the zipper opening.

72. Spread each seam apart and make cross marks on the seam allowances at 3- or 4-inch intervals to serve as stitching guides.

73. Remove the pins from the zipper opening and carefully remove the slipcover from the sofa or chair.

PIN FITTING A SPRING-EDGED SOFA OR CHAIR

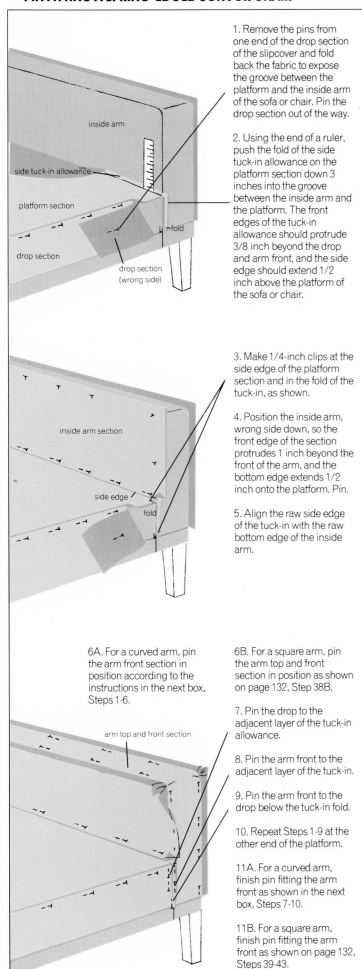

1. Remove the pins from one end of the drop section of the slipcover and fold back the fabric to expose the groove between the platform and the inside arm of the sofa or chair. Pin the drop section out of the way.

2. Using the end of a ruler, push the fold of the side tuck-in allowance on the platform section down 3 inches into the groove between the inside arm and the platform. The front edges of the tuck-in allowance should protrude 3/8 inch beyond the drop and arm front, and the side edge should extend 1/2 inch above the platform of the sofa or chair.

3. Make 1/4-inch clips at the side edge of the platform section and in the fold of the tuck-in, as shown.

4. Position the inside arm, wrong side down, so the front edge of the section protrudes 1 inch beyond the front of the arm, and the bottom edge extends 1/2 inch onto the platform. Pin.

5. Align the raw side edge of the tuck-in with the raw bottom edge of the inside arm.

6A. For a curved arm, pin the arm front section in position according to the instructions in the next box, Steps 1-6.

6B. For a square arm, pin the arm top and front section in position as shown on page 132, Step 38B.

7. Pin the drop to the adjacent layer of the tuck-in allowance.

8. Pin the arm front to the adjacent layer of the tuck-in.

9. Pin the arm front to the drop below the tuck-in fold.

10. Repeat Steps 1-9 at the other end of the platform.

11A. For a curved arm, finish pin fitting the arm front as shown in the next box, Steps 7-10.

11B. For a square arm, finish pin fitting the arm front as shown on page 132, Steps 39-43.

PIN FITTING A CURVED-ARM SOFA OR CHAIR

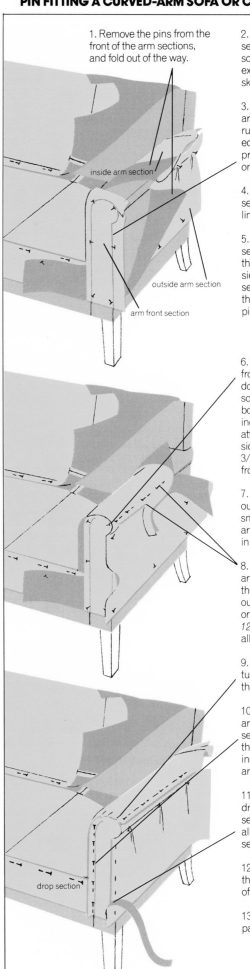

1. Remove the pins from the front of the arm sections, and fold out of the way.

2. Position one arm front section, wrong side down, so that the bottom edge extends 3/8 inch below the skirt attachment line. Pin.

3. Trace the shape of the arm front onto the fabric by running chalk along the edges of the arm front at the prominent edge of the welt or seam.

4. Remove the arm front section. Correct the chalk lines, smoothing the curve.

5. Pin the second arm front section of the slipcover to the chalked section, wrong sides together. Trim the two sections 3/8 inch outside the chalk lines. Remove the pins.

6. Pin one trimmed arm front section, wrong side down, to the arm front of the sofa or chair so that the bottom edge extends 3/8 inch below the skirt attachment line, and the side and top edges protrude 3/8 inch beyond the arm front.

7. Unfold the inside and outside arm sections, and smooth them toward the arm front. Pin the sections in position.

8. Pin the inside and outside arm sections together along the chalk line drawn on the outermost edge of the sofa or chair arm (page 126, Step 12B). Trim the seam allowances to 3/8 inch.

9. Baste three or four small tucks into the top front of the inside arm section.

10. Pin the drop, the inside arm and the outside arm sections of the slipcover to the arm front 3/8 inch inside the raw edges of the arm front section.

11. Trim the inside arm, the drop, and the outside arm section fitting allowances to align with the arm front section seam allowances.

12. Repeat Steps 6-11 on the other arm front section of the slipcover.

13. Proceed with Step 44, page 132.

STITCHING THE SLIPCOVER

A JOINING THE PLATFORM AND INSIDE ARM SECTIONS

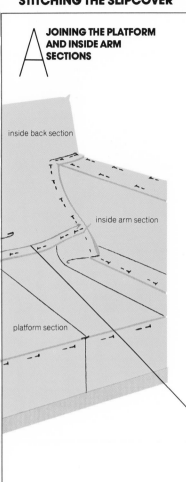

inside back section

inside arm section

platform section

1. If you plan to use welt seams on the slipcover, first make the welting according to the instructions on pages 50-51, Boxes B and C. Then read the section on making welt seams (Boxes D-F).

2. To sew the slipcover, remove the pins from one seam at a time.

3. For an unwelted seam, skip to Step 4. For a seam that is to be welted, attach the welting to the larger of the sections that you plan to join—sewing it to the side of the fabric that will be visible in the finished slipcover.

4. Turn the slipcover, wrong side out, and repin the seam 3/8 inch inside the raw edges.

5. Machine stitch the seam 3/8 inch inside the raw edges of the fabric; remove the pins as you go.

6. Stitch the seam between the inside back section and the platform section from one inside arm to the other.

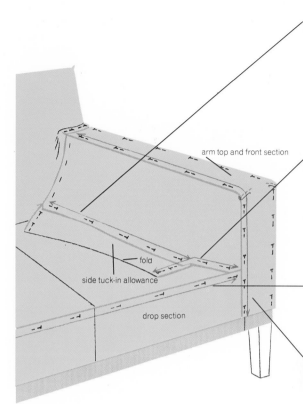

arm top and front section

fold

side tuck-in allowance

drop section

7A. For a hard-edged sofa or chair, stitch the seam between the inside arm and platform sections from the inside back to the indentation at the front of the tuck-in allowance.

8A. Stitch along the front indentation of the platform section— sewing from the fold in the side tuck-in allowance to the front edges of the platform and inside arm sections; pivot (Glossary) at the corner.

9A. Repeat Steps 7A and 8A on the other side of the platform.

10A. Use a welt seam to stitch the drop section to the platform section from one inside arm to the other.

11A. For a curved-arm sofa or chair, skip to Step 13.

12A. Use a welt seam to stitch the arm top and front section to the inside arm and drop sections from the inside back to the bottom of the drop.

7B. For a sofa or chair with a spring edge, stitch the seam between the inside arm section and the side tuck-in allowance of the platform section from the inside back to the drop.

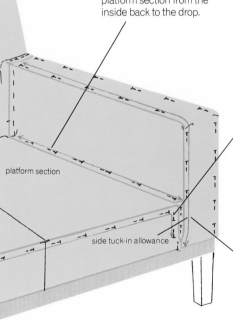

platform section

side tuck-in allowance

8B. Repeat Step 7B on the other side of the slipcover.

9B. Stitch welting to the front edge of the platform section between the clips at the beginning of each side tuck-in allowance.

10B. Stitch the inner layer of the side tuck-in allowance to the adjacent portion of the drop from the fold to the platform edge. Without breaking threads, stitch the front of the platform section to the top of the drop section. Then stitch the inner layer of the other side tuck-in allowance to the other end of the drop.

11B. For a curved-arm sofa or chair, skip to Step 13.

12B. Use a welt seam to stitch the arm top and front section to the inside arm section and the outer layer of the side tuck-in allowance. Then stitch from just beneath the fold in the side tuck-in allowance to the bottom edges of the drop and arm front sections.

13. Stitch the inside back section to the arm top and inside arm sections from the outside arm to the side tuck-in allowance of the platform section. Then stitch together the layers of the tuck-in allowance.

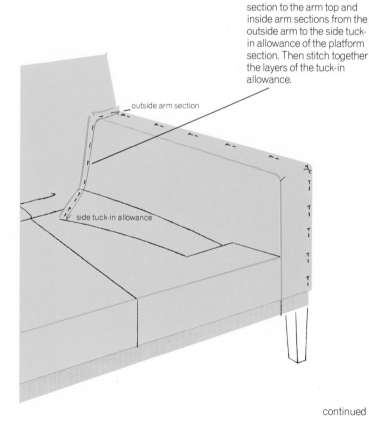

outside arm section

side tuck-in allowance

continued

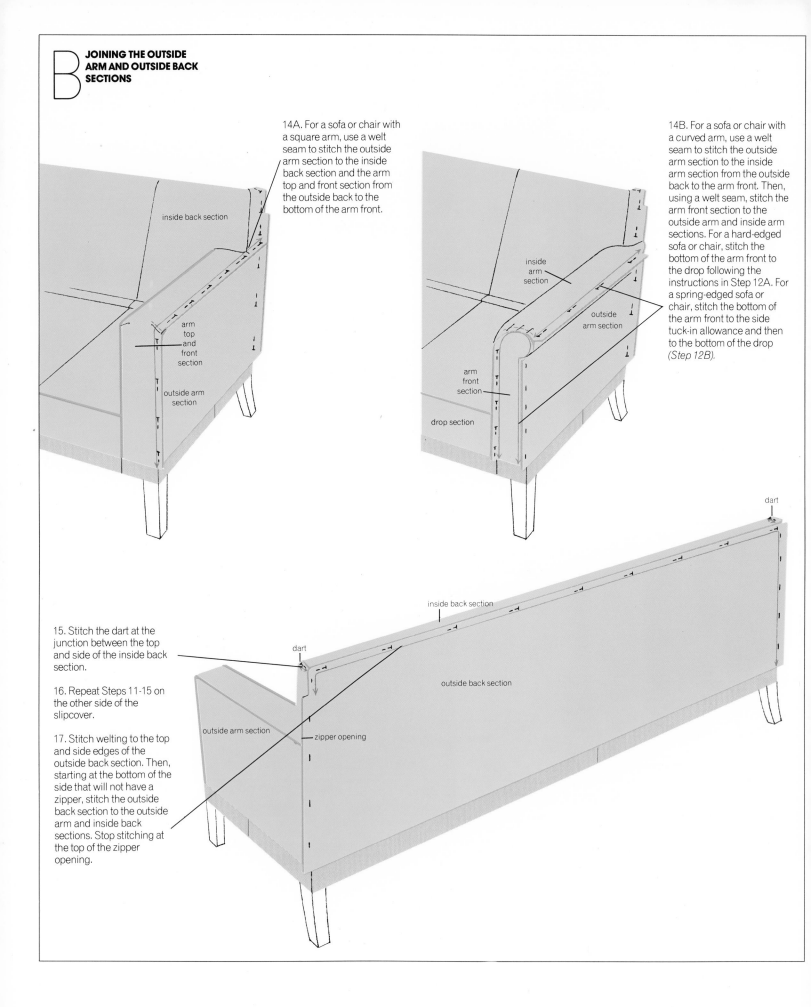

14A. For a sofa or chair with a square arm, use a welt seam to stitch the outside arm section to the inside back section and the arm top and front section from the outside back to the bottom of the arm front.

inside back section

arm top and front section

outside arm section

14B. For a sofa or chair with a curved arm, use a welt seam to stitch the outside arm section to the inside arm section from the outside back to the arm front. Then, using a welt seam, stitch the arm front section to the outside arm and inside arm sections. For a hard-edged sofa or chair, stitch the bottom of the arm front to the drop following the instructions in Step 12A. For a spring-edged sofa or chair, stitch the bottom of the arm front to the side tuck-in allowance and then to the bottom of the drop (Step 12B).

inside arm section

outside arm section

arm front section

drop section

15. Stitch the dart at the junction between the top and side of the inside back section.

16. Repeat Steps 11-15 on the other side of the slipcover.

17. Stitch welting to the top and side edges of the outside back section. Then, starting at the bottom of the side that will not have a zipper, stitch the outside back section to the outside arm and inside back sections. Stop stitching at the top of the zipper opening.

dart

inside back section

dart

outside back section

outside arm section

zipper opening

JOINING THE SKIRT SECTIONS

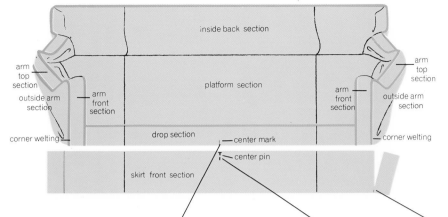

18A. For a pleated skirt, follow the instructions on pages 145-146 to join the skirt sections and plot the pleats. At the zipper opening allow a 1 1/4-inch seam allowance outside the edges of the first and last pleats. Then skip to Box D.

18B. For a ruffled skirt, machine stitch the widths together 1/2 inch inside their raw edges. Then skip to Box D.

18C. For a slipcover with a straight skirt, lay the body of the slipcover wrong side down on a large, flat surface.

19. Replace the pins marking the centers of the outside back, drop and outside arm sections with chalk marks.

20. Align the center pin on one skirt section with the center mark on the corresponding slipcover section.

21. Align the top edge of the skirt section with the bottom edge of the slipcover.

22. At the corners of the slipcover, mark the skirt section 1 inch outside the corner welting. At the corner where the zipper opening will be, mark the skirt section even with the zipper opening seam allowance.

23. Trim the ends of the skirt section even with the marks made in the preceding step.

24. Repeat Steps 20-23 on each skirt section.

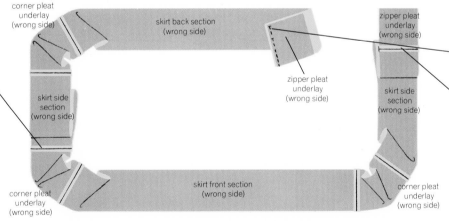

25. To make underlays for pleats at the closed corners of the slipcover, cut scraps of slipcover fabric into three rectangles 16 inches wide and the length of the skirt. Mark the center of one wide edge of each rectangle with chalk.

26. To make underlays for the zipper opening pleat, cut two rectangles 9 1/4 inches wide and the same length as the skirt.

27. Place the skirt front section wrong side down and set a pleat underlay over it, wrong side up.

28. Align one end of the underlay with one end of the skirt section. Pin.

29. Machine stitch 1/2 inch inside the raw edges of the fabric, removing the pins as you go. Press the seam allowances open.

30. Repeat Steps 27 and 29 on the other side of the skirt front section.

31. Pin and stitch the skirt side sections to the unstitched ends of the corner pleat underlays already attached to the skirt front.

32. Pin and stitch one end of the remaining corner pleat underlay to the end of the skirt side section that will not have a zipper. Then pin and stitch the back skirt section to the other end of the underlay.

33. Pin and stitch one end of a zipper pleat underlay to the end of the back skirt section that will have a zipper. Then attach the other zipper pleat underlay to the skirt side section that will have a zipper.

D LINING THE SKIRT

34. Measure the total width of the skirt sections joined in Box C.

35. To make the skirt lining, decide the number of widths needed by dividing the skirt width by the width of the lining fabric. Round the figure to the next highest full number. Subtract 3 inches from the skirt length to find the lining length. Cut out the lining.

36. Machine stitch the lining widths together 1/2 inch inside their raw edges.

37. Place the skirt wrong side down with the lining on top, wrong side up. Align the bottom edges. Pin.

38. Machine stitch 1/2 inch inside the raw edges.

39. Turn the skirt away from the lining, and press the seam allowances toward the skirt.

40. Fold up the lining with its wrong side against the wrong side of the skirt. Match the top edges of the skirt and lining. Pin.

41. Press the bottom edge of the skirt.

42. Stitch the lining and skirt together 1/4 inch inside their top edges, removing the pins as you go.

continued

MAKING THE PLEATS OR RUFFLES

43. For a slipcover with a pleated skirt, make box pleats following the instructions on page 147, Box H, Steps 47-49. Then skip to Box F.

44. For a slipcover with a ruffled skirt, gather the ruffles as described on page 59, Box C, Steps 12A and 12B, but in this case make the gathering stitches 1/4 inch from the top edge of the skirt. Also, start and end the ruffling 2 inches inside the ends of the skirt. Then skip to Box F.

45. For a slipcover with a straight skirt, place the skirt on a flat surface, lining side down.

46. To make an inverted pleat at one closed corner of the skirt, first form a lengthwise crease in one skirt section with your fingers. Make the crease 1/2 inch outside and parallel to the seam between the skirt section and a corner pleat underlay.

47. Fold the fabric to align the crease with the chalk mark in the center of the underlay. Pin the fold in place.

48. Repeat Steps 46 and 47 on the other side of the corner pleat underlay.

49. Press the inverted corner pleat, then machine stitch it in place 1/4 inch inside its top edge.

50. Repeat Steps 46-49 to make the inverted corner pleats on the two remaining closed corners of the slipcover.

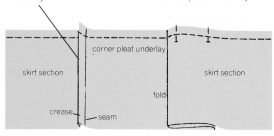

54. Make a half pleat in the manner described in Steps 46, 47 and 49.

51. To make an inverted corner pleat on one edge of the zipper opening of the slipcover, fold the unattached end of one of the zipper pleat underlays under by 1/4 inch.

52. Machine stitch close to the fold.

53. Measure in from the fold 1 inch and make a mark with chalk.

55. Repeat Steps 51-54 to make a half pleat on the other zipper opening edge.

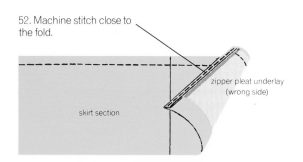

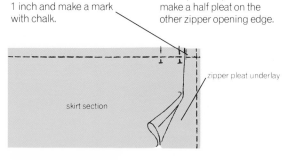

ATTACHING THE SKIRT TO THE BODY OF THE SLIPCOVER

56. Sew welting to the bottom edge of the body of the slipcover. Start the welting on the outside back, at the zipper opening edge. End the welting at the zipper opening seam line marked on the wrong side of the outside arm section.

57. Place the skirt on a flat surface, lining side down, and position the body of the slipcover on top of it, wrong side up. Align the top edge of the skirt with the bottom edge of the slipcover.

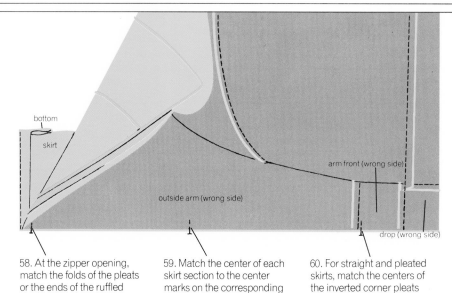

58. At the zipper opening, match the folds of the pleats or the ends of the ruffled portion of the skirt to the ends of the welting sewed around the bottom of the slipcover in Step 56. Pin.

59. Match the center of each skirt section to the center marks on the corresponding slipcover sections. Pin.

60. For straight and pleated skirts, match the centers of the inverted corner pleats with the corners of the slipcover. Pin.

61. Finish pinning the skirt to the slipcover.

62. Machine stitch the skirt to the slipcover 3/8 inch inside their raw edges, removing the pins as you go.

63. Insert the zipper in the zipper opening, following the instructions on page 70, Steps 2-19. For a skirt with pleats at the zipper opening edges, make this exception in Step 19: when sewing the unattached edge of the zipper to the outside arm and side skirt, stop stitching at the welt between the two sections. Break the threads. Then turn the pleat out of the way, and resume stitching below the welt to the bottom edge of the skirt.

G CUTTING THE CUSHION SECTIONS

64A. To separate the front boxing from each seat cushion, measure the depth of the box from the lower edge of the top block. Add a 3/4-inch seam allowance. Draw a chalk line across the block at this point. Then cut along the line.

64B. To separate the top boxing from each back cushion, measure the depth of the box from the upper edge of the top block. Add a 3/4-inch seam allowance. Draw a chalk line across the block at this point. Then cut along the line.

68. Place the cushion bottom block, wrong side up, and set the cushion top section over it, wrong side down. Be sure the arrows on the wrong sides of the sections face the same direction. Pin.

69. Trim around the edges of the cushion top section.

65. Lay the cushion top section, wrong side down, on the cushion with the edge cut in the preceding step protruding 3/8 inch beyond the front edge of a seat cushion or the upper edge of a back cushion. Pin the section to the cushion.

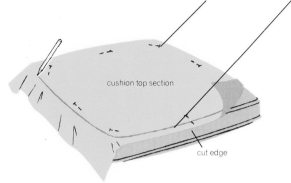

cushion top section

cut edge

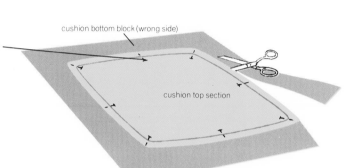

cushion bottom block (wrong side)

cushion top section

66. With dressmaker's chalk, trace around the perimeter of the cushion at the prominent edge of the welt or seam line. Remove the section from the cushion.

67A. For a rectangular cushion, fold the fabric in half—wrong side in—and match up the chalk lines as closely as possible. Then trim 3/8 inch outside the chalk lines on the top layer.

67B. For a cushion that is T-shaped, or semi T-shaped, trim the cushion top section 3/8 inch outside the chalk lines.

70. To make the boxing for the sides of each cushion, cut scrap fabric into two rectangles the depth of the cushion front box and the length of the cushion sides. Label each piece with chalk on its wrong side.

71. Determine the length the zipper should be by measuring the back edge of a seat cushion or the lower edge of a back cushion. Add 8 inches.

72. Cut two strips of fabric that are the depth of the box sides and front and the length of the zipper tapes.

H SEWING THE CUSHION COVERS

73. Stitch welting around the outside edges of the cushion top section and the cushion bottom section.

74. Sew the zipper into the strips cut in Step 72, following the instructions on page 69, Steps 3-13.

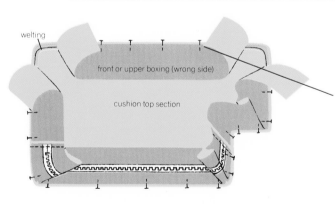

welting

front or upper boxing (wrong side)

cushion top section

79. Stitch the boxing sections to the cushion top section between the pins.

80A. For a rectangular cushion, make seams to connect the sides of the boxing to the front or upper boxing section 2 inches short of the front or upper edge of the cushion top section. Trim the seam allowance to 3/8 inch, and press the seam allowance open.

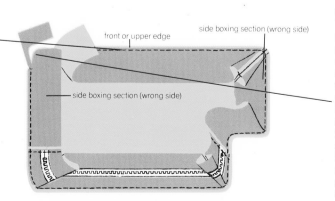

front or upper edge

side boxing section (wrong side)

side boxing section (wrong side)

75. Align the ends of the zippered boxing with the ends of the side boxing. Pin. Follow the instructions on page 69, Steps 15-18.

76. Pin the front or upper boxing to the corresponding edge of the cushion top. For a rectangular cushion, start and stop pinning at the corners. For a T- or semi T-shaped cushion, start and stop pinning 2 inches from the front or upper corners of the cushion top.

80B. For a T-shaped or semi T-shaped cushion, trim the ends of the side boxing sections even with the front or upper edge of the cushion top seam allowance. Then trim the ends of the upper or front boxing section even with the side edges of the cushion top seam allowance. Make seams connecting the boxing at the front or upper corners of the cushion top section. Press the seam allowances open.

77. Center the zippered boxing section along the lower or back edge of the cushion top section.

78. Pin the zippered and side box sections to the edges of the cushion top. For a rectangular cushion, stop pinning the sides 4 inches short of the upper or front edge of the cushion top section. For a T-shaped or semi T-shaped cushion, stop pinning 2 inches short of the upper or front edge of the cushion top section.

81. Finish stitching the boxing to the cushion top section.

82. Pin and machine stitch the cushion bottom to the unattached edges of the box.

Tailored
to the bed

Beds, like the people who sleep in them, have idiosyncrasies of height and girth; that is why making a bedspread requires such accurate measurements and careful estimates of yardage, which vary with the style of the spread—fitted, ruffled or pleated (following pages).

On the bed shown at right, peppermint stripes on a crisp pleated skirt and matching headboard are combined with flowers and dots on a quilted removable cover; the result is a trim but cozy look. The mock pleats at the corners allow the cover to slip off easily at night.

Calculations for bedcovers and skirts

The chart below lists the fabric and lining yardage needed for a fitted bedcover and a bed skirt, and the drawings at right show how to measure your bed to make them. The chart estimates are generous and provide ample fabric for welting and even for non-standard sizes.

With plain fabric, simply find the figures on the chart that best correspond to your bed. With patterned fabric, measure the depth of the skirt or drop (C, F or G at right) and add 2 1/2 inches for a bed skirt, 5 1/2 inches for a bedcover. Then measure the pattern repeat lengthwise from one design detail to the next one. If the repeat is longer than the total depth, use the column headed Long Repeats. If the repeat is shorter, use the column headed Short Repeats.

ESTIMATING YARDAGE

STYLE OF COVER	BED SIZES	PLAIN FABRIC 48-INCH WIDTH*	FABRIC WITH DESIGN REPEATS 48-INCH WIDTH*		LINING 48-INCH WIDTH
			LONG REPEATS	**SHORT REPEATS**	
FITTED BEDCOVER	TWIN	8	7 × REPEAT ÷ 36 (THEN ADD 3½)	14 × REPEAT ÷ 36 (THEN ADD 3½)	8
	DOUBLE	12	8 × REPEAT ÷ 36 (THEN ADD 7)	16 × REPEAT ÷ 36 (THEN ADD 7)	12
	QUEEN	12	8 × REPEAT ÷ 36 (THEN ADD 7)	16 × REPEAT ÷ 36 (THEN ADD 7)	12
	KING	12	8 × REPEAT ÷ 36 (THEN ADD 7)	16 × REPEAT ÷ 36 (THEN ADD 7)	12
FITTED BED SKIRT	TWIN	4½	6 × REPEAT ÷ 36 (THEN ADD 2½)	12 × REPEAT ÷ 36 (THEN ADD 2½)	7
	DOUBLE	6	6 × REPEAT ÷ 36 (THEN ADD 2½)	12 × REPEAT ÷ 36 (THEN ADD 2½)	8½
	QUEEN	6	7 × REPEAT ÷ 36 (THEN ADD 2½)	14 × REPEAT ÷ 36 (THEN ADD 2½)	11
	KING	8	7 × REPEAT ÷ 36 (THEN ADD 2½)	14 × REPEAT ÷ 36 (THEN ADD 2½)	13
PLEATED BED SKIRT	TWIN	10	14 × REPEAT ÷ 36 (THEN ADD 2½)	28 × REPEAT ÷ 36 (THEN ADD 2½)	12½
	DOUBLE	12	14 × REPEAT ÷ 36 (THEN ADD 2½)	28 × REPEAT ÷ 36 (THEN ADD 2½)	17
	QUEEN	12	15 × REPEAT ÷ 36 (THEN ADD 2½)	30 × REPEAT ÷ 36 (THEN ADD 2½)	17
	KING	13	15 × REPEAT ÷ 36 (THEN ADD 2½)	30 × REPEAT ÷ 36 (THEN ADD 2½)	18
RUFFLED BED SKIRT	TWIN	8	10 × REPEAT ÷ 36 (THEN ADD 2½)	20 × REPEAT ÷ 36 (THEN ADD 2½)	10½
	DOUBLE	10	10 × REPEAT ÷ 36 (THEN ADD 2½)	20 × REPEAT ÷ 36 (THEN ADD 2½)	12½
	QUEEN	10	12 × REPEAT ÷ 36 (THEN ADD 2½)	24 × REPEAT ÷ 36 (THEN ADD 2½)	15
	KING	11	12 × REPEAT ÷ 36 (THEN ADD 2½)	24 × REPEAT ÷ 36 (THEN ADD 2½)	16

*For 36-inch-wide fabric, multiply the total yardage by 1½.

BASIC BED MEASUREMENTS

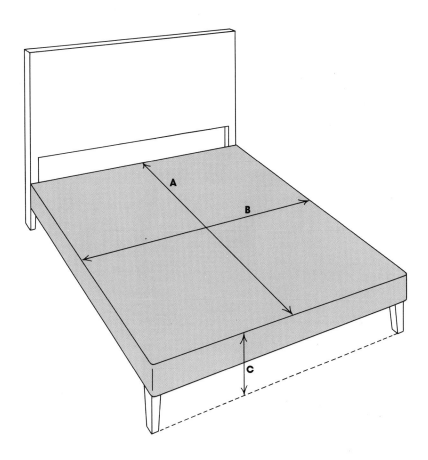

MEASURING THE BOX SPRING FOR A BED SKIRT

Before measuring the box spring, remove the mattress. For accuracy, use a steel measuring tape or a yardstick.

Measuring platform length: Measure the platform—the top surface of the box spring—from the foot to the head of the bed (*measurement A on the diagram at left*).

Measuring platform width: Measure across the platform from one side edge to the other (*B*).

Measuring platform height: Measure down from the top edge of the platform to within 1/2 inch of the floor (*C*).

Calculating the fabric for the platform cover: For the length of the platform fabric, add 9 1/2 inches to A (this includes a 6-inch overhang and a 3-inch fold-over hem at the head and a 1/2-inch seam at the foot). To find the width of the platform fabric if your fabric is wider than the bed, add 1 inch to B. To achieve the width of the platform fabric if your fabric is narrower than the bed, you will have to add two side panels equally on each side of a central panel. The central panel will be the width of your fabric. To find the width of each side panel, subtract 1 inch from the width of your fabric, then subtract the result from B. Divide this figure by two and add 1 inch for seam allowances.

Calculating the fabric for the facings: The foot and side edges of the platform require 5-inch-wide facings. To find the length of each side facing, add 9 1/2 inches to A. To find the length of the foot-end facing, add 1 inch to B.

Calculating the fabric for the skirt: For the length of the skirt, first multiply A by two and add B. Then add at least 7 inches for hems. For a pleated skirt, multiply this figure by three; for a ruffled skirt, multiply by two; for a fitted skirt, add 32 inches for corner pleats. To determine the number of fabric widths you should cut, divide the final skirt-length figure by the width of your fabric. To find the depth of the skirt, add 2 1/2 inches for hem and seam to C.

MEASURING THE BED FOR A FITTED BEDCOVER

Before measuring, make the bed with the sheets and blankets you normally use but leave the pillows off. For accuracy, use a steel measuring tape or a yardstick.

Measuring the mattress length: Measure the top of the made-up mattress from the foot of the bed to the head (*measurement D in the diagram at right*).

Measuring the mattress width: Measure across the top of the made-up mattress from one side edge to the other (*E*).

Measuring the bed height: For a short bedcover, measure down one side from the top of the made-up mattress to at least 2 inches below the point where the mattress meets the box spring (*F*). For a full-length bedcover, measure from the top of the mattress to within 1/2 inch of the floor (*G*).

Calculating the fabric for the bedcover top: For the bedcover-top fabric length, add 27 1/2 inches to D (this includes a 24-inch tuck-in under the pillows, a 3-inch hem at the top and a 1/2-inch seam allowance at the foot). To find the width of the top if your fabric is wider than the bed, add 1 inch to E. If your fabric is narrower than the bed, add two side panels equally on each side of a central panel. The central panel will be the width of your fabric. To find the width of each side panel, first subtract 1 inch from the width of your fabric, then subtract the result from E. Divide this figure by two and add 1 inch for seam allowances.

Calculating the fabric for the drops: The foot and side edges require three panels of fabric called drops. To find the length of the two side drops, add 34 inches to D (for a 24-inch pillow tuck-in and 5-inch hems at the head and foot ends). To find the length of the foot drop, add 10 inches to E. To find the depth of each drop if you are making a short bedcover, add 5 1/2 inches to F (for 5-inch hems at the bottom and a 1/2-inch seam allowance at the top). If you are making a full-length bedcover, add the 5 1/2 inches to G.

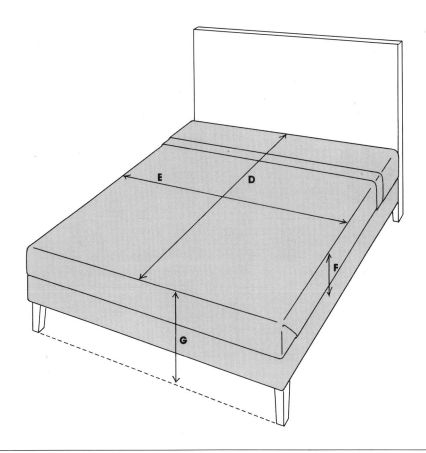

THE PLEATED BED SKIRT

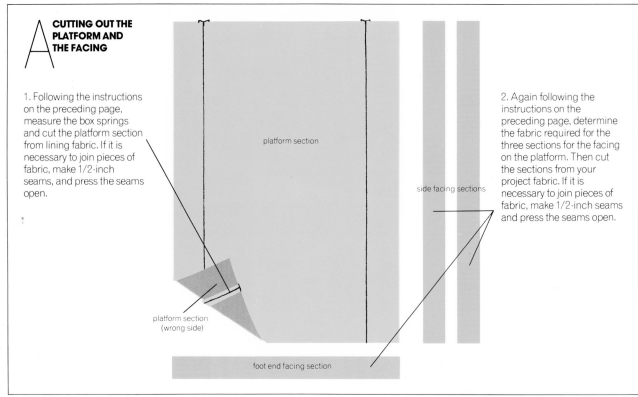

A CUTTING OUT THE PLATFORM AND THE FACING

1. Following the instructions on the preceding page, measure the box springs and cut the platform section from lining fabric. If it is necessary to join pieces of fabric, make 1/2-inch seams, and press the seams open.

2. Again following the instructions on the preceding page, determine the fabric required for the three sections for the facing on the platform. Then cut the sections from your project fabric. If it is necessary to join pieces of fabric, make 1/2-inch seams and press the seams open.

platform section

side facing sections

platform section (wrong side)

foot end facing section

B PREPARING THE FACING

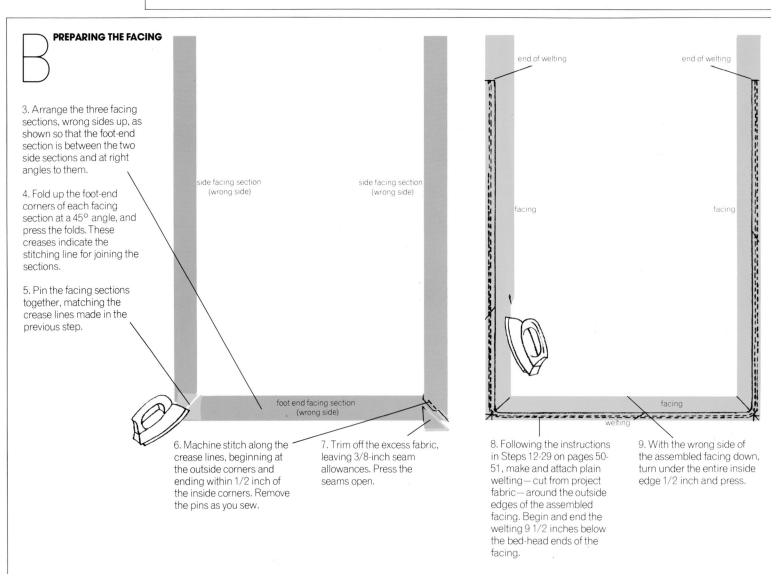

3. Arrange the three facing sections, wrong sides up, as shown so that the foot-end section is between the two side sections and at right angles to them.

4. Fold up the foot-end corners of each facing section at a 45° angle, and press the folds. These creases indicate the stitching line for joining the sections.

5. Pin the facing sections together, matching the crease lines made in the previous step.

side facing section (wrong side)

side facing section (wrong side)

end of welting

end of welting

facing

facing

foot end facing section (wrong side)

facing

welting

6. Machine stitch along the crease lines, beginning at the outside corners and ending within 1/2 inch of the inside corners. Remove the pins as you sew.

7. Trim off the excess fabric, leaving 3/8-inch seam allowances. Press the seams open.

8. Following the instructions in Steps 12-29 on pages 50-51, make and attach plain welting—cut from project fabric—around the outside edges of the assembled facing. Begin and end the welting 9 1/2 inches below the bed-head ends of the facing.

9. With the wrong side of the assembled facing down, turn under the entire inside edge 1/2 inch and press.

C PLANNING THE PLEATS

10. Following the instructions on page 143, cut as many widths of project fabric as you will need for the skirt. If you are using fabric with a design repeat, cut each width of fabric at the same point on the design so that the pattern can be matched.

11. Join two widths, or skirt pieces, together just inside the selvages. If the fabric is patterned, make sure to match the design. First pin, then machine stitch, removing the pins as you sew. Press the seam open.

12. To determine the width of the skirt pleats and the spaces between them, experiment with the joined pieces by folding in a few box pleats (Steps 1 and 2, page 79). If you are using a fabric with a prominent motif, be sure to center the motifs on the pleats.

13. When you are satisfied with the result, measure the width of the finished pleat and the width of the space.

14. Now determine the number of pleats you can fit across the foot of the bed, making sure you end up with a pleat—not a space—at each end. To do this, first subtract the width of one finished pleat (Step 13) from the platform width (measurement B, page 143).

15. Divide the combined width of one finished pleat plus one space into the figure. Add 1 to this result to obtain the total number of pleats at the foot of the bed. (If the division in this step does not come out even, you can either divide the remainder in half and add it to each end pleat or repeat the calculations with slightly different figures.)

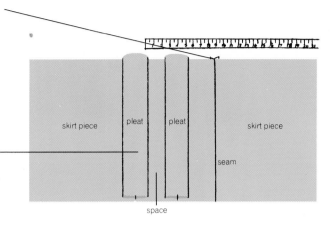

D BEGINNING THE MARKING OF THE PLEATS

16. Place a pin 1/2 inch to the left of the seam joining the two skirt pieces. Make a chalk mark at this pin.

17. Working to the left of the pin, measure a distance equal to twice the width of a finished pleat. Insert another pin at this point. This distance, shown bracketed, is the fabric needed for one pleat. The two pins will be matched up when folding the pleat, and the seam will be hidden on the underside of the pleat.

18. Still working to the left, measure a distance equal to the combined width of one finished pleat and one space. Insert another pin at this point.

19. Continue pin-marking twice the width of one finished pleat and then the combined width of one pleat and one space until you are near the left-hand end of the fabric. End by marking twice the width of a finished pleat for the left-hand corner pleat at the foot end. (If you had a remainder in Step 15, be sure to add it.)

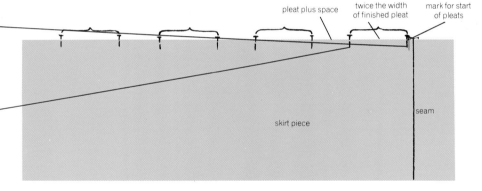

20. Return to the first pin you inserted beside the seam in Step 16. Measure out to the right of the pin a distance equal to the combined width of one finished pleat and one space. Place a pin there.

21. Working to the right, measure and pin-mark a distance equal to twice the width of a finished pleat. Continue pin-marking in this sequence until you are near the end of the fabric.

22. Count the number of pleats you have marked. If you have enough pleats for the foot of the bed, make sure you ended with a pleat, not a space, for the corner, and skip to Step 32.

continued

ATTACHING NEW SKIRT PIECES

23. If you do not have enough pleats, join another skirt piece at the end of the piece you were just working with. Turn the fabric wrong side up. Matching the selvages, pin the new piece on temporarily since you may have to move the seam if it is not hidden. Insert the pins vertically to simulate a seam, taking 1/2-inch seam allowances.

24. To determine if the seam will be hidden, first pin-mark one more sequence, continuing onto the new skirt piece.

25. Fold in the pleat closest to the pinned seam, matching the pin markers.

26. If, as in this example, the seam falls on top of the pleat, fold back the left-hand side of the pleat as shown. Then make a chalk mark 1/2 inch to the left of the point at which the folds of the pleat meet to indicate where you must cut.

27. If the seam falls in a space, fold back the right-hand side of the pleat. Then make a chalk mark 1 inch to the right of the point at which the pleat folds meet.

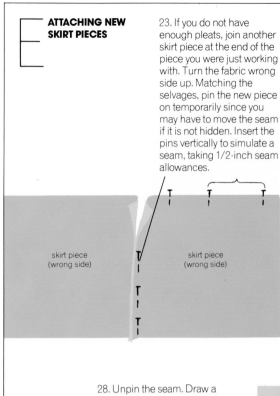

skirt piece (wrong side)

skirt piece (wrong side)

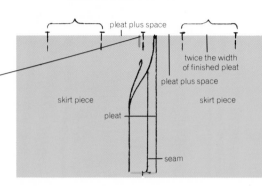

pleat plus space

twice the width of finished pleat

pleat plus space

skirt piece

skirt piece

pleat

seam

28. Unpin the seam. Draw a vertical chalk line, starting at the chalk mark.

29. Trim the fabric along the line.

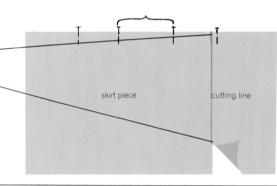

skirt piece

cutting line

30. Turn the fabric wrong side up and repin the new skirt piece to the trimmed edge with a temporary seam, as you did in Step 23. Pin-mark the last pleat or space again. Follow this procedure whenever you join new skirt pieces.

FINISHING THE MARKING OF THE PLEATS

31. Continue to pin-mark until you have the number of pleats needed for the foot of the bed. Make sure you end with a pleat. Be sure to add any remainder from Step 15.

32. To make the inverted pleat at the corner, mark the width of only a single finished pleat.

33. Now pin-mark the pleats for the right-hand side of the bed. To determine the number of pleats you will need, divide the combined width of one finished pleat and one space into the length of the platform (measurement A, page 143). Ignore any remainder.

34. For the first pleat on the right-hand side of the bed, pin-mark twice the width of a finished pleat. Then mark the combined width of a finished pleat and a space.

35. Continue pin-marking in this manner until you have the number of pleats determined in Step 33. Join new skirt pieces, as needed, repeating Steps 23-30 to hide the seam.

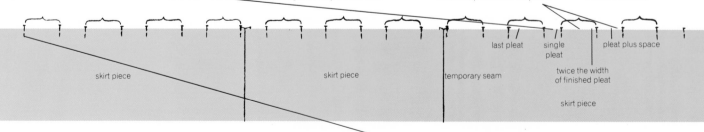

skirt piece

skirt piece

temporary seam

last pleat

single pleat

twice the width of finished pleat

pleat plus space

skirt piece

36. After marking the last pleat near the bed-head end, leave at least 12 inches of extra fabric at the end for a hem and, if necessary, an extended space.

37. To join and mark the left-hand side of the skirt, return to the pin marking the end of the last pleat you made in Step 19. Then repeat Steps 32-36 to mark the inverted pleat at the corner and the pleats for this side of the bed.

38. When the entire bed skirt has been marked, remove all the pins marking the pleats.

39. Machine stitch all the pinned seams, removing the pins as you sew. Press the seams open.

G LINING THE SKIRT

40. Cut enough widths of lining fabric to equal the length of the skirt. Make the depth of each lining piece 2 inches less than the depth of the skirt.

41. Pin the lining pieces together at the selvages, taking 1/2-inch seam allowances. Then stitch, removing the pins as you sew. Press the seams open.

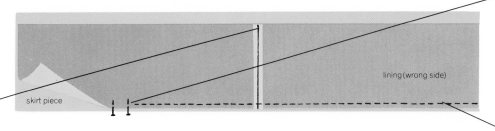

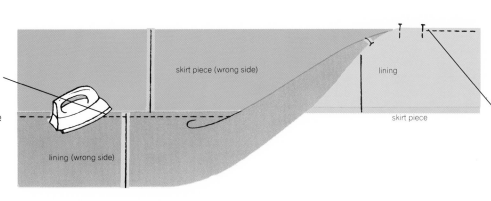

skirt piece

lining (wrong side)

42. Place the assembled skirt wrong side down. Cover it with the assembled lining, wrong side up. Pin them together, matching one long raw edge of the lining with the bottom edge of the skirt.

43. Machine stitch the two pieces together 1 inch in from the bottom. Remove the pins as you sew.

44. Bring the skirt out from underneath the lining. Spread the two pieces apart so that the skirt is at the top and both extend away from the seam and are facing wrong sides up. Press both seam allowances toward the skirt.

skirt piece (wrong side)

lining

skirt piece

lining (wrong side)

45. Turn the lining up over the skirt and match the raw edges at the top. Doing this will create a 1-inch hem of skirt fabric at the bottom. Press the hem.

46. Pin the raw edges together at the top. Then machine stitch 1/4 inch in from the edges, removing the pins as you sew.

H MAKING THE PLEATS

47. Place the lined skirt wrong side down. Go back to the mark made in Step 16 indicating the starting point for forming the pleats. Then repeat Steps 17-21 and Steps 31-37 to pin-mark all the pleats, including the two inverted pleats at the corners.

48. When all the pleats are marked, fold, pin and machine stitch following the instructions for the box pleat on page 79, Steps 1 and 2, and 4-8.

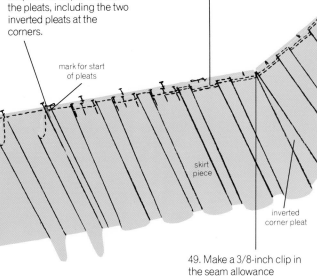

mark for start of pleats

skirt piece

inverted corner pleat

49. Make a 3/8-inch clip in the seam allowance between each inverted corner pleat, cutting up to —but not through—the stitching.

I PINNING THE FACING TO THE SKIRT

50. With the skirt wrong side down, and the assembled facing wrong side up, align the bed-foot section of the facing with the bed-foot section of the skirt between the inverted corner pleats.

51. Match the raw outside edge of the facing—the edge with the welting—with the top edge of the skirt. At each end of the bed-foot sections, match the corner of the stitching on the facing with the bottom of the clip on the skirt made in Step 49.

52. Pin the facing securely to the skirt, first pinning at the corners and then between them. Finally pin each long side section of the facing to the sides of the skirt, stopping just before the ends of the welting.

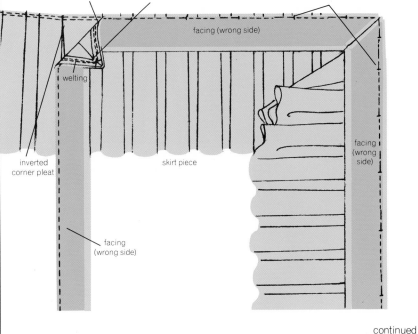

facing (wrong side)

welting

inverted corner pleat

skirt piece

facing (wrong side)

facing (wrong side)

facing (wrong side)

continued

FINISHING THE BED-HEAD ENDS OF THE SKIRT

J

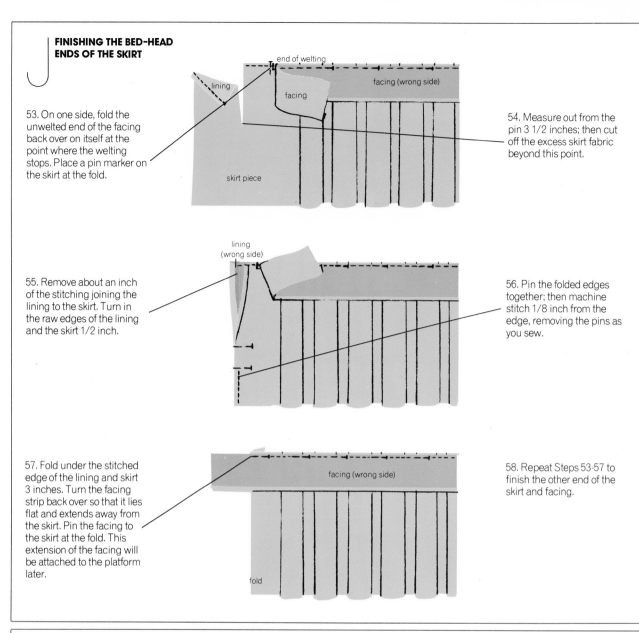

53. On one side, fold the unwelted end of the facing back over on itself at the point where the welting stops. Place a pin marker on the skirt at the fold.

54. Measure out from the pin 3 1/2 inches; then cut off the excess skirt fabric beyond this point.

55. Remove about an inch of the stitching joining the lining to the skirt. Turn in the raw edges of the lining and the skirt 1/2 inch.

56. Pin the folded edges together; then machine stitch 1/8 inch from the edge, removing the pins as you sew.

57. Fold under the stitched edge of the lining and skirt 3 inches. Turn the facing strip back over so that it lies flat and extends away from the skirt. Pin the facing to the skirt at the fold. This extension of the facing will be attached to the platform later.

58. Repeat Steps 53-57 to finish the other end of the skirt and facing.

SEWING THE FACING TO THE SKIRT

K

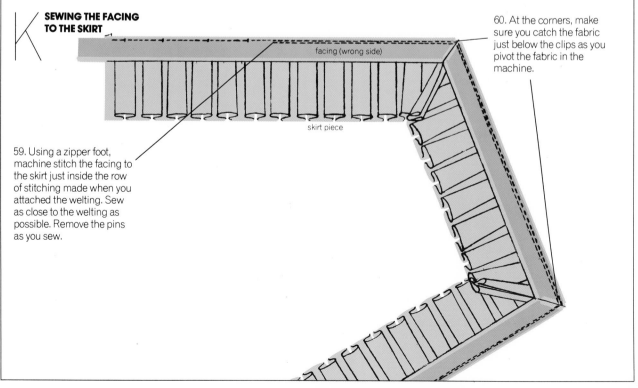

60. At the corners, make sure you catch the fabric just below the clips as you pivot the fabric in the machine.

59. Using a zipper foot, machine stitch the facing to the skirt just inside the row of stitching made when you attached the welting. Sew as close to the welting as possible. Remove the pins as you sew.

ATTACHING THE SKIRT TO THE PLATFORM

61. Place the platform section wrong side up on a flat surface — in most cases, this will have to be the floor. Place the skirt, wrong side down, over the platform, as shown, making sure the attached facing is still wrong side up.

62. Match the ends of the two extensions of the facing to the bed-head end of the platform. Pin.

63. Match the corners of the skirt with the foot-end corners of the platform. Pin.

64. On all three sides, match the raw edges of the platform with the raw edges of the skirt and facing; then pin all around the three sides.

65. Turn the entire project over so that the platform side is on top.

66. Making sure the skirt is out of the way and still using the zipper foot, machine stitch the platform section to the skirt and facing. Start at the right-hand bed-head corner, stitching 1/2 inch in from the edge.

67. When you reach the welting, which is not visible but can be felt to the left of the needle, stitch as close to it as possible. Remove the pins as you sew, and pivot carefully at the corners.

68. When all three sides are stitched, trim the two corners diagonally.

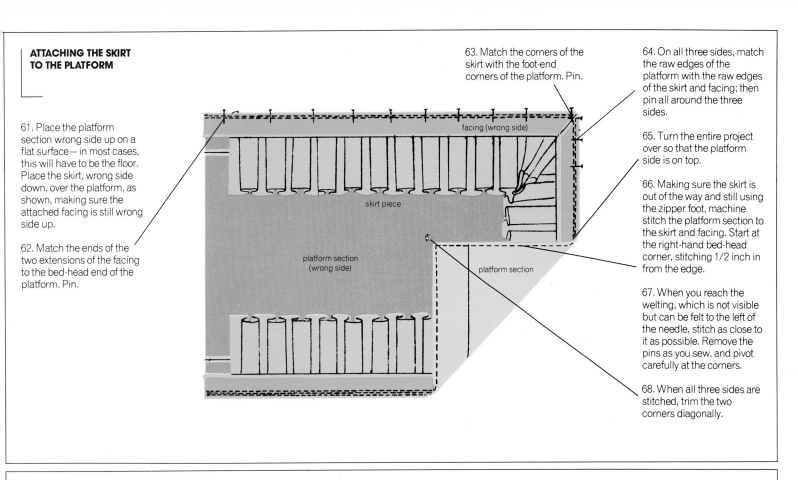

facing (wrong side)

skirt piece

platform section (wrong side)

platform section

M FINISHING THE BED SKIRT

69. With the project still wrong side down, bring the skirt and the facing out from under the platform section so that the skirt extends away from the platform.

70. Turn the unattached folded edge of the facing over onto the platform. Use a pencil to push out the corners. Press the facing flat against the platform.

71. Pin the folded edge of the facing to the platform section.

72. Machine stitch just inside the fold, going around all three sides. Remove the pins as you sew.

73. At the bed-head end of the platform section, turn under the edge 1 1/2 inches. Press the fold.

74. Turn the edge under once more 1 1/2 inches and press this fold.

75. Pin the folded edge in place; then machine stitch on the underside, sewing 1/8 inch in from the inside fold, removing the pins as you sew.

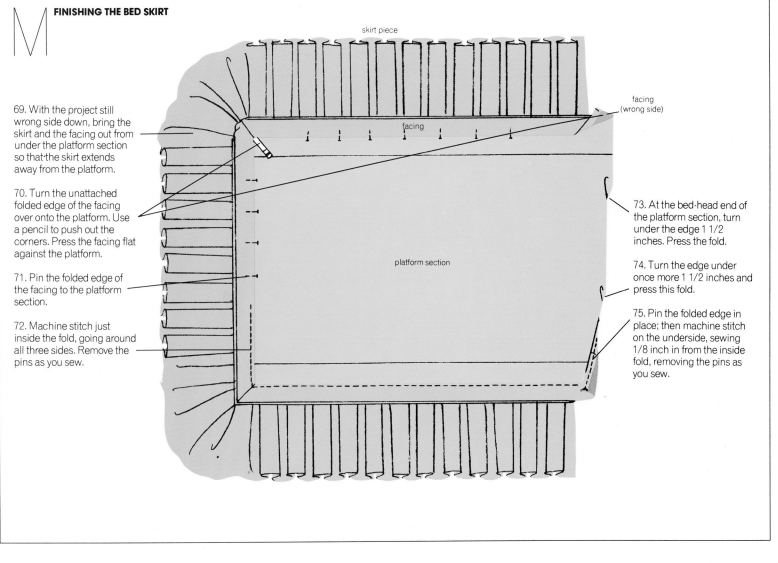

skirt piece

facing

facing (wrong side)

platform section

A LINING THE SIDE AND FOOT DROPS

1. Following the instructions on page 143, measure the bed. Then using the dimensions indicated on that page, cut from project fabric the two side drops and the foot drop for the bedcover. If your fabric's design requires it, sew fabric widths together, matching the pattern at the selvages, and press the seams open. Otherwise, cut the fabric parallel to the selvages to avoid joining the fabric.

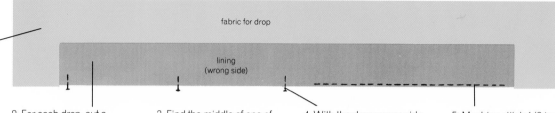

2. For each drop, cut a section of lining fabric that measures 18 inches less in length and 9 inches less in depth than the drop.

3. Find the middle of one of the drops by folding it in half lengthwise. Repeat with a corresponding lining section.

4. With the drop wrong side down, place the lining strip, wrong side up, over the drop, matching the midpoints. Align the bottom edges and pin them together.

5. Machine stitch 1/2 inch in from the bottom edges, beginning and ending 1 inch from the end of the lining. Remove the pins as you sew.

6. Spread out the joined sections so that they are both wrong side up. Press both seam allowances toward the drop.

7. Turn the lining section up over the drop, and match the raw edges at the top. Doing this will create a 4-inch hem of fabric at the bottom. Press the hem.

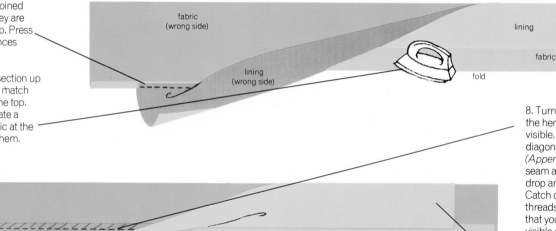

8. Turn the lining back over the hem so that the seam is visible. Make a row of diagonal basting stitches (Appendix) to attach the seam allowances of both the drop and lining to the drop. Catch only one or two threads of the drop fabric so that your stitches will not be visible on the outside of the drop.

9. Turn the lining up over the drop again.

B HEMMING THE ENDS OF THE DROPS

10. Working on one end of the drop, fold back the unstitched end of the lining 1 inch. Then fold over the end of the drop so that the raw edge of the drop meets the folded edge of the lining. Press the drop at the fold.

11. Unfold the end of the drop. Fold up the bottom corner of the drop diagonally as shown. Then refold the drop along the crease made in Step 10.

12. Turn under the end of the lining 1/2 inch, and place the folded edge over the raw edge of the drop. Pin along the diagonal fold of the drop and then along the folded edge of the lining.

13. Using a slip stitch (Appendix), sew the diagonal fold in place. Sew the folded lining edge to the drop. Remove the pins. Finish the other end.

14. Repeat Steps 3-13 to attach the lining and finish the ends of the two remaining drops.

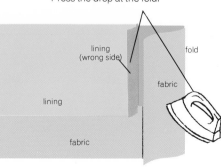

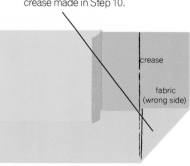

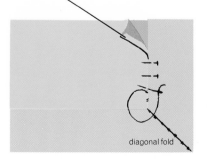

C PREPARING THE TOP OF THE BEDCOVER

15. Using the dimension given on page 143, cut the top for the bedcover from project fabric. If it is necessary to join panels on each side of the central panel to obtain the width needed, match the fabric at the selvages, then make seams wide enough to hide the selvages. Press the seams open.

16. Following the instructions in Steps 12-29 on pages 50-51, make and attach plain welting around the edges of the two sides and the foot end of the bedcover top. Begin and end the welting 3 inches in from the head end of the cover.

D ATTACHING THE DROPS TO THE BEDCOVER TOP

17. With the bedcover top wrong side down, place the two side drops, wrong sides up, over the top. Align the raw open edges of the drops with the side edges of the top. Position the ends of the drops so that they are 1/2 inch in from the foot end of the bedcover top.

18. Pin the drops to the top, with the pinheads extending away from the edges of the fabric.

19. Turn the entire cover wrong side up. Using a zipper foot, machine stitch the drops to the top just inside the row of stitches made when you attached the welting. Remove the pins as you stitch, and make sure to keep the bottom edges of the drops out of the way.

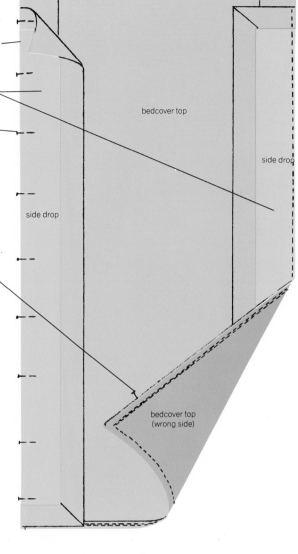

20. Turn the cover wrong side down again. Fold the foot-end corners of the side drops out of the way.

21. Place the foot drop, wrong side up, over the foot end of the top, again aligning the raw open edges of the drop with the outside edge of the top. Pin, with the heads facing out as before.

22. Machine stitch as you did on the side drops, sewing on the wrong side of the top and 1/2 inch in from the edge, just inside the welting stitches. Remove the pins as you sew.

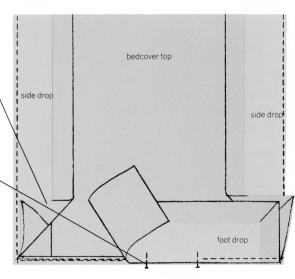

continued

QUILTED FABRIC

23A. If you are working with quilted project fabric, cut two pieces of the fabric. Make the width of each 16 inches. Make the depth of each the same as the depth of the drops (as they now measure). Also cut two pieces of lining with exactly the same dimensions.

24A. Place a project fabric section wrong side down and cover it with a lining section, wrong side up. Pin the pieces together.

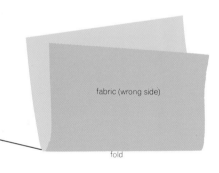

fabric

lining (wrong side)

25A. Machine stitch the pieces together around three sides, leaving one long side open. Sew 1/2 inch in from the edges, and remove the pins as you sew. Trim the stitched corners diagonally.

26A. Turn the pieces right side out through the open end. Push out the corners with a ruler. Press the seamed edge on the wrong side.

27A. Repeat Steps 23A-26A to make the other corner panel.

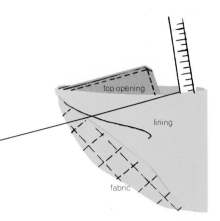

top opening

lining

fabric

UNQUILTED FABRIC

23B. If you are using unquilted fabric, cut two pieces of the fabric. Make the width of each 16 inches. Make the depth of each 1 inch less than twice the depth of the drops (as the drops now measure).

24B. Fold one of the fabric sections in half, wrong sides out, so that two 16-inch edges are together.

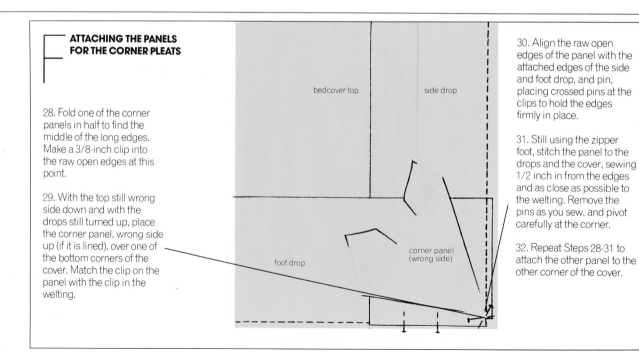

fabric (wrong side)

fold

25B. Pin along the two short sides. Then machine stitch 1/2 inch in from the edges. Clip the corners at the fold diagonally.

26B. Turn the panel right side out through the open end. Press along the folded and seamed edges.

27B. Repeat Steps 23B-26B to make the other corner panel.

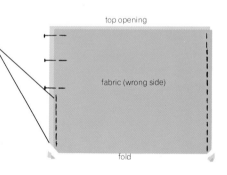

top opening

fabric (wrong side)

fold

28. Fold one of the corner panels in half to find the middle of the long edges. Make a 3/8-inch clip into the raw open edges at this point.

29. With the top still wrong side down and with the drops still turned up, place the corner panel, wrong side up (if it is lined), over one of the bottom corners of the cover. Match the clip on the panel with the clip in the welting.

bedcover top

side drop

corner panel
(wrong side)

foot drop

30. Align the raw open edges of the panel with the attached edges of the side and foot drop, and pin, placing crossed pins at the clips to hold the edges firmly in place.

31. Still using the zipper foot, stitch the panel to the drops and the cover, sewing 1/2 inch in from the edges and as close as possible to the welting. Remove the pins as you sew, and pivot carefully at the corner.

32. Repeat Steps 28-31 to attach the other panel to the other corner of the cover.

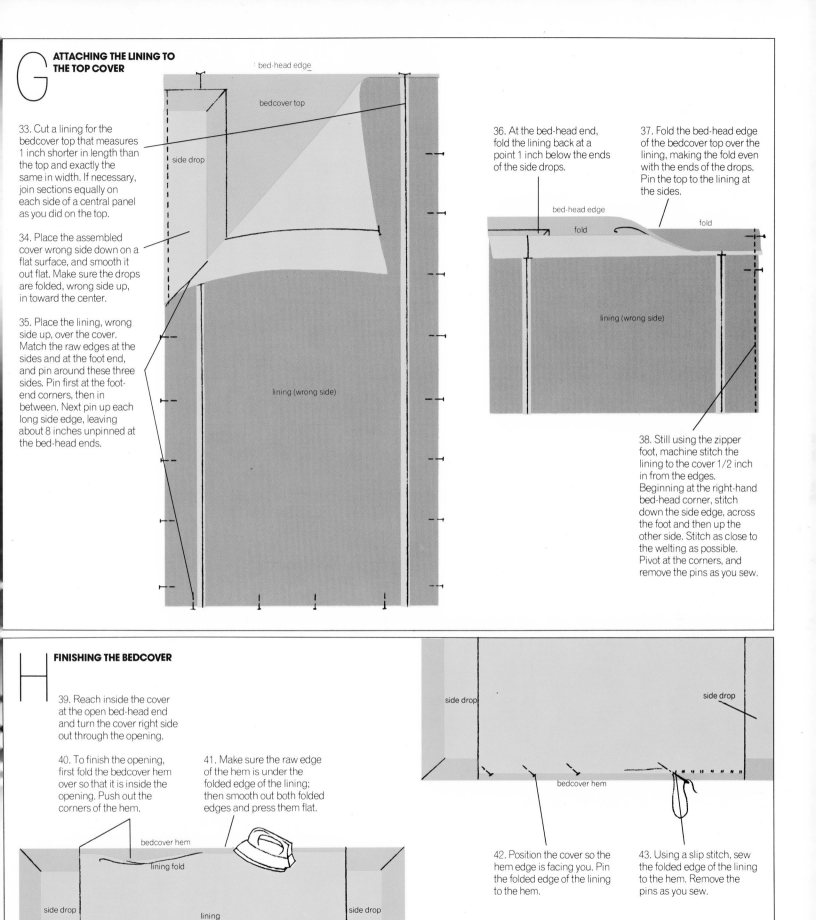

G ATTACHING THE LINING TO THE TOP COVER

33. Cut a lining for the bedcover top that measures 1 inch shorter in length than the top and exactly the same in width. If necessary, join sections equally on each side of a central panel as you did on the top.

34. Place the assembled cover wrong side down on a flat surface, and smooth it out flat. Make sure the drops are folded, wrong side up, in toward the center.

35. Place the lining, wrong side up, over the cover. Match the raw edges at the sides and at the foot end, and pin around these three sides. Pin first at the foot-end corners, then in between. Next pin up each long side edge, leaving about 8 inches unpinned at the bed-head ends.

36. At the bed-head end, fold the lining back at a point 1 inch below the ends of the side drops.

37. Fold the bed-head edge of the bedcover top over the lining, making the fold even with the ends of the drops. Pin the top to the lining at the sides.

38. Still using the zipper foot, machine stitch the lining to the cover 1/2 inch in from the edges. Beginning at the right-hand bed-head corner, stitch down the side edge, across the foot and then up the other side. Stitch as close to the welting as possible. Pivot at the corners, and remove the pins as you sew.

bed-head edge
bedcover top
side drop
lining (wrong side)

bed-head edge
fold
fold
lining (wrong side)

H FINISHING THE BEDCOVER

39. Reach inside the cover at the open bed-head end and turn the cover right side out through the opening.

40. To finish the opening, first fold the bedcover hem over so that it is inside the opening. Push out the corners of the hem.

41. Make sure the raw edge of the hem is under the folded edge of the lining; then smooth out both folded edges and press them flat.

42. Position the cover so the hem edge is facing you. Pin the folded edge of the lining to the hem.

43. Using a slip stitch, sew the folded edge of the lining to the hem. Remove the pins as you sew.

bedcover hem
lining fold
side drop
side drop
lining

side drop
side drop
bedcover hem

6
NEEDLEWORK
THAT MAKES
HEIRLOOMS

When advertising man Herbert Bippart died in 1966, he bequeathed to his son Charles, a New Jersey obstetrician, two half-finished needlepoint covers for a set of dining-room chairs. Dr. Bippart inquired about the cost of having them completed professionally and was horrified. He took a second look and decided, "Anyone who can do simple math can do this!" Picking up needle and yarn, he fin-

A RENAISSANCE OF NEEDLEPOINT DECORATION

ished them himself, and has never looked back. In the seven years that followed he made eight additional dining-room chair covers to complete the set, a cover for a piano bench and a petit point chair cover. He then turned to making a needlepoint rug and covering a wing chair in bargello.

Charles Bippart is one of thousands of needlepoint devotees who have moved on from small exhibition pieces to pillows, bench and footstool covers, even to upholstery for entire chairs—in short, to all the furnishings for which needlepoint was used originally. For once upon a time needlepoint was not only a hobby and a means of decoration, but also very functional.

In the 16th Century, when needlepoint as it is now known began to emerge as a distinctive type of embroidery, women used it much as medieval tapestries had been used —for wall hangings, bed hangings and bed coverlets. Needlepoint was also used for large cushions to upholster the seats of wooden benches and chairs—so much so that it was known as "cushion work."

Mary Queen of Scots, imprisoned for 18 years by her cousin Queen Elizabeth I, completed untold numbers of bed hangings, cushions and tapestries, designed for her by the "imbroiderer" she was allowed to keep "to plan out such needleworkes as she would be about."

Needlepoint furnishings continued to occupy the time of needlewomen throughout the 17th Century, causing diarist Samuel Pepys to note sympathetically, "Home to my poor wife, who works all day like a horse, at the making of her hangings for our chamber and bed." By this time the technique was also being used to make fitted covers for the upholstered furniture that was part of the domestic scene. One of the most popular stitches of the day was a vertical stitch worked over several threads, identical to the stitch known today as bargello—or less frequently, as Florentine, flame or Hungarian stitch. Many fanciful legends have grown up to explain bargello's history and the manner in which it acquired its various names. It

was enormously popular in Eastern Europe, especially Hungary, and according to one account it was brought to Florence by a Hungarian noblewoman who married a Medici prince. Another story has her teaching the stitch to prisoners in the dungeon of Florence's Bargello palace, today the Bargello Museum—although all that is known for certain about the museum's connection with bargello is that it owns a set of chairs worked in the stitch.

Bargello traveled early to the North American colonies, where it was used for everything from purses to draperies. Its popularity may have sprung from the fact that it needs less yarn than any other form of needlepoint —and the colonists had to import all their yarn, as well as needles, scissors and thimbles, from Europe. Ship captains were implored to bring back needles in "oyled paper" to protect them from rust.

Today the jagged flame patterns of bargello are once again back in style after a hiatus that began in the 1800s and lasted into the early years of this century. Needlepoint enthusiasts are attracted to its free-form designs and the speed with which it can be worked. For similar reasons they are also making furnishings of quick-point, a very modern form of needlepoint that is really a jumbo stitch done in thick rug yarn on large-sized canvas.

Needlepoint for furnishings can be fast and easy to do, like the project on pages 158-159 for a matching rug, pillow and footstool done in quick-point. And, like the bargello designs on pages 168-169 and 176-177, it can be vibrantly colorful.

Quick variations in needlepoint

Inspired by Portuguese tiles, a single motif serves for a needlepoint area rug, pillow and footstool. The pattern and colors on each are the same —they are simply switched from one element of the design to another.

All three pieces are done in the cross stitch, employing a form of needlepoint eminently suitable for home furnishings and aptly named quickpoint. Made with sturdy rug yarn on a canvas having a widely spaced mesh, quickpoint is worked in oversized stitches that cover large areas with relative speed. The directions start overleaf—including instructions for assembling and backing the rug, stuffing the pillow, and covering the footstool.

A big stitch for handsome covering

"Quick-point" needlework is an invention of recent years dreamed up to achieve embroidery effects quickly and easily. It adapts embroidery's cross-stitch (so-called because it looks like a cross or an X) to needlepoint materials: thick rug yarn and a large-gauge rug, or penelope, canvas, which has three to five squares to the inch.

The quick-point stitch is worked out in rows from right to left, by either of two methods. In one, each cross is completed before the next is begun. The other *(opposite)* completes a row in half crosses, one leg of each cross being made at a time; the same row is repeated (this time left to right) to complete the crosses. The second method is the quicker of the two; and because the hands can work up a rhythm by going straight ahead, without having to switch directions stitch by stitch, it is easier to make stitches come out regular and even. In either case, left-handers and right-handers work the same way.

A PREPARING PENELOPE CANVAS

1. Using a light-colored waterproof marker, mark off a rectangle around the design area. Mark each line between two threads, letting the indentation between them guide the marker.

2. Trim the canvas, leaving at least a 2-inch border outside the design area.

3. Bind the edges of the canvas with masking tape.

4. If your design starts at the center of the canvas, fold the canvas first in half crosswise and then in half lengthwise. Mark a dot on the center point of the two folds with the waterproof marker.

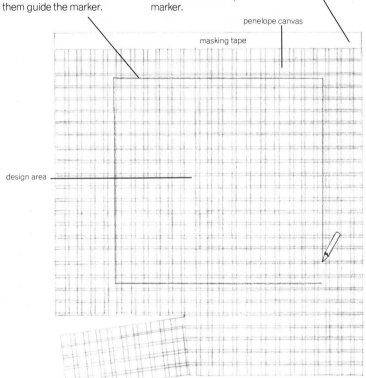

penelope canvas

masking tape

design area

B ANCHORING THE YARN

5. Whether you are right-handed or left-handed, start the row at the right edge of the design area. Knot one end of the yarn. Then insert the needle from the front of the canvas three or four holes to the left of the beginning hole (marked here with an X) and bring the needle out through that hole.

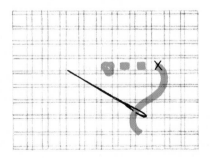

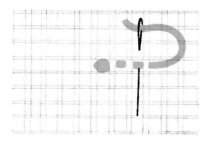

6. To make the first half cross-stitch, insert the needle into the canvas one hole above and one hole to the left of the hole from which the yarn last emerged. Turn the needle downward and bring it out one hole to the left of the hole from which the yarn last emerged. Pull the yarn through.

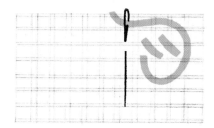

7. Repeat Step 6 to make each of the remaining half cross-stitches across the row, tightening the stitches evenly. When the stitches reach the knot and anchor the yarn on the back of the canvas, cut off the knot.

8. To complete the first cross-stitch, insert the needle one hole to the right and one hole above the hole from which the yarn emerged after the last half cross-stitch. Turn the needle downward and bring the needle out one hole to the right of the hole from which the yarn last emerged. Keep the yarn in front of the needle as you pull the needle through.

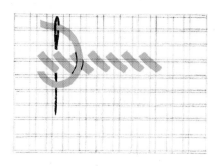

9. Repeat Step 8 back across the row to form the remaining cross-stitches. Tighten the stitches evenly.

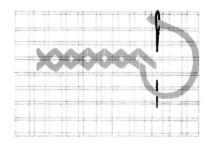

10. To complete the last stitch on the row, bring the needle out two holes below and one hole to the right of the hole from which the yarn last emerged. Keep the yarn in front of the needle as you pull the needle through.

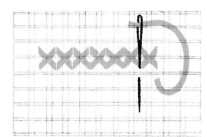

11. Repeat Steps 6-10 as many times as necessary to complete subsequent rows.

12. When you reach the end of the yarn or finish a pattern, turn the canvas wrong side up. Slide the needle under the nearest stitches and pull it through. Snip off the excess yarn.

BLOCKING NEEDLEPOINT

1A. For a project that uses only one piece of needlepoint, clean the needlepoint before blocking it. Have it dry-cleaned but not pressed, or wipe it with a sponge that has picked up cold-water suds but no water.

1B. For a project that uses two or more pieces of needlepoint, block each piece separately but do not clean the needlepoint until after the pieces are assembled.

2. Pad a board with a folded piece of muslin or a folded towel to avoid flattening the stitches.

3. Place the needlepoint face down on the padding. Align one edge with one edge of the board, and pin down the corners of that edge with rustproof carpet tacks.

4. Work around the canvas to align the remaining edges with the edges of the board and pin down the other two corners.

5. Pulling the canvas with pliers as necessary, tack along each edge at 1- to 2-inch intervals.

6. Using a sponge and cold clear water, thoroughly wet the needlepoint.

7. Place a plastic dry-cleaner's bag over the needlepoint to hold the moisture in. Then place a wet towel on top to weight the plastic down.

8. Leave the needlepoint on the board for at least 24 hours. Then remove the towel and the plastic.

9A. For a needlepoint project worked with standard yarn, let the piece dry for 24 hours or until it is dry to the touch.

9B. For a project worked with rug yarn, let the piece dry for 48 hours or more.

10. Take out the tacks and remove the needlepoint from the padded board. If the needlepoint is still askew, repeat Steps 3-9.

needlepoint

folded muslin

board

Making the quick-point design

To make a quick-point pillow, rug or footstool cover like the one on pages 158-159, use 4-mesh penelope canvas (i.e., canvas made up of doubled threads), Size 2 3/4-inch steel yarn needles or Size 13 tapestry needles and rug yarn.

The amount of yarn you need will depend on the number of squares required by the project. Each square takes 40 yards of yarn for the background color (*shown as triangles on the chart at right*), 12 yards for the predominant cross color and the color accents on the flowers (*rectangles on the chart*) and 17 yards for the predominant flower color and the color accents in the crosses (*circles on the chart*).

The footstool cover will require only one square that can be enlarged on the outside edges, if necessary, to fit the stool (*pages 166-167*); the pillow will require four squares and the rug 15.

To finish each of the projects you will also need special fabrics. Allow 1 yard of a heavyweight material such as velvet or duck to back the quick-point pillow—1 1/2 yards if you want to have welting around the edges of the pillow.

Allow 2 yards of burlap or duck for backing the 33-inch-by-55-inch finished rug. The skirt around the sides of the quick-point footstool cover will require 1 1/2 yards of silk or other upholstery fabric.

Preparing the canvas: Cut the canvas at least 2 inches wider on each side than the area to be worked. The finished design as outlined on the chart will measure 11 inches on each side.

In enlarging the design outside the border for the footstool, estimate that each extra row will add 1/4 inch to the length or the width of the rectangle—depending on where it is used.

Bind the nonselvage edges with masking tape so that the canvas will not ravel as you work.

Handling the yarn: Cut the yarn into lengths of no more than 30 inches each; longer strands will tend to fray. If possible, use a different needle for each color to minimize rethreading the needle. When working with any given color of yarn, you can jump to the next area of that same color if it is no more than 1 inch away; otherwise you should finish off and begin with a new strand.

Stitching the design: The design is worked in the cross-stitch from the center of the canvas (*page 160*).

First make a single cross-stitch at the center point. Next work the stylized central motif—first the cross and then the flowers—by working cross-stitch rows that use one stitch on the canvas for each square of the chart. Use the symbols in the color key below to determine the placement of each color.

Then make the border and the corner designs in the same manner. Finally fill in the background around the design and outside the border.

When working squares that will be stitched together for the pillow, alternate colors within the elements of the motif on adjacent squares as shown on the color key below.

For the pillow and rug, leave 2 rows of the border unstitched along any edge of a square that will be joined to another square so that the edges can be overlapped and stitched together later (*pages 164-165*).

Blocking the finished work: Press the canvas square on the wrong side using a damp cloth and a dry iron. If the canvas is badly distorted, you may need to block the finished piece following the instructions on page 161.

COLOR KEY

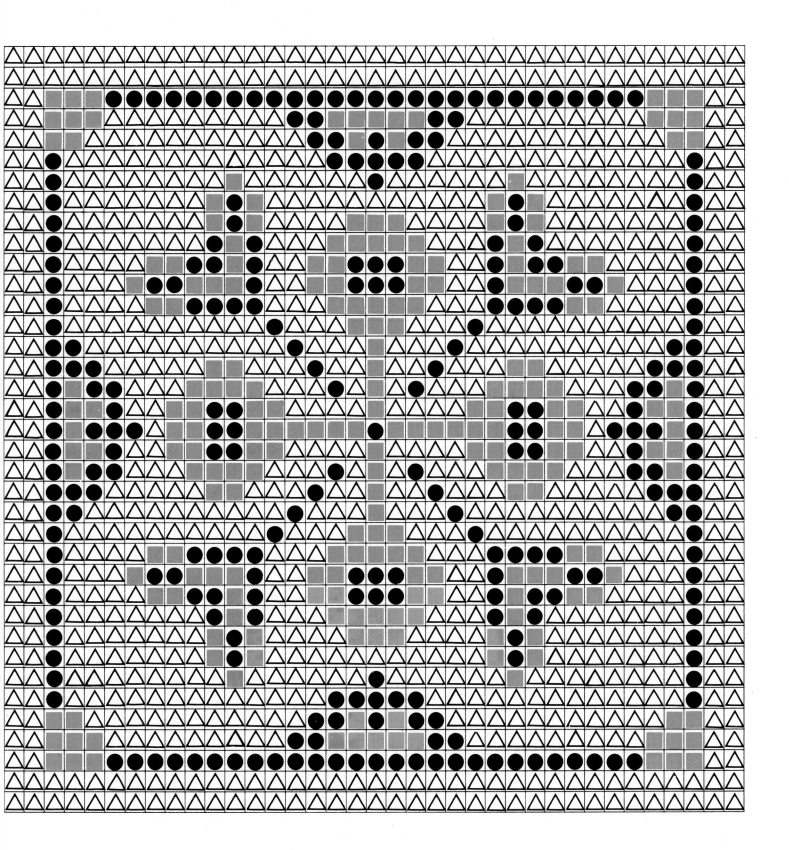

MAKING THE QUICK-POINT PILLOW

A PREPARING THE PILLOW

1. Work four 11-inch design squares *(pages 162-163),* leaving two meshes unstitched on two adjacent edges of each square. To duplicate the pillow on pages 158-159, work a blue background; make the crosses predominantly beige and the flowers predominantly red on two squares and reverse the other two squares.

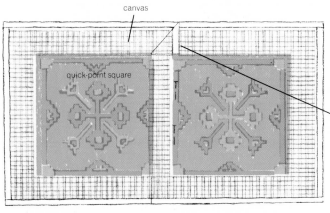

2. On one square, trim the canvas border just outside the fourth mesh on the edge that will be joined to an adjacent square.

3. Align the trimmed and untrimmed squares. Place the unworked canvas meshes of the trimmed square over the unfinished edge of the other. Butt the trimmed edge of the first against the stitching on the second. Pin.

4. To join the squares, use the background color and cross-stitch through the layers of canvas.

5. Turn the canvas wrong side up and trim the excess meshes close to the stitching.

6. Join the remaining squares by repeating Steps 2-5 as required.

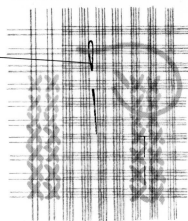

7. To back the quick-point pillow, cut a 24-inch square out of a fabric such as velvet or other heavyweight upholstery fabric.

8. Run a line of machine stitching along one side 1 inch from the raw edge to mark the seam allowance.

backing fabric

9. If you want to add a welting of the backing fabric to the pillow, attach it to the quick-point. Follow the instructions on pages 50-51 for making plain welting.

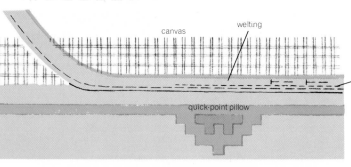

10. Attach the welting as for a continuous edge, catching about half the yarn along the outside rows of quick-point in the machine stitching.

11. To attach the backing to the quick-point, pin the canvas to the fabric with the wrong sides facing out, leaving open the machine-stitched edge of the fabric.

12. Using a zipper foot and a setting of 15 stitches to the inch, machine stitch one side of the pillow perpendicular to the open end. Start at the open end and stitch just inside the quick-point, catching part of the yarn from the outside row in the stitching. If the quick-point is welted, stitch just inside the line of stitching made in Step 9.

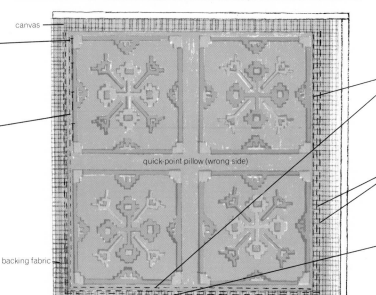

quick-point pillow (wrong side)

13. Stitch the other side of the pillow perpendicular to the open end—sewing in the same direction. Finally, stitch the third side of the pillow—the side parallel to the open end.

14. Run a continuous row of machine stitching just outside the first row, pivoting *(Glossary)* at the corners. Then make a third row just outside the second.

15. Trim the sides of the canvas flush with the raw edge of the fabric backing and trim the corners diagonally.

B | MAKING THE INNER PILLOW

16. Cut out two 22 3/8-inch squares of muslin.

17. Place one square on top of the other, wrong sides together, and pin the squares around three sides.

18. Machine stitch 5/8 inch from the pinned raw edges and remove the pins.

19. Stitch the seam allowances together close to the raw edges with a zigzag stitch.

20. Stuff the muslin pillow, making sure that the stuffing is firmly packed.

21. Machine stitch the fourth side of the pillow to close it, then stitch the seam allowances together with zigzag stitches.

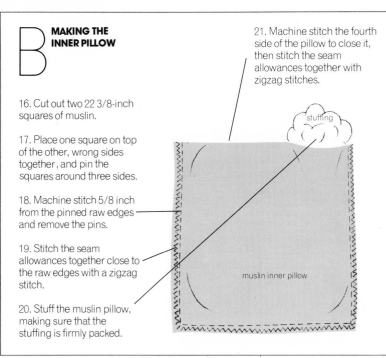

C | FINISHING THE PILLOW

22. Turn the quick-point pillow right side out, pushing out the corners with the eraser end of a pencil.

23. Insert the inner pillow into the quick-point pillow.

24. Turn under the backing fabric along the machine stitching at the open edge and turn the unstitched canvas under the quick-point. Then close the edge with a slip stitch (Appendix).

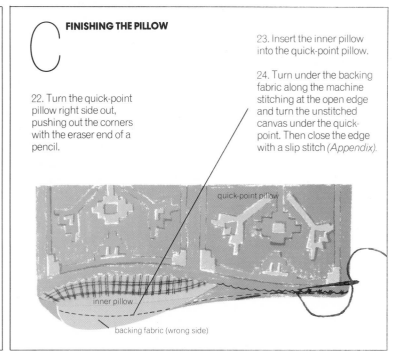

MAKING THE QUICK-POINT RUG

1. Work the fifteen 11-inch design squares (pages 162-163). To duplicate the rug shown on pages 158-159, work all of the squares with a beige background, making the flowers predominantly red and the crosses predominantly blue. Leave two meshes of the background unstitched along each edge that will be joined to another square; that is, leave unstitched four sides of the center squares, two sides of each corner square and three sides of each of the other outside squares.

2. Join the squares as for the quick-point pillow (Box A, Steps 2-6).

3. Press the finished rug on the wrong side with a damp cloth and a dry iron.

4. Trim the canvas border around the outside of the rug to 2 inches and cut the corners diagonally.

5. Turn under the canvas border all around the rug.

6. With a long, large-eyed needle and heavy carpet thread, stitch the canvas to the back of the rug using a hemming stitch (Appendix).

7. Cut a fabric backing of burlap, heavy duck or canvas; it should equal the dimensions of the rug plus 2 inches for a seam allowance on each side.

8. With the backing fabric wrong side up, turn up the 2-inch seam allowance and press in creases.

9. Trim the corners diagonally.

10. Pin the backing fabric to the rug, wrong sides together.

11. Join the backing to the rug with a hemming stitch (Appendix).

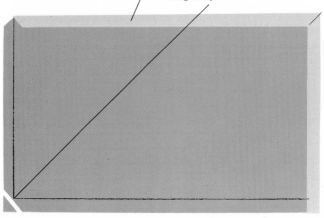

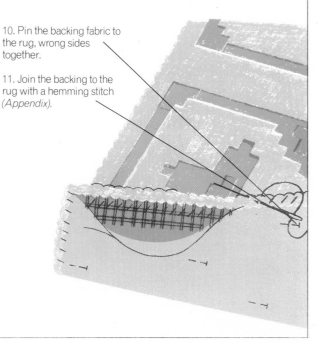

THE QUICK-POINT FOOTSTOOL

A ESTIMATING THE FABRIC

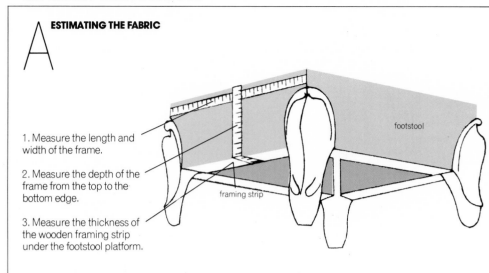

1. Measure the length and width of the frame.

2. Measure the depth of the frame from the top to the bottom edge.

3. Measure the thickness of the wooden framing strip under the footstool platform.

framing strip

footstool

4. To determine the length and width of the design area for the quick-point cover, add 1/4 inch to the length and width (Step 1) of the stool. Make the design, following the directions on page 162.

5. Determine the length of each pair of fabric bands for the skirt around the quick-point by adding 2 inches to the length and width of the stool (Step 1).

6. To determine the width of each fabric band, multiply the width of the framing strip (Step 3) by two. Then add the depth of the frame (Step 2) plus 1 inch for a seam allowance.

B PREPARING THE FABRIC

7. Place the skirt fabric wrong side up and chalk four skirt bands of the length and width required. Draw the lengthwise sides parallel to the selvage edge. Cut out the skirt.

8. Pin one band of fabric wrong side out to one side of the stool, so the 1-inch seam allowances at the top and sides of the fabric extend beyond the edges. Insert pins at an angle, smoothing the fabric taut.

9. Pin the other three bands to the stool similarly.

10. Pin the edges of the bands together at the corners of the stool.

11. Chalk a seam line on both sides of each corner just outside the pins.

12. Mark the seam line at the top of each band by folding the fabric over the edge of the footstool and running a piece of chalk along the fold. Then fold the fabric under the footstool at the bottom edge and mark the fold line with chalk.

13. If the legs extend onto the body of the stool as shown in Box A, outline the tops of the legs on the fabric with chalk.

14. Unpin the fabric and use a ruler to straighten the chalk lines made in Steps 11-13.

15. Draw cutting lines 3/8 inch outside the chalked seam lines at the ends of each band and around the curves of the legs. Extend the curved lines down to the bottom of the bands.

16. To indicate the hemline of the skirt, first multiply the measurement made in Step 3 by two. Measure this distance from the bottom seam line of the skirt on both sides of each band and make a chalk mark. Cut out the fabric bands along the cutting lines.

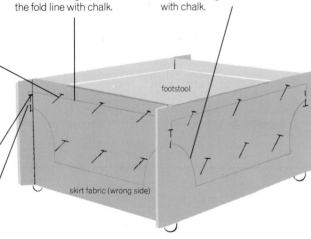

footstool

skirt fabric (wrong side)

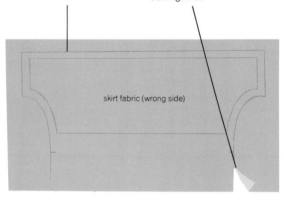

skirt fabric (wrong side)

17. Place one fabric band for the length of the stool on top of one for the width, wrong sides out, and align the seam lines at one end. Pin just outside the seam line. Then machine stitch and remove the pins. Do not stitch beyond the end of the chalked seam line.

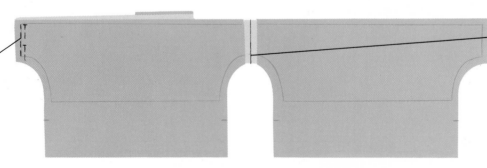

18. Add each of the remaining bands, pinning and stitching them in the same manner to make a continuous skirt. Press the seam allowances flat.

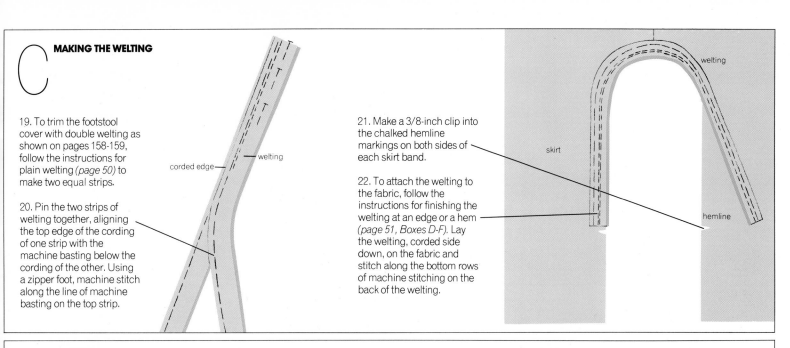

C MAKING THE WELTING

19. To trim the footstool cover with double welting as shown on pages 158-159, follow the instructions for plain welting *(page 50)* to make two equal strips.

20. Pin the two strips of welting together, aligning the top edge of the cording of one strip with the machine basting below the cording of the other. Using a zipper foot, machine stitch along the line of machine basting on the top strip.

21. Make a 3/8-inch clip into the chalked hemline markings on both sides of each skirt band.

22. To attach the welting to the fabric, follow the instructions for finishing the welting at an edge or a hem *(page 51, Boxes D-F)*. Lay the welting, corded side down, on the fabric and stitch along the bottom rows of machine stitching on the back of the welting.

D FINISHING THE FOOTSTOOL

23. Place the quick-point wrong side down, then pin one side of the skirt to it, wrong side up. Align the top seam line with the center of the outer stitches.

24. Baste outside the seam line and remove the pins.

25. Repeat Steps 23 and 24 to baste the other three bands of the skirt to the quick-point.

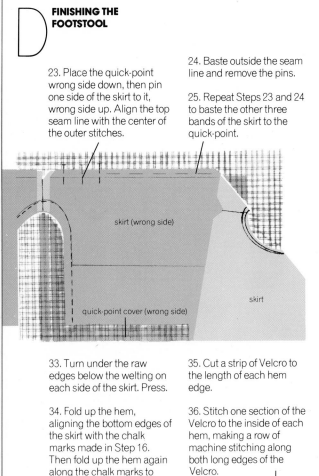

26. Machine stitch along one side of the skirt, catching half of the outer row of quick-point in the stitching. Begin and end the stitching 1/4 inch from the end of the chalked seam line.

27. Repeat Step 26 to machine stitch the parallel side. Begin at the same end of the seam line that you did on the first side and stitch in the same direction.

28. Repeat Steps 26 and 27 to stitch the other two sides of the skirt to the quick-point.

29. Finally, stitch around all four corners, overlapping the stitches at the beginning and end along the edges and pivoting at the corners.

30. Run a continuing row of machine stitching just inside the previous row and remove the bastings.

31. Trim the canvas close to the raw edge of the fabric.

32. Clip the corners of the canvas diagonally to within one mesh of the stitching.

33. Turn under the raw edges below the welting on each side of the skirt. Press.

34. Fold up the hem, aligning the bottom edges of the skirt with the chalk marks made in Step 16. Then fold up the hem again along the chalk marks to enclose the raw edges. Press.

35. Cut a strip of Velcro to the length of each hem edge.

36. Stitch one section of the Velcro to the inside of each hem, making a row of machine stitching along both long edges of the Velcro.

37. Staple the other section of each Velcro strip to the underside of the framing beneath the edges of the footstool.

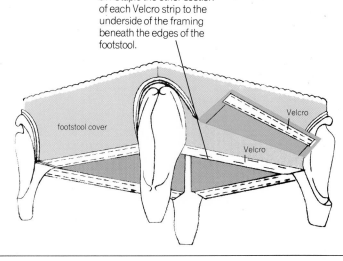

Bargello—
a Florentine
fantasy

Bargello is a specialized form of needlepoint used mainly for repetitive geometric patterns. Unlike conventional needlepoint, in which stitches fill in a printed design, bargello is created on blank canvas by working one row of color across the canvas to act as an outline for each succeeding row. Rows of vertical stitches in vividly contrasting or harmoniously blended colors are stitched over varying numbers of threads, and flow across the canvas in brilliant arcs, zigzags and diagonals.

Though the instructions on the following pages describe how to duplicate the designs shown here, you can achieve a totally new effect by using different colors. Or, with graph paper and colored pencils, you can design a pattern of your own.

Illustrating the wide variety of possible design sources for bargello, this sampler contains a scallop from an English quilt and a diamond *(near right)* from an ancient Egyptian tomb. The zigzag *(center panel)* derives from a Peruvian tapestry, and the triangular patch intersecting it is based on an American quilt. African raffia work supplied the motif for the pattern of interlocking rectangles *(far right)*, while the "Baby Block" pattern in the four corners is derived from another American quilt.

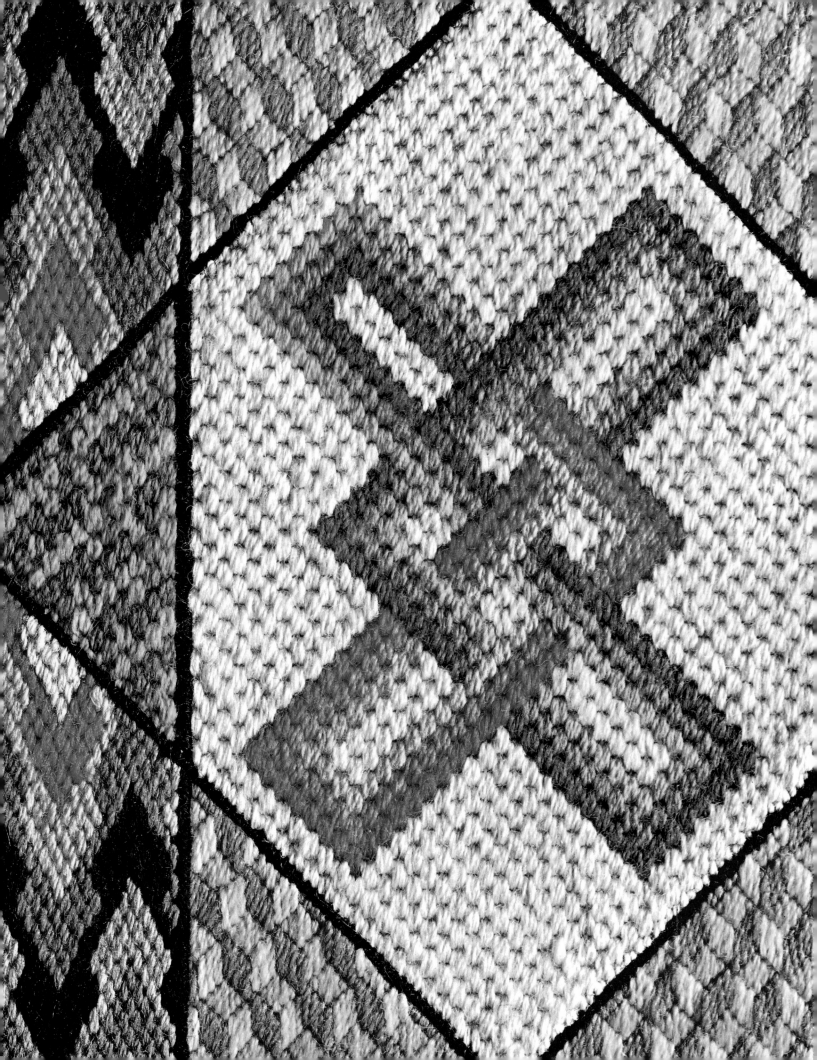

The basic techniques of bargello

For all their diversity, the six bargello patterns illustrated by the sampler on the preceding page were worked in one basic needlepoint stitch—the Gobelin stitch shown opposite. The stitch is done vertically in clusters of varying sizes—and colors—that rise and fall across the canvas to create the desired effect.

Like the sampler patterns, for which instructions are given on the following pages, most bargello begins with a single pattern row—or several rows that are repeated sequentially to establish the pattern. The pattern rows must be carefully counted. Subsequent rows, which are worked from the pattern row, are either simple repetitions of the pattern row—changed only in color—or they are filling stitches for spaces within the pattern.

The first pattern row is usually worked from a starting point in the center of the canvas, in order to center the design—or it is worked from the mid-point on the edge of the canvas. After you have completed a pattern row, pivot the canvas, so that you keep working in the same, most comfortable direction.

A PREPARING THE CANVAS

1. Using a light-colored waterproof marker, draw a square or rectangle to define the design area. Mark each line between two threads, letting the indentation between them guide the marker.

2. Trim the canvas, making sure to leave at least a 2-inch border outside the design area.

3. Bind the edges of the canvas with masking tape.

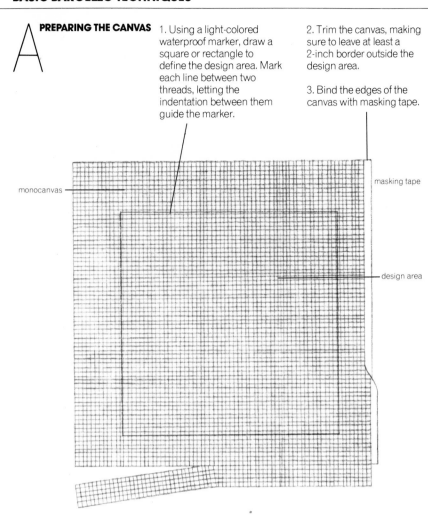

monocanvas

masking tape

design area

4. The pattern or outline row of a bargello design, which serves as a guide for subsequent rows, usually starts at a point midway along one side of the canvas. To determine that point, fold the canvas in half.

5. If the pattern row starts near the center of the design area, fold the canvas in half again in the other direction to locate the center.

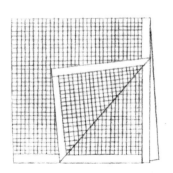

MAKING THE GOBELIN STITCHES FOR THE PATTERN ROW

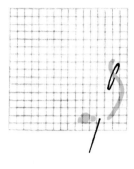

6. Determine the position of the bottom hole for the first Gobelin stitch by counting the required number of holes from the mid-point on one edge, the center or any other reference given in your design directions. Anchor the yarn (page 160). Then bring the needle out through the beginning hole and pull the yarn through.

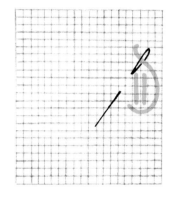

7. To finish a single Gobelin stitch, insert the needle the required number of holes above the hole from which the yarn last emerged (four in this example). If the segment will be made up of only one stitch, skip to Step 11 to start an ascending segment or Step 13 to start a descending segment.

8. To make a segment of several Gobelin stitches, first slant the needle downward and bring it out one hole to the left of the hole from which the yarn last emerged. Pull the yarn through.

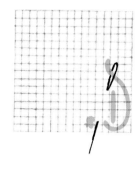

9. Insert the needle on a line with the top of the previous stitch.

10. Repeat Steps 8 and 9 until you reach the last stitch required for the segment.

11. To ascend to the next segment of stitches, slant the needle downward and bring it out one hole to the left and the required number of holes above the hole from which the yarn last emerged (two in this example). This will be the bottom point of the next stitch. Pull the yarn through.

12. Repeat Steps 7-10, making as many segments of ascending stitches as your design requires.

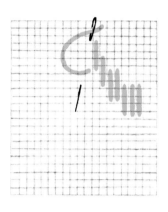

13. To descend to the next segment of stitches, slant the needle downward and bring it out one hole to the left and the required number of holes below the hole from which the yarn last emerged (two in this example). This will be the bottom point of the next stitch. Pull the yarn through.

14. Repeat Steps 7-10, making as many segments of descending stitches as your design requires.

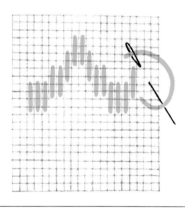

15. Complete the pattern row, ascending and descending as required. If necessary, turn the canvas so that you will always be working from right to left.

16. To end off the pattern row—or change colors—turn the canvas wrong side up. Then slide the needle under a few of the nearest stitches and pull it through. Snip off the excess yarn.

IF YOU ARE LEFT-HANDED...
Establish the beginning hole by counting toward the left rather than toward the right of the reference point specified by your design —or on the left-hand edge if the right-hand edge is specified. Always work from left to right as shown.

C **FILLING IN THE REMAINING ROWS**

17. After the pattern or outline row, work subsequent rows away from it. On these rows, insert the needle for the top of each stitch into the same hole used for the bottom of the stitch above it.

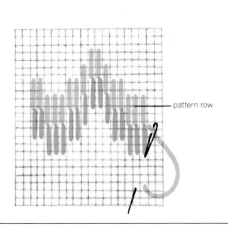

— pattern row

18. To square off the design at the top and bottom edges, reduce the length of the stitches as necessary.

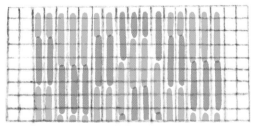

Making the bargello patterns

To make a project such as a pillow with any of the six bargello patterns shown in the sampler on pages 168-169, you will need a 14-mesh monocanvas—i.e., canvas with a single-thread grid containing 14 holes to the inch—that is 2 inches wider on each side than the finished piece. Use Size 20 blunt tapestry needles and three strands of Persian wool yarn cut into 30-inch lengths to prevent fraying. One ounce of yarn produces about 48 such lengths and covers about 48 square inches of canvas. Allow 10 per cent extra yarn to make sure you have enough for your project.

For each pattern, use the chart that accompanies it to determine the starting point for the first stitch in each color, and also to count stitches. Block the finished canvas following the directions on page 161. To use the piece for a pillow or footstool cover, follow the directions on pages 164-167.

SCALLOPED ENGLISH QUILT PATTERN

This pattern is shown in the upper left-hand corner of the sampler on pages 168-169. When working the pattern, make Gobelin stitches *(page 171)* going over four threads of the canvas except when stitches going over two threads are needed to fill in between the pattern rows and to square off the top and bottom edges *(Step 18, page 171)*.

Making the pattern rows: On the sampler, the color A rows are the pattern rows for the motifs. These scalloped rows are worked one above the other across the canvas and form an X when they touch. A complete motif is shown at the center of this design on the sampler. Make the first stitch *(identified as A 1 on the chart at left)* at a point midway along the bottom edge of the design area. (Or if you want to leave room for a partial motif, as shown at the bottom of the design on the sampler, count up 13 holes from the bottom mid-point.) Following the chart and ascending and descending two holes as required *(Steps 11-14, page 171)*, work to the left as indicated by the arrows on the chart if you are right-handed—or to the right if you are left-handed. Repeat the pattern as necessary until you reach the edge of the design area. Then pivot the canvas 180° and complete the first pattern row, working from the first stitch to the opposite edge of the design area. Start subsequent pattern rows from the right-hand side of the design area (the left-hand side if you are left-handed). Make the first stitch of each pattern row *(identified as A 2 on the chart)* above the center stitch of the highest segment on the preceding pattern row.

Filling in the design: After all of the pattern rows have been completed, work subsequent rows—starting at an inside corner of the motif where two pattern rows meet. Fill in colors B through G in sequence as shown on the chart. Then end by repeating colors D and E at the lowest point of the motif. Make stitches over two threads of the canvas when necessary to fill in the motif.

EGYPTIAN DIAMOND PATTERN

This pattern is shown in the lower left-hand corner of the sampler on pages 168-169. When making the pattern, use Gobelin stitches *(page 171)* going over either two or four threads of the canvas as indicated by the chart at right. Stitches going over two threads are also needed when filling in the top and bottom edges of the design area *(Step 18, page 171)*.

Making the pattern rows: The color A blocks and color B diagonals that connect the blocks are the pattern rows for the diamond-shaped motifs of this pattern on the sampler. To find the center of the first block, count up 24 holes from the center of the canvas and start the first block two holes to the right of that point *(identified with an A on the chart at right)*. Start two holes to the left, if you are left-handed. Then complete the block, alternating one long and two short stitches as shown. Change to color B and make the first diagonal pattern row, following the chart and descending *(Steps 13 and 14, page 171)* from the second stitch of the block (if you are left-handed, descend from the fourth stitch). Note that stitches covering only two threads are

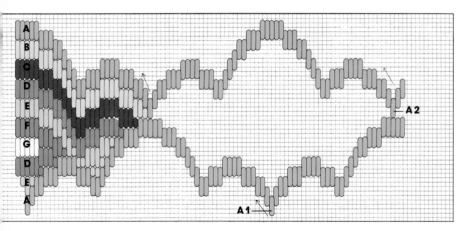

used at the top and bottom of the diagonal row. Each of the other stitches descends two holes. Make another color A block at the end of the diagonal row. Then starting above the second stitch of that block (the fourth stitch if you are left-handed), make an ascending diagonal row (Steps 11 and 12, page 171) and make a third block at the upper end of that diagonal row. Continue making color A blocks and color B diagonal rows in this zigzag fashion until you reach the side edge of the design area. Then starting below the second block, make another descending diagonal row and another block at the end of that row. Make diagonal rows and blocks in the same zigzag manner to complete the diamond shapes and as many similar pattern rows as needed to reach the upper and lower edges of the design area. Then rotate the canvas 180° and make pattern rows on the other half of the canvas in the same way.

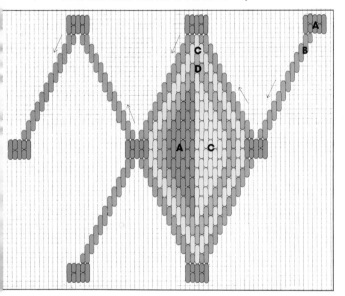

Filling in the design: When all of the pattern rows have been completed, fill in the diamond-shaped openings, working inward. First make diamonds with color C, starting below the center stitch of each block. Then work a diamond with color D inside each color C diamond. Finally, fill in half of each diamond with color A and half with color C as shown.

PERUVIAN ZIGZAG FLAME PATTERN
This pattern is shown on the narrow panel at the center of the sampler on pages 168-169. Although six colors appear on the sampler, this pattern can be worked with as many colors as desired. In this chart only four colors are shown. Make Gobelin stitches (page 171) going over four threads of the canvas, except where stitches over two threads are needed to fill in at the top and bottom edges of the design area (Step 18, page 171).
Making the pattern rows: Each flame motif has a pattern row —a zigzag row outlining the sides of the motif and both the upper and lower points. Using color A, make the first stitch—the upper point of a flame motif—at the center of

the canvas (identified with an A on the chart below). Then follow the chart and work down to the lowest point of the flame motif, descending two holes after each stitch (Steps 13 and 14, page 171). If you are right-handed, work toward the left side of the canvas; if you are left-handed, work toward the right. At some points you will be descending in the reverse of the usual direction—going back in toward the center. These reverse descents can be made easily without turning the canvas. When you reach the lowest point of the flame motif, work back up to the highest point of the next flame, making corresponding ascending stitches (Steps 11 and 12, page 171). Continue the row—descending and ascending in the same pattern—until you reach the side edge of the design area.

To start the second pattern row with color B below the first row—count down 12 holes from the bottom of the first stitch of the previous row. Then make the row in the same manner. Work subsequent rows with colors C and D—and as many additional colors as desired. When the pattern rows on the bottom left quarter section of the canvas (or bottom right quarter if you are left-handed) are complete, rotate the canvas 180° and continue the rows across the section that is now the top left (top right) quarter to finish the top half of the canvas. Then without turning the canvas, work the remaining pattern rows across the bottom half from the right-hand edge. Make the first stitch of each row by counting down 12 holes from the stitch at the edge of the row above. Work from the left-hand edge across the bottom of the canvas, if you are left-handed.

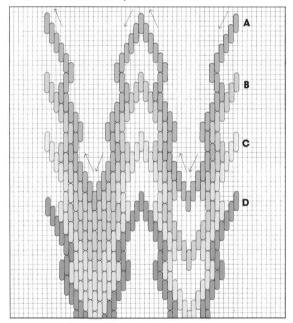

Filling in the design: Fill in each of the open spaces separately with rows of ascending and descending stitches using the same color that was used for the pattern row. Start next to the pattern row of the same color. If necessary, rotate the canvas 180°

19th CENTURY AMERICAN QUILT PATTERN

This pattern is shown in the triangle at the center of the sampler on pages 168-169. Make Gobelin stitches *(page 171)* over four threads of the canvas except when stitches going over two threads are needed to fill in at the top and bottom edges of the design area *(Step 18, page 171)*. All of the stitches are worked in rows of 3 pairs, forming vertical and diagonal segments of each color.

Making the first sequence of pattern rows: On the sampler, this sequence consists of short vertical rows of color A and color B running diagonally across the canvas. If you are right-handed, start with color A at the lower right-hand corner of the design area and make the first pair of stitches *(marked with an A on the chart below)*. Make 2 more pairs of stitches worked vertically one above the other just above the first pair to complete the first row. Then ascend two holes *(Steps 11 and 12, page 171)* and make another group of 3 pairs of stitches one above the other. These two groups form one vertical segment. To start the next segment of color A—which is made exactly the same way as the first segment—bring the needle out three holes to the left of the preceding stitch and four holes below the bottom of the stitch. Continue to make color A segments in this manner—working diagonally from right to left across the canvas—until you reach the edge of the design area. Then fill in the spaces between the color A segments with short vertical rows of color B. Each of these rows also consists of 3 pairs of stitches worked one above the other. Make the first

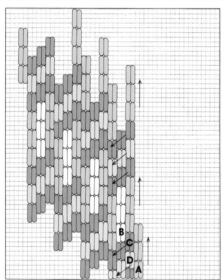

stitch of color B next to the first color A segment, two holes below and one hole to the left of the bottom stitch *(marked with a B on the chart above)*. Then work the color B rows between the color A segments across the canvas.

If you are left-handed, follow the instructions above, but start at the upper left-hand corner, making pairs of stitches one below the other. Work descending color A segments and color B rows from left to right across the canvas.

Making the second sequence of pattern rows: This se-

quence consists of the short diagonal rows of color C and color D worked under the first pattern sequence. Start with color C and make 3 pairs of stitches under each cluster of three vertical rows across the canvas. If you are right-handed, work from right to left starting under the lowest cluster *(marked with a C on the chart)* and descending two holes between each pair of stitches. If you are left-handed, work from left to right, starting under the upper cluster and ascending two holes between each pair of stitches. Then using color D, work a second series of diagonal rows across the canvas just below the first series of diagonal rows. Finally, make a third series of diagonal rows below the second, using color C again. Square off the design *(Step 18, page 171)* at the bottom edge.

Filling in the design: The canvas is filled in by alternately repeating the pattern sequences—working toward the edges of the design area. If you are right-handed, start by repeating the sequence of diagonal rows just above each cluster of vertical rows. Then alternately add sequences of vertical and diagonal rows up the canvas, squaring off the design at the top edge. Rotate the canvas 180° and work the second half of the canvas in the same manner. If you are left-handed, first make diagonal segments below the vertical rows and add sequences of vertical and diagonal rows down the canvas, squaring off the design at the bottom edge, then pivot the canvas and fill in the other half of the canvas.

AFRICAN INTERLOCKING RECTANGLES PATTERN

This pattern is shown in the center of the right-hand panel of the sampler on pages 168-169. Use Gobelin stitches *(page 171)* going over four threads, except when it is necessary to make stitches going over two threads to fill in the background at the top and bottom edges of the design area *(Step 18, page 171)*. All of the stitches are worked in pairs.

Making the first sequence of pattern rows: This sequence is made up of three rows, worked next to each other in a pattern that forms three arms of the design. If you are right-handed, determine the beginning hole for the first row by counting up 24 holes from the center of the canvas and two holes to the left *(marked with an A on the chart at right)*. Then use color A to work the first pattern row. Ascend and descend *(Steps 11-14, page 171)* two holes after each pair of stitches, following the arrows on the chart. Whenever necessary, rotate the canvas 180° so that you will always be working from right to left. To leave room for subsequent rows, interrupt the row that you are working on and carefully count the number of holes that will be taken up by the row that will cross it as shown on the chart. To guarantee the proper placement of the stitches, temporarily fill in the skipped holes with stitches using another color yarn and remove them as you complete the pattern.

If you are left-handed, begin with the chart turned so that the top edge is toward you. Count down 24 holes from the center of the canvas and two holes to the right to find the beginning hole. Then work the first pattern row following the instructions above, but working from left to right.

Make the second row of this pattern sequence using color B. Start the row just below the second pair of stitches of the first row; then work next to the first row, using it as a guide. Be sure to skip holes in the same places. Using color C make the third row in the same manner, starting just below the second pair of stitches of the second row.

Making the second sequence of pattern rows: This sequence is also made up of three rows worked next to each other. The pattern forms the fourth arm of the design. If you are right-handed, begin with the canvas and the chart turned so that the top edge is toward you. Count down 16 holes from the center of the canvas and one hole to the left to find the beginning hole *(marked with a D on the chart);* then work the color D pattern row, following the arrows on

within the design. Then fill in the rest of the background, starting at the design and working toward the edges.

"BABY BLOCKS" AMERICAN QUILT PATTERN

This pattern is shown in triangular segments at the corners of the right-hand panel on the sampler *(pages 168-169).* When making the pattern, use Gobelin stitches *(page 171)* going over six threads on the pattern rows and over two, four and six threads on the fill-in rows.

Making the pattern rows: On the sampler, the color A rows that—together with the adjacent color B rows—form the V-shaped side of each block serve as the pattern rows. If you are right-handed, start with color A at the center of the top edge of the design area *(identified with an A on the chart below).* To form the first block, make 4 stitches, descending one hole after each stitch *(Steps 13 and 14, page 171).* Then descend five holes and make another block of 4 stitches. Continue making blocks in a diagonal row to the bottom edge of the design area. Starting on the left side of each color A block make ascending rows of color B blocks. Make 3 stitches ascending one hole between them *(Steps 11 and 12, page 171),* then ascend eight holes (one hole above the top of the previous stitch) to start the next block. Work to the top of the design area. Rotate the canvas 180°, and make ascending rows of color B blocks from the other side of the color A row. Rotate the canvas back to the starting position and make the remaining color A rows, starting on the left side of each color B block.

If you are left-handed, make the first stitch at the center of the bottom edge of the design area. Work the pattern

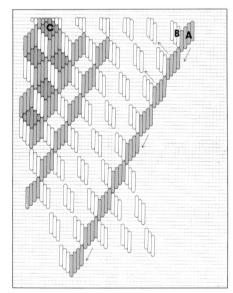

the chart and turning the canvas so that you are always working from right to left. Be sure to skip over the pattern rows you have already worked. If you are left-handed, start with the canvas in its normal position and count up 12 holes from the center of the canvas and one hole to the right to find the beginning hole. Then work the color D pattern row following the arrows and turning the canvas so that you are always working from left to right.

Make the second row of this sequence with color E, using the first row as a guide. Then make the third row with color F, using the second row as a guide.

Filling in the design: Using color G and ascending and descending between pairs of stitches, fill in the open areas

rows following the instructions above, but make ascending stitches with color A and descending stitches with color B from the right side of the color A blocks.

Filling in the design: With color C, fill in the open spaces between the pattern rows with stitches that cover two, four and six threads, as shown on the chart.

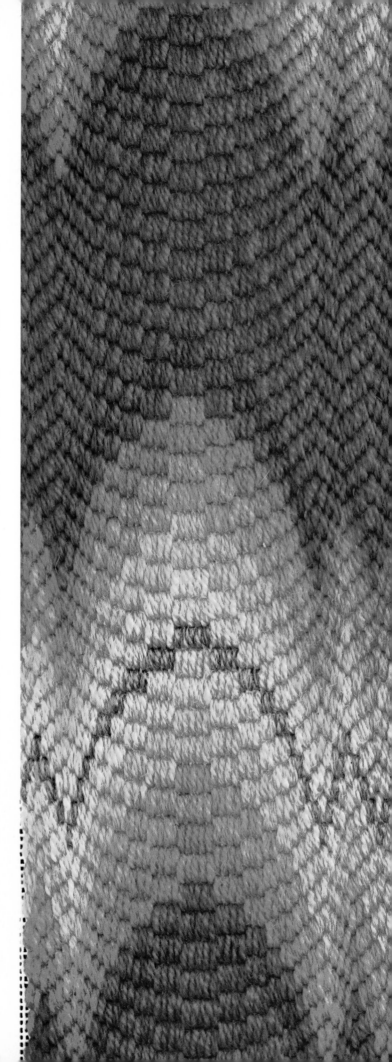

A blaze of contemporary bargello

The fiery radiance and vibrant depth of the uncommon bargello pattern shown here is achieved by subtle changes in yarn color. Seven shades are used, and all but the surprising rows of cool green are closely related tones ranging across the hot end of the spectrum from deep red to light yellow.

Unlike traditional bargello patterns, which are completely symmetrical, this design is modern, with liberated, free-form lines suggestive of flickering flames. Yet it is made in the same way as all other bargello.

The undulating rows are created by ascending and descending groups of stitches. Decreasing the number of stitches in the groups forms the sharp jagged peaks, while increasing them gives the smooth gradual sweeps. Complete directions for this design—which can be used for a pillow or even framed —start on the following page.

Making the bargello design

To make the free-form bargello design shown on the preceding pages, use the materials for the sampler patterns *(pages 172-175):* 14-mesh monocanvas, seven colors of Persian wool yarn in the amounts on the color key *(below the chart on the facing page),* and Size 20 blunt tapestry needles—preferably one for each color.

The design area measures 13 3/4 by 11 3/8 inches. If you use the design for a pillow or footstool, several threads on the outer edges will be taken up in the seams.

Preparing the canvas: Trim the canvas to a rectangle measuring at least 15 3/4 by 13 3/8 inches to allow a 2-inch-wide border all around. Bind the edges with masking tape.

Handling the yarn: Leave all three strands of the yarn together and cut 30-inch lengths; longer strands tend to fray. Using a different needle for each color minimizes the amount of rethreading you will need to do.

Making the pattern row: The pattern row—which determines the sequence of stitches for all other rows—is the uppermost complete row of color DO (dark orange).

If you are right-handed, determine the starting point by first measuring 2 inches down from the top edge of the canvas and 2 inches in from the right edge. Then count down 20 holes to find the beginning hole for the first stitch. Make 3 Gobelin stitches *(Steps 6-10, page 171)* with each stitch going over four threads of the canvas. Continuing to make Gobelin stitches over four threads, complete the row. Follow the chart for the number of stitches in each segment. Ascend or descend as required by bringing the needle out one hole to the left and three holes above or below the point from which the yarn last emerged *(Steps 11-14, page 171).*

If you are left-handed, turn the chart upside down and determine the starting point by first measuring 2 inches up from the bottom edge of the canvas and 2 inches in from the left edge. Then count up 16 holes to find the beginning hole for the first stitch. Make 3 Gobelin stitches *(page 171),* going over four threads of the canvas. Following the chart for the number of stitches, each going over four threads, ascend and descend as required by bringing the needle out one hole to the right and three holes above or below the point from which the yarn last emerged.

Making the remaining rows: Again starting on the right if you are right-handed—or on the left if you are left-handed—work the next row immediately below the pattern row, following the stitch pattern established by the pattern row *(Step 17, page 171).* In the same manner, make each subsequent row—working in sequence toward the bottom of the canvas. Use the letters at the edges of the chart and the color key to determine the placement of each color. Make stitches over four threads with each color except G (green), which should cover only three threads. To fill in the design at the bottom edge, follow the established sequence of colors, but cover only enough threads to reach the lower edge of the design, as shown in the diagram below. When the portion of the canvas below the pattern row is finished, rotate the canvas 180° and finish the rows above the pattern row in the same manner.

Finishing the piece: Press the bargello on the wrong side with a damp cloth and a dry iron; if the canvas is badly distorted, block it—following the instructions on page 161—and tack the edges at 1-inch intervals. To make a pillow, follow the directions for assembling the quick-point pillow on pages 164-165.

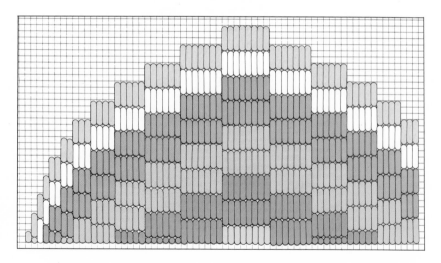

When you reach the bottom of the design area (the lower right-hand corner on the chart shown in detail at left), fill in the remaining open areas by making rows in the established color sequence. As you make the stitches, cover only as many holes as needed to fill the area. Fill in the top of the design in the same way.

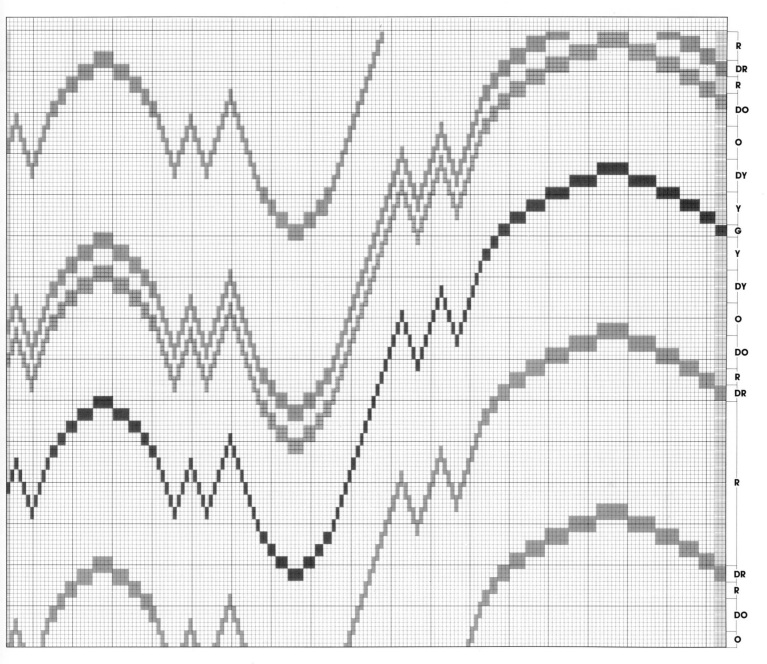

This chart shows the bargello design in schematic form. The dark orange pattern row is shown in color since it is worked first to establish the pattern of stitches for all of the other rows. The dark red and green rows are also outlined because both of them will stand out prominently in the design and will furnish reference points for other colors, indicated on the chart by stitches along the side edges. The color of each row is identified by letters along the edge of the chart, and keyed to the list at right.

DO dark orange—1 ounce   **G** green—1 ounce

O orange—1 ounce   **DR** dark red—1 ounce

DY yellow—1 ounce   **R** red—2 ounces

Y light yellow—1 ounce

GLOSSARY

BARGELLO: A form of needlepoint worked in rows of vertical stitches over varying numbers of canvas threads, usually to create repetitive geometric patterns. Most bargello begins with one or several pattern rows that act as guides for succeeding rows of stitches.

BIAS: A direction diagonal to that of the threads in woven fabric, i.e., the warp and woof, or "grains." A true bias is at a 45° angle to the grains.

BINDER: See PRESSER FOOT.

BLOCKING: In making slipcovers, a system of measuring and cutting fabric into rectangles slightly larger than the furniture sections they are to cover. In needlepoint, the process of setting the final shape of the finished work by tacking it face down on a padded board, dampening and rubbing it, and then allowing it to dry.

CLIP: A short cut made with scissors into a seam allowance to help the seam lie flat around curves and corners.

EASE: An even distribution of fullness in fabric, without perceptible gathers or tucks, that enables one section of a garment to be smoothly joined to another slightly smaller section.

FRENCH SEAM: A finished seam with enclosed seam allowances. It is made by placing two fabric pieces wrong sides together, stitching outside the seam line and trimming the seam allowances. Then the fabric is folded wrong sides out and stitched along the seam line to enclose the seam allowances.

GRADING: Trimming each seam allowance within a multilayer seam to a different width to reduce bulk and make the seam lie flat.

GRAIN: In woven fabric, grain is the direction of the threads: the warp (the threads running from one cut end to the other) forms the lengthwise grain; the woof, or weft (the threads running across the lengthwise grain from one finished edge to the other), forms the crosswise grain.

GRAIN-LINE ARROW: The double-ended arrow that is always marked on a pattern piece to indicate how the piece should be aligned with the fabric grains.

HEMMER: See PRESSER FOOT.

INTERLOCKING FELL SEAM: A finished seam that is especially suitable for unlined draperies and opaque curtains. It is made by placing two pieces of fabric together wrong sides out with the edge of the bottom fabric extending 1/4 to 1/2 inch beyond the edge of the top fabric. The bottom edge is folded over along the top edge and both layers are then folded together along the visible raw edge of the bottom piece. Next, the fold is pinned

and stitched just inside the inner fold line; finally, it is pressed.

LINING: Fabric covering the inside of part or all of a project to give it body or to prevent the outer fabric from fading.

MITER: A diagonal fold at a corner.

NAP: On the surface of a fabric, the short fibers that are pulled and brushed in one direction. Pattern pieces for fabrics with nap are usually laid out and cut in one direction—with the nap.

NATURAL FIBERS: Fibers of vegetable and animal origin that are used to make fabrics, most commonly cotton, linen, silk and wool.

NOTCH: A triangular cut made into the seam allowance of a curved seam to help it lie flat.

PATTERN REPEAT: The space occupied by each complete unit of the design motif in a printed, plaid or striped fabric.

PILE: A surface of upright fibers found on such material as velvet. Because the pile of a fabric tends to lie in a particular direction, the way that fabric is positioned for sewing affects the appearance of the finished project.

PIVOT: A technique for machine stitching around angular corners that involves stopping the machine with the needle down at the apex of a corner, raising the presser foot, pivoting the fabric and then lowering the presser foot before continuing to stitch.

PLEATS: Fabric folds used to control fullness and add a decorative element.

PRESSER FOOT: The part of a sewing machine that holds down fabric while it is being stitched. A general-purpose foot has two prongs of equal length and is used for most stitching. A binder foot has a special scroll-shaped slot and is used for attaching bias binding to the edge of fabric with either a straight or zigzag stitch. A hemmer foot has a slot that turns a fabric edge into a narrow hem as it is being stitched with either a straight or zigzag stitch. A roller presser foot has rollers that prevent bulky or sheer fabric from sticking or slipping while being stitched. A ruffler foot has special blades and a guide that make evenly gathered or pleated ruffles in light- to medium-weight fabric; some rufflers make and attach the ruffle at the same time. A straight-stitch foot has one long and one short prong and can be used for straight stitching and for stitching fabrics of varying thicknesses. A two-pronged even-feed foot, for use on zigzag machines, has teeth on the bottom to move two or more layers of fuzzy, slippery or heavy fabric at the same speed. A zipper foot has only one prong and is used to stitch zippers and welting.

QUICK-POINT: A modern form of needlepoint worked on large-meshed canvas with thick rug yarn.

RUFFLER: See PRESSER FOOT.

SEAM: The joint between two or more pieces of fabric, or the line of stitching that makes a fold in a single fabric piece.

SEAM ALLOWANCE: The extra fabric that extends outside a seam line.

SELVAGE: The lengthwise finished edge in woven fabric.

SHANK: A short length of several strands of thread, used to link two pieces of fabric permanently but loosely together.

SHIRRING: Decorative gathering of fabric, used primarily to control fullness. Shirring is made by drawing up material along two or more parallel lines of stitching or along one or more cords that have been stitched between layers of fabric.

SIZING: A coating applied to fabric to stiffen it, give it strength and add a smooth or shiny finish.

SOLUTION DYEING: The dyeing of synthetics in a liquid state before they are spun into fibers. This technique gives uniform color.

SYNTHETIC FIBERS: Man-made fibers used to make fabrics. Cellulose-based fibers (such as acetate and rayon) are made from chemically treated plant materials reduced to a chemical liquid and then spun into fibers. Noncellulosic fibers (such as acrylic, nylon and polyester) are made by creating wholly new molecules, unknown in nature, primarily from mineral materials, such as petroleum.

TACKING STITCH: Several stitches made in the same place to hold pieces of fabric permanently in position.

WEAVE: The manner in which yarns are interlaced to make fabric. In a plain weave, the crosswise and lengthwise yarns crisscross one another in a simple checkerboard fashion, producing a sturdy, durable fabric. In twill and satin weaves, the yarns running in one direction pass or "float" over several yarns running in the other direction, thus creating a diagonal ribbed pattern in twill fabrics, or a smooth, delicate surface in satin weaves.

WELTING: Fabric-covered cording with exposed seam allowances that can be sewed into seams for decoration, and to reinforce the seams of furniture covers.

ZIGZAG STITCH: A serrated line of machine stitching.

BASIC STITCHES

The diagrams below show how to make the elementary hand stitches in this volume.

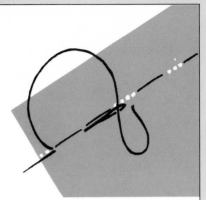

THE FASTENING STITCH

To end a row with a fastening stitch, insert the needle back 1/4 inch and bring it out at the point at which the thread last emerged. Make another stitch through these same points for extra firmness. To begin a row with a fastening stitch, leave a 4-inch loose end and make the initial stitch the same way as an ending stitch.

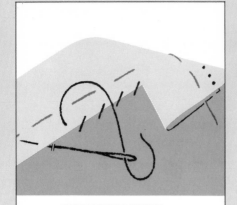

THE HEMMING STITCH

Anchor the first stitch with a knot inside the hem; then, pointing the needle up and to the left, pick up one or two threads of the garment fabric close to the hem. Push the needle up through the hem 1/8 inch above the edge; pull the thread through. Continue picking up one or two threads and making 1/8-inch stitches in the hem at intervals of 1/4 inch. End with a fastening stitch.

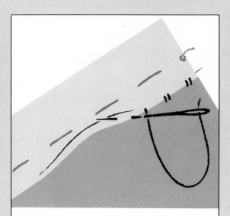

THE SLIP STITCH

Fold under the hem edge and anchor the first stitch with a knot inside the fold. Point the needle to the left. Pick up one or two threads of the garment fabric close to the hem edge, directly below the first stitch, and slide the needle horizontally through the folded edge of the hem 1/8 inch to the left of the previous stitch. Continue across in the same manner and end with a fastening stitch.

THE OVERCAST STITCH

Draw the needle, with knotted thread, through from the wrong side of the fabric 1/8 to 1/4 inch down from the top edge. With the thread to the right, insert the needle under the fabric from the wrong side 1/8 to 1/4 inch to the left of the first stitch. Continue to make evenly spaced stitches over the fabric edge and end with a fastening stitch.

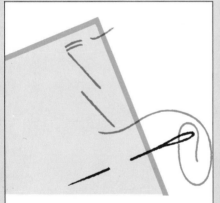

THE DIAGONAL BASTING STITCH

Anchor the basting with a fastening stitch *(above)* through all fabric layers. Keeping the thread to the right of the needle, make a 3/8-inch stitch from right to left, 1 inch directly below the fastening stitch. Continue making diagonal stitches, ending with a backstitch if the basting is to be left in, or a 4-inch-long loose end if the basting is to be removed.

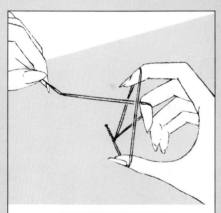

THE CHAIN STITCH LOOP

Using a knotted double thread, make a fastening stitch on the wrong side of the fabric. Then take a small stitch through the fabric leaving an 8-inch loop. Holding the needle in the left hand, insert three fingers of the right hand through the loop. Still holding the needle, draw the needle end of the thread through the loop with the middle finger, releasing the first loop and creating another. Pull the new loop tight to form a chain stitch. Repeat as many times as needed. Anchor with a fastening stitch.

 # CREDITS

Sources for illustrations, interiors and furnishings in this book are shown below. Credits from left to right are separated by semicolons, from top to bottom by dashes.

ILLUSTRATIONS: Cover design by Allumé Handprints, Inc. 6,7—Ryszard Horowitz. 11—From the book *History of Furnishing* by Mario Praz, published by George Braziller and Longanesi. 12 through 21—Alen MacWeeney. 22,23—Ryszard Horowitz. 26 through 39—Ben Rose. 42 through 45—Richard Jeffery. 46—Jack Escaloni. 47 through 53—Drawings by John Sagan. 54—Jack Escaloni. 55 through 59—Drawings by John Sagan. 60—Jack Escaloni. 61 through 67—Drawings by Raymond Skibinski. 68—Jack Escaloni. 69,70,71—Drawings by John Sagan. 72—Jack Escaloni. 73 through 79—Drawings by John Sagan. 80 through 85—Tom Yee. 86 through 97—Drawings by John Sagan. 98,99—Tom Yee. 100 through 107—Drawings by Raymond Skibinski. 108,109—Tom Yee. 110 through 117—Drawings by John Sagan. 118,119—Ben Rose. 122,123—Bernie Gold. Drawing by Oni. 124 through 139—Drawings by John Sagan. 140,141—Bernie Gold. Drawing by Oni. 142,143—Drawings by John Sagan. 144 through 153—Drawings by Raymond Skibinski. 154 through 159—Al Freni. 160,161—Drawings by Carolyn Mazzello. 163—Drawing by Elaine Zeitsoff. 164 through 167—Drawings by Carolyn Mazzello. 168,169—Al Freni. 170 through 175—Drawings by Carolyn Mazzello. 176, 177—Al Freni. 178—Drawing by Carolyn Mazzello. 179—Drawing by Patricia Byrne.

181—Drawings by John Sagan.
INTERIORS AND FURNISHINGS: 6,7—Fabrics from & Vice Versa, sofa designed by Angelo Donghia from & Vice Versa. 12,13—Room designed by Kevin McNamara, Inc.; slipcover fabric from Brunschwig & Fils, Inc.; table cover fabric from Colefax and Fowler (London); flowers from Jean Jacques Bloos, Ltd. 14,15—Room designed by Tom Morrow; wall covering and fabrics from Hannett. Morrow.Fischer, Inc. 16,17—Slipcover, curtain and matching pillow cover fabric from Hannett.Morrow.Fischer, Inc.; needlepoint pillows on sofas from Mazaltov's Inc. Custom Needlework; needlepoint pillow on chair from Woolworks, Inc. 18,19—Room designed by Tom Morrow; wall covering and fabrics from Hannett.Morrow.Fischer, Inc. 20,21—Room designed by Tom Morrow; wall covering and fabric from Hannett. Morrow.Fischer, Inc.; needlepoint rug from A. Morjikian Co. 26,27—Fabrics from Woodson Wallpapers; Boussac of France, Inc.; Margowan Fabrics; Clarence House; Cyrus Clark Co., Inc.; Decorators Walk. 28,29—Fabrics from Henry Cassen, Inc.; Scalamandré Silks, Inc.; Scalamandré Silks, Inc.; Isabel Scott Fabrics; Patterson-Piazza Fabrics. 30,31—Fabrics from Isabel Scott Fabrics—Decorators Walk—Lee/Jofa—Fabrications, by Kaufman—Bloomingdale's. 32, 33—Fabrics from Scalamandré Silks, Inc.—Isabel Scott Fabrics—Decorators Walk

—Patterson-Piazza Fabrics—Stroheim and Romann. 46—Fabric from Bergamo Fabrics, Inc.; pillow cover made by Delta Upholsterers, Inc. 54—Fabric from Henry Cassen, Inc.; shirring made by Delta Upholsterers, Inc. 60—Fabric from Fabrications, Inc. by Kendix of Holland; decorative edge made by Delta Upholsterers, Inc. 68—Fabric from Scalamandré Silks, Inc., cushion cover made by Delta Upholsterers, Inc. 72—Fabric from Brunschwig & Fils, Inc., pleat made by Delta Upholsterers, Inc. 84,85—Fabric from F. Schumacher & Co.; draperies made by Delta Upholsterers, Inc. 98,99—Fabric from F. Schumacher & Co.; shades made by Delta Upholsterers, Inc. 108,109—Blue stripe and check fabrics from F. Schumacher & Co.; red print fabric from Allumé Handprints, Inc.; curtains made by Delta Upholsterers, Inc. 122—Fabric from Carleton V, Ltd.; slipcover made by Delta Upholsterers, Inc. 140,141—Fabrics from F. Schumacher & Co.; bedcovers made by Delta Upholsterers, Inc. 154,155—Needlepoint pillows made by Nikki Scheuer; Mazaltov's Inc. Custom Needlework; Granny's Knitting Bag; Granny's Knitting Bag; Nikki Scheuer. Blouse courtesy of Blousecraft. 158,159—Needlepoint pillow and stool cover made by Lucy Ciancia; stool covered by Delta Upholsterers, Inc. 168—Bargello sampler made by Nikki Scheuer. 176—Bargello by Harry Schmidt.

ACKNOWLEDGMENTS

For help in preparing this book the editors thank the following: *in Hamburg, Germany:* Ilex Ness, *Schöner Wohnen; in London, England:* David Hicks, Michael Inchbald, David Mlinaric, Tom Parr; *in Milan, Italy:* Mary Annovazzi, *Casa Viva;* Maria Vittoria Carloni, *Casa Vogue;* Franca Santi Gualteri, *Arbitare; in Morristown, N.J.:* Dr. Charles Bippart; *in New York City:* Jacqueline Beymer, ASID; Lucy Ciancia; Lois Coleman, Conso Products Co.; Jesse Dalzell, Singer Co., Inc.; Ruth De Luca and Charles E. Lico, Delta Upholsterers, Inc.; Joel Ergas; Mr. and

Mrs. Richard Feldstein; Mr. and Mrs. Arthur Klein; Kevin McNamara; Tom Morrow; Donna Reynolds, Velcro Corporation; Belle Rivers, Donahue Sales, Ltd.; Christine Roth; Nikki Scheuer; Harry Schmidt; Jeanne Weeks; John E. Winters, ASID; *in Paris, France:* Joël Feau, Jacques Grange, Françoise Siriex, Corinne Trincano; *in Rome, Italy:* Howard Dilday, Stefano Mantovani; *in San Francisco, Calif.:* Mack McDowell, Robert McNie, Michael Taylor; *in Stuttgart, Germany:* Antoinette Goltermann De Boers.

The editors would also like to thank the

following: *in New York City:* B. Altman & Co.; Bloomcraft; Bloomingdale's; Boris Kroll; Butterick Fashion Marketing Co.; The Camel; Conso Products Co.; Duffy Mayer Needlework; Granny's Knitting Bag; Greenberg & Hammer; Greentex Upholstery Supplies; Lord & Taylor; Mazaltov's Inc. Custom Needlework; Riverdale Division—United Merchants & Manufacturers, Inc.; Sears, Roebuck and Company; F. Schumacher & Co.; W. & J. Sloane; Stroheim & Romann; Surefit Products, Inc.; & Vice Versa; *in Wilmington, Delaware:* E. I. Dupont de Nemours & Co.

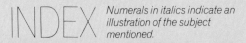